The Seamstress

The Seamstress

A Memoir of Survival

SARA TUVEL BERNSTEIN

INTRODUCTION BY EDGAR M. BRONFMAN

G. P. PUTNAM'S SONS
New York

G. P. Putnam's Sons
Publishers Since 1838
a member of
Penguin Putnam Inc.
200 Madison Avenue
New York, NY 10016

Library of Congress Cataloging-in-Publication Data

Bernstein, Sara Tuvel, 1918–83
The seamstress / by Sara Tuvel Bernstein ; introduction by
Edgar M. Bronfman.
p.   cm.
Includes index.
ISBN 0-399-14322-X
1. Bernstein, Sara Tuvel, 1918–83.   2. Jews—Romania—Biography.
3. Holocaust, Jewish (1939–45—Romania—Personal narratives).
4. Auschwitz (Concentration camp).   I. Title.
DS135.R73B47   1997   97-9461 CIP
940.53'18'092—dc21
[B]

Printed in the United States of America
1   3   5   7   9   10   8   6   4   2

This book is printed on acid-free paper. ∞

BOOK DESIGN BY AMANDA DEWEY
MAPS BY JEFFREY L. WARD

To my sister Esther and my friend Ellen, who despite their youth so courageously survived the horror and the pain, and to the memory of all the men and women who died locked in the cars when our train was bombed at Schwabhausen, Bavaria, on April 29, 1945.

Contents

Introduction

After reading *The Seamstress* by Sara Tuvel Bernstein, my great regret is that I never met this remarkable woman. Her autobiography is a brilliantly told story about, basically, survival. It's also about cruelty, about women, about love and family, and about the terrible anti-Semitism that infested not only Germany but all of central and eastern Europe, becoming so manifest between the two World Wars, reaching its inevitable conclusion during the Holocaust.

Seren Tuvel was born in Romania, one of the younger children of a lumber mill manager and his second wife, who brought up his first children and then her own, a very large family. Seren was naturally bright and independent. She won a contest enabling her to go to a gymnasium in Bucharest—a great educational opportunity—but quit when the priest who was teaching her class kept making horrid remarks about Jews. So angered was she that she threw her inkwell at him, striking out on her own at the age of thirteen. She became an apprentice seamstress and worked her way into expertise in her field, which would stand her in good stead as her life progressed.

As Nazism swept Germany, so did similarly disgusting waves of hatred of Jews sweep her native Romania. During the course of World War II, the part of Transylvania where her family lived was transferred to Hungary. On a visit to her family, she and her father were arrested and imprisoned. Now, as she starts her slide into the camp for women at Ravensbrück, we see a new, heroic Seren Tuvel. Strong, and at the same time so loving of her mother and father, her siblings, her people.

I will not reveal any more of the story. What is so fantastic about this tale of persecution, of cruelty, of horror is that it is told in such a matter-of-fact style. With few if any superlatives, Seren tells her story with a light, and therefore an incredibly incisive, touch. One feels her pain, her wisdom, and moreover her determination to survive.

—EDGAR M. BRONFMAN

Central Europe, 1923

LATVIA

LITHUANIA

Baltic Sea

GERMANY

SOVIET

UNION

Berlin •

• Warsaw

GERMANY

POLAND

• Kiev

• Prague

CZECHOSLOVAKIA

CARPATHIAN

Vienna •

• Satu-Mare

• Budapest

AUSTRIA

HUNGARY

Cluj • Tirgu-Mures •

• Moinesti

TRANSYLVANIA

• Galati

ROMANIA

• Brasov

MOUNTAINS • Ploiesti

Bucharest
•

*Black
Sea*

BULGARIA

• Sofia

0   100   200   300

Scale of Miles

© 1997 Jeffry L. Ward

Central Europe, 1942

Baltic Sea

SOVIET UNION

□ RAVENSBRÜCK

Berlin •

Warsaw •

• Kiev

GERMANY

Prague •   AUSCHWITZ □

□ DACHAU   Vienna •   HUNGARY

• Budapest   Satu-Mare

Cluj • Tirgu-Mures • Moinesti

CARPATHIAN

BESSARABIA

TRANSYLVANIA   • Brasov   Galati

ROMANIA   • Ploiesti

MOUNTAINS   DOBRUJA

Bucharest •

BULGARIA   Black

Sea

• Sofia

© 1997 Jeffrey L. Ward

0   100   200   300

Scale of Miles

Part One

One of two existing pictures of Seren prior to the war, when she was
living in Romania. She was sixteen when this was taken. It is this particular
photograph that her nephew carried in his shoe and then sent to her when he
learned, from friends, that they had seen her alive in Germany after the war.

Prologue

*L*ATE ONE EVENING MY MOTHER WAS SURPRISED TO hear the tramping of many feet on the path outside her front door and loud, excited voices. Exhausted after a long day of cooking and cleaning and heavy with her third pregnancy, she rose slowly from her bed and stumbled to the door. Opening it, she was confronted by several workers from my father's lumber mill.

"Is your husband here?" asked one of the men anxiously. "There's another peasant revolt. They're threatening to attack us and all the other Jews again."

"He isn't here," my mother answered. "He's in the northern part of Transylvania buying lumber."

"But we need Mr. Tuvel's help!" the man exclaimed. His voice turned suspicious. "Are you sure he's not here?"

"Yes, I'm positive. I'm here all alone with my two little boys."

The man turned abruptly to the others. "I'm not so sure he's gone," he said. "He's probably in bed and doesn't want to get up—the old man!"

After more angry mutterings, the men left. My mother climbed back into bed and tried to calm herself. But, the angry millworkers, the threats of the peasants, had frightened her and she could not rest. Within half an hour she felt the stab of a contraction and then another, even though she was still in the eighth month of her pregnancy. She thought about who she might summon for help, but quickly realized that there was no one; the midwife could be reached only by horse and wagon and the closest neighbor lived three miles up and around the mountainside.

As the contractions came closer and closer, the cold night wind crashed against the windows. With each new gust, my mother realized that she could not risk going out into the darkness. Within several hours she gave birth to me by herself as the wind howled all around the house isolated at the foot of the mountain, howled through the trees bending over the roof in low, swishing arcs. I was born gasping, my small, frail cry rising above the wind, on April 25, 1918, and was named Seren.

One

ROUNDING A CURVE IN THE PATH, I SAW IT—A LONG
caravan of gaily colored covered wagons. They were slowly winding their
way down to the outskirts of the village. An old man turbaned in black,
smoking a long black pipe, strolled beside the lead horse. Behind him jan-
gled eleven more horses and wagons, the pots and pans inside bouncing up
and down.

At the edge of the field I stopped and hid behind the largest tree. A
wagon was pulling up only a few meters away. A man with wavy dark hair
and a bushy beard jumped down and looked around quickly with glistening eyes. I ducked back behind the tree. *What if he's seen me!* I thought, my
heart bumping wildly in my chest. My father's warnings rang in my ears.
"Don't go near the Gypsies!" he had shouted at breakfast. "They kidnap
children. Do you want us to find you dead in some ravine?"

The Gypsy man said something in a language I did not understand. A
woman's soft voice answered him. A baby's laughter rippled through the
warm, still air. I peeked out again. The man was pulling wooden poles from

the rear of the wagon, his white smock and loose trousers flowing with the quick movements. In a few minutes he had crossed the poles to form a large frame for a tent. The woman draped heavy green-and-gold rugs over the framework. The baby was placed in a cradle which now swung gently from one of the cross poles.

It grew dark. The woman hung a black kettle on an iron frame and began to stir something in it, the man standing to one side, a violin in his hands. As the flames began to crackle and spit under the cooking pot, the man pulled his bow across the violin. Melancholy notes eased into the gathering blackness. Then the music suddenly turned more festive. The man bent his body into the fire and then away from it again in a slow dance; he beckoned the other men to come. They drifted from their wagons, violins in hand, blending with the same tune, varying from it in high, lilting arcs and then merging with it once more.

Suddenly I realized that it must be quite late. Father was surely home from the mill; my older half sisters and half brothers as well as my full brothers and sister must be sitting around the table, the prayer already said, my mother wringing her hands and asking, "What has happened to her now?"

I crept away from the tree and ran, the lanterns from the villagers' houses lighting my way.

"Whoa!" someone yelled.

I looked up. My oldest half brother, Herman, was standing in the path. "You almost knocked me over!" he said. I knew he had been sent to look for me, and I was glad it had been him. Although Herman was tall and fair like my father, he did not have his disposition. "I bet I know where you've been," he teased. "You've been to see the Gypsies and one has asked you to marry him and run away forever!"

I did not answer.

"And may I ask what is his name?" he continued.

"He didn't tell me," I answered. "I didn't ask."

Herman laughed, a rich laugh coming from deep within his chest. "Well, Father will have something to say about this, I'm sure."

"Is he angry?"

"Let's say he is not in the best of moods. Come! I'll race you back!"

When I arrived at the long red house the lumber company provided for us, everyone was sitting by the table stretching almost the entire length of the kitchen. "Look who's here!" yelled Mendel, my second-oldest half brother. "It's about time you came home!"

"She should be spanked!" said Rose, my youngest half sister. "If she were my child I'd give her a good whipping. Thank goodness I don't ever plan to have any children!"

"She's not even wearing a sweater!" said Louise, the middle half sister. "No wonder she's always sick! She doesn't dress properly. Then she runs off until it's pitch-dark. Who knows where she goes or what she does?"

If only Father didn't have all these older children, I wished for the hundredth time. *If only he had been young and alone when he met my mother, instead of an old man with seven spoiled children. If only they were all married and gone . . .*

"Silence!" my father roared then. Quiet hung in the usually clanging kitchen.

"Where . . . have . . . you . . . been?" he said then, spacing each word separately.

I looked at the floor; I could think of nothing to say. I could not tell about going to see the Gypsies after he had forbidden me to go.

"Since you will not answer me, you will go to bed without supper," my father said. "Now!"

I went feeling alone, friendless. Later Mama came quietly to the bed I shared with my little sister, Zipporah, and whispered, "I've brought you some bread and cheese and a little milk."

"Thank you, Mama," I whispered back.

"You must not disobey your father. Do you know that?"

"Yes, Mama."

"Do you promise?"

"Yes, Mama."

"Good! Sleep well," she said as she bent to kiss me good night. As she left the room I thought, *I will never leave Mama. Never!*

————

THE NEXT MORNING WHEN I CAME INTO THE KITCHEN I was expecting everyone to scold me again. Instead, Mama and my three half sisters were talking, seemingly all at once.

"It's only two more weeks until the wedding!" Louise was saying.

"It will be fine!" Mama answered. "I'm starting the pies today. They'll keep in the pantry. It's still ice-cold in there! The cakes I'll do next week. The invitations have been sent and the neighbors have all agreed to take in guests during the wedding."

"Where will Bela's family be staying?" Louise asked.

"With the Goodmans."

"He'll probably break their bed," Mendel laughed.

"Oh, be quiet!" Rose yelled. "Bela is big, but at least he's not a lazy oaf like you!"

"Please don't talk about my fiancé like that," Louise said, her voice trembling. She was the most delicate and tiny of my three half sisters. No one could understand why she had picked huge, burly Bela for a husband.

"It's all r-r-right," Berta said, putting her arm around Louise. "B-B-Bela is a good man. We all like him. A-A-And you found him without a m-m-m-m-matchmaker!"

While Berta was my oldest half sister, the fairest of them all in my opinion, she was still at home, single and nearing thirty in a time when many girls married at the age of fifteen or sixteen. As I grew older I realized how intelligent she was. Yet she was not as beautiful as Louise or Rose, her face broad, her speech halting.

"The dressmaker still has to do the final fitting on my gown," Louise said then. "I think she's ready for me now."

"Oh, can I watch?" Rose asked. "I wish it were me. I can't wait until it's me!"

The three girls went to the spare bedroom where the dressmaker had been working for weeks, sewing Louise's gown and all of her trousseau in addition to the rest of the family's wedding apparel and any other new clothes we had needed.

My three half brothers, Herman, Meyer, and Mendel, ambled into the front yard. My mother was left alone with all of the work. She would not think of asking one of her stepsons to bring in a pail of water or one of her step daughters to knead some bread, lest she be regarded as a cruel stepmother. Since she did not ask for help, they did not volunteer any. Instead my mother would assign many tasks to us, the four children born to my father and her after their marriage. "Pick some beans for supper," she could tell Eliezer, the brother two years old than I, "and have Seren help you." Shlomo, the first child born to my mother and father, had been sent to the yeshiva to become a rabbi. He was home only on holidays. He was now nine years old; Eliezer, seven; I, five; and Zipporah, three. In another year Esther, the last child, would be born.

On this particular morning I was sure I'd be asked to help out. Tucking my doll under my sweater, I began to edge toward the front door, planning to escape to my new hiding place high in the hayloft. There the yellow shafts of light fell on me, on my doll cradled in one arm, on the sacks of goose down all around me. I liked nothing more than to lie in the sweet hay, dreaming of the time when I would be able to go to school and learn how to become someone very important.

"Seren," my mother called as I was almost out of the door.

My heart sank. So she had seen me. "Yes, Mama?" I answered.

"I know you would like to play, but I need your help. I have to make five different kinds of pies today. Would you watch Zipporah for me this morning?"

"Yes, Mama."

"What a sweet child you are!"

No, I'm not a sweet child, I thought to myself. I did not always like Zipporah. She would never listen to me, even though I was two years older than she. When I told her to stop chasing the geese or to stay away from the mill yard she laughed and went right on doing what she wanted. It made me furious.

For the next two weeks I supervised Zipporah almost constantly while the pies and cakes and breads piled up high on the pantry shelves. The wedding celebration would last for three days and nights—enough time to eat all of these and more. My mother's aged mother and one brother, my Uncle

Louie, were coming. All the people from the temple at the mill were coming, the ones my father invited home for a glass of wine and cake after every service. Even distant cousins were coming, planning to make a vacation of the event by staying as long as possible.

THE FIRST DAY OF THE WEDDING WAS CLEAR AND dazzling. The *chuppah* was set up in the spacious side yard near the garden, the fragrance of lilacs wafting through the still air during the ceremony. *Louise is so beautiful,* I thought as she drifted around and around under the *chuppah* seven times, Rose on one arm and Berta on the other, her long black hair a shadow under the veil that covered her head and eyes. *I don't know whether or not I would like to get married someday,* I thought, gazing at the silken, glistening dress, *but I would love a gown like that.*

When the ceremony was over, the feasting and music began. For three days and nights I wandered about, mostly listening to Uncle Louie argue with my father. It amazed me that anyone would dare to disagree with anything my father said. That Uncle Louie said things like, "Temple is a complete waste of time. I believe none of it!" utterly shocked me. My father would listen to this sacrilege and declare, "If you were not my wife's brother I would forbid you to enter my house!" Uncle Louie simply smiled and helped himself to another piece of challah, slathering it with a thick layer of butter.

In the evenings the Gypsies came. We all gathered in the large, open hall at the mill where the Saturday night dances were held. The lead violinist would strike up a fast dance tune. The accordionist would join him and in an instant all of my brothers and sisters were dancing: Herman with his new young wife, Tamara, the ribbons from her newest hat fluttering around her long, flying hair; Mendel, the Casanova of the family, invariably holding the prettiest girl of the village in his arms; Meyer, my quiet brother, dancing with an equally silent girl; Berta, slowly gliding back and forth with some kind uncle who had asked her to dance; Rose, passing from one young man to another all evening long; and Louise, held like a porcelain doll in the arms of her new husband, Bela. My mother sat on the side happily watching, Zipporah asleep on her lap. My father kept his tradition of dancing only at weddings and performed his special dance, which we called the Tuvel Wedding Dance, in the middle of the evening.

Shlomo, home from the yeshiva, darted around the dance floor, often pummeling a cousin with his fists until an uncle came along and lifted him up by the seat of his pants. Eliezer sat quite still beside my mother, not saying more than two words all evening. Mama often called him her *la ceas o lingurița* (teaspoonful every hour). He talked so seldom that it was as if his words were doled out one by one. Although Eliezer and I had very different personalities, I loved him dearly.

On the last night of the wedding, a Thursday, I went up to him sitting alone and said, "Come, Eliezer. Dance with me!"

He looked down at his shoes, the back of his neck turning a deep red.

"Will you?" I asked again.

He continued to look at the floor, not moving. "No, thank you," he finally said.

"All right," I answered. "I'll go outside and find something else to do."

I wandered from wagon to wagon parked along the road to the mill, the horses already harnessed for the trips home. At the end of the evening the guests would all begin their journeys back, some traveling all night. I stopped behind one wagon, intrigued by the soft down comforters piled up at one end of the straw bedding. Exhausted after the long days and late nights, I decided to climb into the wagon for a minute and rest. Lying down in the space under the high seat at the front end of the wagon, I pulled a comforter over me. Through a knothole in the boards a single star twinkled.

"DAVID!" A WOMAN WAS CALLING. "OH, DAVID! Who is this?"

I opened my eyes. The bright sun was shining in them, making me blink. Hurriedly I pulled the comforter off and climbed out from under the seat. I did not seem to be at home.

"Isn't she a Tuvel child?" a man was saying.

"Why, yes. That's who she is—Miriam and Abraham's little girl. But how did she get there?"

"She must have crawled in there last night and fallen asleep. We had a stowaway!"

"We must take her right back!" the woman answered.

"We can't do that, Rebeccah. If we start back now we'll have to travel on Shabbat. It's forbidden."

"But what will we do? Miriam and Abraham will be so worried, won't they? Won't your mother and father worry?" the woman asked me.

"Maybe they won't miss me," I answered. "I have so many brothers and sisters."

The man laughed and lifted me from the wagon with big, heavy arms. "Are you hungry?" he asked.

"A little," I answered.

"Come, child. What is your name?" the woman asked.

"Seren."

"Come, Seren. I'll get you some breakfast. We won't be able to take you home until Sunday, the day after tomorrow. I do hope your poor mother doesn't make herself sick with worry."

For two days I stuffed myself with potato dumplings and chocolate cake. In the afternoons I spent long hours playing with a litter of kittens in the barn, their furry bodies like soft balls in my hands. It was wonderful to be an only child, to have Rebeccah offer me dessert even if I had not finished all my carrots, to have David pull me onto his lap before the fire in the evenings and tell me funny stories.

Finally, early on Sunday morning, we set out for Fulehaza, hoping to reach our house before dark. By dusk we were bouncing into the yard. Although it had been only three days since I left, the house looked unfamiliar. I felt like a stranger seeing it for the first time—the wide wooden house with the kitchen running all along one side, the mill beyond, the piles of lumber, the long, low dormitories for the workers, and the river, the Mures, ever flowing down the mountainside.

I ran to the house while David was still tying up the horse and Rebeccah gathering some boxes from the wagon. I opened the door quietly and walked softly into the hall, hoping I could listen for a moment to everyone chattering over supper and see if Father was angry. However, the clinking of silverware, the scraping of bowls, did not greet me. Instead I heard a low droning coming from the sitting room opposite the kitchen and across the hall. I recognized some of the words of the Kaddish, the prayer for the dead. *Someone has died!* I realized with a shock. *Maybe it was Grandmother. She was so old. It must have been her.*

I crept to the doorway. All of my older sisters and brothers, my mother and father, sat on low stools, their feet covered only by stockings, heads bowed. My father's suit coat was torn, Meyer's, Herman's, and Mendel's coats as well. Mama and my sisters were crying, the tears running down onto their collars, collecting on the torn edges of their sleeves. They were surely in mourning. It was Grandmother who had died; I was convinced. A tear slid down one cheek.

Quietly I tiptoed into the room, sinking down at my mother's feet. As I entered I heard a gasp. Before I knew what was happening Mama had grabbed me from behind, holding me so tight that I could hardly breathe.

"Seren . . . Seren . . . Seren . . ." she was saying over and over, the tears washing down her face.

My father's face loomed before me, strangely pale. "Where did you come from?" he asked, his voice much quieter than I had remembered.

By then Rebeccah and David had entered the room. "You're in mourning," Rebeccah said. "Please forgive us for disturbing you. May I ask who has died?"

Herman began to shake with deep, rolling laughter. Then he burst out, exploding with joy, his laughs bouncing all around the quiet room. David and Rebeccah stared at him as if he had gone berserk with grief. "Don't you know what happened?" Herman finally asked.

David and Rebeccah shook their heads silently.

"Seren just disappeared!" Herman shouted between bouts of laughter. "We couldn't find a trace of her!"

"And since the Gypsies were here when she disappeared and were gone the next morning," Tamara added, "we were sure they had kidnapped her for spying on them. We thought she was dead—thrown in some ditch where we would never find her."

I looked at my mother, at the deep circles beneath her red eyes. "Did you really think I was dead, Mama?" I asked.

She hugged me to her again. "I'm afraid so. I'm afraid I did," she said. "But you're back. That's all that matters!"

Two

THE SUMMER DAY IN 1924 WHEN I WAS SIX BEGAN like any other in Fulehaza—clear and slightly chilly. However, by mid-morning when the sun had crested the mountaintops and warmed the air, I was to feel for the first time the fear and sorrow that came from being one of the relatively few Jewish people in the midst of a nation where Greek Orthodoxy was the state religion.

As I was running outside to play on the swing in the backyard that day, one of the men from the mill came running up to the house. "Where's your father?" he asked me in one, sharp burst of breath. Hearing the voice, my mother came out quickly and said, "What is it? Is it Mr. Tuvel? Is he hurt?"

"No, no, I have to find him. Isn't he here?"

"He left early this morning to look at some timber. He should be back soon. What's wrong?" asked my mother.

"I just saw all the men from the sheriff's office board the train going out of town. The students must be on their way here. We've got to decide what to do!"

The color quickly drained from my mother's face.

"I'll be back in a few minutes," the man yelled as he ran toward the mill.

"Who are the students?" I asked my mother, following her back into the house. "Are they from the school in the village?"

"No," she answered. "These are older students from the gymnasium in Bucharest. When they get bored during summer vacation they form a mob and go from village to village."

"What do they do in the villages?" I asked.

My mother looked into the distance, saying nothing. Finally, she pulled me to her and said, "It's all right. Don't worry. It's all right."

I didn't believe her of course and pretended to return to the swing. Instead I edged around behind the mill, where I saw a whole group of men standing together. Now I knew something was seriously wrong. My father's presence was felt at the mill even when he was not there; no one simply stood around during working hours.

"Look what happened in my cousin's village!" a worker named Albert was shouting. "When the mob came they rampaged through the village for the entire night. Not one Jewish household was left unharmed. My cousin and his family barely escaped with their lives. After they had run away from their homes with only the clothes they were wearing, they climbed to the top of the hill overlooking the village. Flames burned through the darkness where moments before their homes had been. The only houses left standing were the non-Jewish peasant huts on the outskirts of the village. Thank God my brother had room to take them all in."

"But do you think they will really bother with us?" asked one of the new workers. "In my village the Jews were never burned out. We are so remote here at the mill, and there are not many of us. They might think we are not worth their trouble."

"Worth their trouble?" yelled Albert. "A handful of Jews is worth their trouble! One solitary Jew is worth their trouble! We can't just stand here and do nothing. Why do you think the sheriff and his men left town? To give the students free rein—that's why! They can have a day off and the Jews can learn a lesson, all at the same time."

This was far more than I wanted to hear. I did not want to picture my home going up in flames, my family and me left with nowhere to go. There were so many of us. Who could take us in? Suddenly I remembered my doll and all of the clothes I had carefully made for her. Running as fast as I could, I hurried back to the house and to my room. She was still there! But where could I hide her where the students would not find her? Eliminating one place after another, I finally settled on the hole in one of the apple trees in the garden. I ran to the tree, taking along only her finest dresses, wrapped my doll and her clothes in an old cloth, and stuck the bundle down into the hole. "Don't worry," I said to her. "It's all right."

When I got back to the house I was relieved to see that my father was talking to some of the men from the mill. My father was not one to simply allow anyone to destroy everything we had. The men at the mill were the same. I had heard my father say how fortunate he was to be able to hire dedicated, hardworking Jewish men. Since Jews were forbidden by law to own land or hold a government position, many of the young men who could not afford to go out of the country for a college education worked at my father's mill, learning the trade from one of the best mill managers in Romania.

Our family and the millworkers were particularly vulnerable to the student mobs, as there were no longer any other Jewish families in Fulehaza or nearby; they had all escaped to large cities like Tirgu-Mures, where they could live with a number of other Jews and feel safer.

"The best thing to do," my father said, "is for everyone to gather inside our house once it begins to grow dark. The small children will be taken away from the house in case they set it on fire. But I don't think that will happen. We'll barricade ourselves inside. If they do break down the front door we'll throw pots of scalding water on them. That should slow them down! Now let's get to work and bring in all the water we can."

The rest of the day went by in a flurry. Men ran in and out of the kitchen constantly. Immediately after supper, Eliezer, Zipporah, baby Esther, and I were taken outside to the garden by Herman's wife, Tamara. She placed some blankets under the large, spreading oak tree at the far end of the garden. "Lie down and try to go to sleep," she said. "Would you like me to sing to you? It's a lovely evening—I'll sing you a song about the evening." She sang to us there under the tree, a slow, quiet song about the setting of the sun over the still meadows.

I had no intention of falling asleep. Eliezer and Zipporah were sprawled next to me on one blanket and Tamara was curled around the baby on another, all sound asleep, their heavy, peaceful breathing mingling with the rustling of the leaves in the cool night wind. If only I could see something! All the lights inside the house had been turned off to make it appear as if everyone were in bed asleep. The only light still burning was the one outside the front door, as it was controlled by a switch at the mill and turned off automatically at midnight.

Hour after hour went by as I watched that light flickering hesitantly in the darkness. Sometimes I thought it had stopped shining altogether, but then it would appear again from behind a cluster of leaves swaying in the breeze. Finally, I decided that I could not stay away any longer. Very quietly I crawled off the blanket while everyone slept on peacefully.

Quickly, I ran out of the garden and down to the house. Everything was still; even the crickets on the lawn had stopped their chirping. Then a terrifying thought overcame me: The students had come in through a back window and taken everyone by surprise. Everyone inside was dead! Frantically, I reached for the door latch, but it was high above my outstretched arm. With little leaps I jumped up and down on the porch, my hand thumping against the door with each try.

Suddenly, the door opened inward. In the instant it took me to fall across the doorsill I saw a huge, steaming kettle of water poised above my head.

"Stop! Stop! Don't throw it!" yelled my brother Meyer. It's Seren."

"Seren!" shouted my father. "What on earth are you doing here? Why didn't you stay in the garden like you were told? You could have been scalded if the porch light hadn't been on!"

He pulled me inside. While they were relieved that it was only me, they did not give up their vigil. The rest of the night was spent keeping watch while I slept peacefully in my bed. Once I awoke with a start, thinking, *My doll! She's still in the tree!* Just as suddenly I fell asleep again. The students never came, but later we heard that they had totally destroyed a nearby village heavily populated by Jews that very same night.

ALL DURING THE REMAINDER OF THAT YEAR I thought, *Only one more year and I will be able to go to school in Fulehaza!* The thought of leaving my mother and being with other, strange children all day frightened me somewhat. But I could not wait to learn as much as possible about everything there was to know.

When I was eight, my mother finally allowed me to go to school. Before then she thought I was too small. But now I eagerly joined Eliezer in his four-kilometer walk.

Finally, one crisp fall morning in 1926, we started off for the village school together. "What is the teacher like?" I said. "Is he terribly strict?"

After what seemed forever, Eliezer answered in his slow, quiet voice, "He's all right."

"How are the other children?" I asked. "Are they friendly?"

Again he hesitated, this time for longer. "They're . . . You'll see." So much for him. I would soon be at school myself and see everything at last.

When we reached the one-room school the other children were playing in the schoolyard. I recognized five or six girls and boys from temple. They were several years older than I was, so I did not walk up to them. All of the other students were children of either the Romanian or the Hungarian peasants living in the foothills of the mountains. One peasant girl stuck out her tongue at me when I walked by her. *I wonder why she did that,* I thought. *She doesn't even know me.* I decided to ignore her. Soon the children began to file into the school. I followed behind, sliding into a wooden bench by a long table near the back of the room.

I looked around the room. Across the entire front was a raised platform, and above it, a large wooden cross with a plaster man hanging from it. He looked lifeless and had barely any clothes on. *Why do they have a dead man for us to look at?* I wondered. In front of me stretched other rows of benches and tables.

As I was counting them, a man in a long, black robe wearing what looked like several necklaces around his neck came out of the side door in the front of the room and strode to the platform. "Silence!" he shouted. I immediately pressed my lips together so I would not even think of talking. The teacher was very thin and pale. I hoped that he would like me.

After he had taken down our names and told us how much money to bring for our books, the teacher began the first class of the day. "How many of you remembered to bring your Bibles with you today?" he asked. About half of the children raised their hands. "Good. At least not all of you are idiots. We will begin," he continued, "by turning to the first chapter of Corinthians, verses twenty-two and twenty-three."

He went on with what I came to understand was religion class. The other Jewish children and I were required to sit through an hour of this class every day, although we did not have to participate.

School was far less exciting than I had thought it would be. The other young children and I were placed in the front row, the ones a year older directly behind us, and so on to the back of the room. Then we began our regular lessons of math, history, reading, and geography, the teacher moving from one age group to another all day long.

Finally, after I thought the first day would never end, we were excused. When I got outside a group of peasant boys in torn, muddy clothes were waiting at the end of the schoolyard. "Stinkin' Jew!" they yelled at me. "Dirty, stinkin' Jew!" They ran off laughing. I hurried to catch up with Eliezer but he was far ahead of me, and I barely kept him in sight all the way home.

As soon as I entered the house I lifted up the hem of my dress and began to smell it, next sniffing my sleeves. The clean, cool odors of sky and rain were embedded in the fabric, lingering from the day the dress was washed and dried on the river's shore.

My mother came into the room. "Seren, you're home!" she said. Then she paused, watching me. "What in heaven's name are you doing?"

"Do my clothes smell bad?" I asked.

"How can they smell bad? You just put on a clean dress this morning."

"Some of the peasant children called me a 'stinkin' Jew.'"

"Oh, that," she answered with a wave. "Don't even listen to it. It's nothing. Here, sit down and have a snack and then off you go to the Hebrew school."

I did as I was told and joined the other seven or eight Jewish children whose fathers worked at the mill. The families had hired a Hebrew teacher for us, and the mill provided a room. We went there immediately after breakfast to say our morning prayers before going to school in the village. After school we went again, to learn how to read and write in Hebrew and to study the Torah.

For weeks at a time the same group of large, rowdy peasant boys followed Eliezer and me home, taunting us all the way. I grew to dread even the sight of them. Then one day in spring none of the boys appeared at school. I could not believe our good luck. "Where do you think those boys have gone?" I finally asked Eliezer.

"I think they have to work in the fields," he answered. "It's spring planting time."

"Then they'll be gone until next year!" I said.

While this source of torment vanished every spring and sometimes in the fall during harvest time, the rantings of our priest teacher never ceased. We were required to attend school every single day, even on Saturday. If we stayed home to celebrate our Sabbath on Saturday we were marked absent and given failing marks in all of our subjects for that day. Often we went to school on Shabbat to avoid the teacher's wrath, even though we could do no writing, as all work is forbidden on Shabbat. If a Jewish holiday such as Rosh Hashanah or Yom Kippur occurred, the rabbi went to the school to petition for us to be excused for that particular day. I remember seeing the rabbi marching out of the classroom in anger, his robes flapping noisily, while the priest stood firm almost without exception.

On Sundays the other children and I congregated in the schoolroom in the morning and then went as a group to church. I did not mind the singing and chanting, but I did not like the container which hung on a long golden chain and held a strongly scented substance. The priest swung it back and forth as he walked down the aisle to the front of the church, often aiming it in my direction. The odor always gave me a headache.

When the sermon began, the priest would look directly into the eyes of one of the peasant farmers sitting with his wife. She wore only a very thin, faded, cotton dress even in the middle of winter. "Do you ever wonder why your life is so hard?" the priest would ask. "Do you ever wonder why you never seem to have enough food, why you have to sell all of your grain for very little money and live on cornmeal? Why you work from before sunrise until after dark and can still barely maintain your simple, cold huts? Why only one or two of your many children have warm shoes for the winter? I am sure you wonder how God can be so unmindful of you, how He can let you live in such conditions with no hope for the future. Well, let me assure you that God is blameless. He has been bountiful in His blessings. Praise ye the Lord! The blame for your sufferings can all be placed on the killers of Christ, the Jews!"

He pronounced "Jews" as if the word were a synonym for snake. This is exactly how he made me feel—like a snake, like the serpent in the story of Adam and Eve. I wanted to crawl under the pew and hide there until it was time to go home. I did not want anyone to look at my clean, warm clothing and then compare it to the torn dress of the peasant girl sitting beside me.

A year later Zipporah joined us. One day in the late fall when we were on our way home, we came to the long bridge spanning the river between the village and our house. Since we had not so much as glimpsed the gang that day, we felt that we were safe. Then we saw them: four rough-looking, rowdy boys standing right in the middle of the bridge. For an instant we started to back away. Then, as if each of us had decided at the same moment, we walked out on the bridge directly up to the boys. Quickly we took our book bags off our backs, placed them on the bridge floor, and stood with legs far apart and hands up, ready for anything.

The boys looked at us for a moment or two with sneers on their faces. Then one of them said, "Dirty J—" Before he could finish the phrase Eliezer slammed the side of the boy's face with his fist. Immediately I began to pummel another boy with my hands. Luckily, I had spotted one as small as I was, so I had no difficulty in reaching his ears, which I hit as hard as I could. Zipporah had on her good thick boots, so she began to kick out with them, hitting one boy in the knee, another in the legs.

"Oh! Stop! Ow! Ow!" the boy I was hitting began to yell. I stopped hitting him just long enough to see my book bag and all my books go sailing over the railing of the bridge and into the fast-moving river below. *My books!* I thought. *Oh, my books!* I decided to worry about them later and started attacking the boy once more, hitting him so hard that my hands stung. In another moment or two the four of them took off at a fast run and rapidly disappeared down a path at the other end of the bridge. We could not believe it. We had won!

When we arrived home, one look at our disheveled clothes and bloody faces was more than enough evidence to give us away. My mother quickly shepherded us to the basin to wash off the blood and dirt, but my father said very little. Yet I could tell that he was secretly pleased that we had successfully defended ourselves. When I asked him the next morning for money to replace the books I had lost, he gave it to me without any hesitation, even though it was all the money he had in his pocket.

However, when I tried to give the money to the teacher the next morning, he looked at me with narrowed eyes and said, "You may not buy books during the school year, only at the beginning of the term. Perhaps that will teach you to be more careful!" The rest of the whole year I went without books. But, that group of boys never bothered us again.

Three

THE SPRING OF MY ELEVENTH YEAR, THE LAST ONE
our family spent at the mill near the little village of Fulehaza, was ushered
in by a swelling, raging river. As Passover was near, our house was filled
with all the married children and their families. On the second morning of
the Seder we looked out and found that our house had become an island. A
week of warm weather followed by heavy rains had washed the melting
snow down out of the mountains in a rush.

We ran from window to window, looking out at the gray, muddy water. Zipporah and I stood at the front windows staring at the trees protruding from the water, fallen twigs and leaves swirling around their trunks.
Suddenly our geese swam by.

"Look!" I said. "They love it! Don't you wish you were a goose now? I do!"

"You *are* a goose!" she said, running from the window.

"You're an old cow!" I yelled, but she was already in the next room and
pretended not to hear me.

Then Esther, four years old at the time and the adored baby of the family with her long blond curls, came running up to me. "Come and see!" she said. "Houses are on the river."

We ran to the back of the house, to my mother and father's room facing the river. My older half sisters were all around the back window, crowded together.

"Look at that hut over there!" said Berta. "A man and a woman are sitting on the roof! I hope they don't fall in." I tried squeezing into one place first and then another, but no one would let me see.

"There's a chicken house going by!" said Rose. "The chickens are still in it!"

"Oh, I see it!" said Tamara. "Can't you imagine the eggs rolling around all over inside."

I tried jumping like Esther; our two heads bobbed up and down, up and down, behind our tall sisters.

"Do you see that?" Louise asked then in an incredulous tone. That did it. I took Esther by the hand, and we got on our hands and knees and soon wiggled our way to the window. Getting up on our knees slowly so no one would notice us, we drew away the lower curtains and looked at last. All across the muddy plain of water were whole households being swept quickly downstream.

As soon as one little hut with several people on its roof went by, it was followed by a barn turned on its side and then a shed bobbing up and down in the current. In between all of the huts and coops and barns, the horses and cows desperately swimming along, were enormous chunks of ice broken loose from the glacier fields high up in the mountains. I stared at it for a long time, hypnotized. One morning you woke up and the quiet, peaceful life you knew had changed overnight.

AS THE DEPRESSION SPREAD ACROSS ROMANIA IN 1929, the huge lumber company that owned the mill my father managed, as well as most of the other mills in the country, began closing down individual mills. At my father's mill, men were dismissed from their jobs, one by one, until finally the mill was shut down completely.

But soon came good news that the lumber company so valued my father's expertise that they were transferring him to a new, modern mill located about a hundred and fifty kilometers north of us in the village of Lunca de Mijloc, "the field in the middle." I wondered what it would be like, this middle field. Were there no mountains there, only fields? Would our house be as pleasant as the one we were leaving by the river I so loved?

As soon as we arrived at the village I knew that although I would miss Fulehaza, I would like living in Lunca de Mijloc very much. It was a bigger village, lying in a broad plain between two mountain ranges. We had piled all of our belongings onto a train, climbed aboard, and ridden to the new village. When we arrived at our house we began walking behind my father around the huge yard. He pointed to all the apple and pear trees, to the wide garden plot, to the nearby houses. As the mill was on the edge of the village, we were going to live in town and I would not have to walk a long way to school.

On the first day of school I was surprised at how our teacher smiled and welcomed us. *Could this be our regular teacher?* I wondered. *He is too young,* I decided, *and the real teacher will be back tomorrow.* The next day, however, the young man was there again and every day after that. His kindness and enthusiasm seemed to affect the children as well, for no one tormented us. After school one day several girls came up to me. One asked me my name.

"My name is Seren Tuvel," I said. "What is yours?"

"Annie Lietze," she answered. "Where do you live?"

"At the edge of the village near the mill. My father is the manager there. He's an expert!"

"That's a Jew mill," she said. " Isn't it?"

I looked down at my brown leather shoes.

"Isn't it?" she repeated.

"Yes," I answered, looking up at her.

"You couldn't be a Jew," Annie continued. "You have blond hair and blue eyes. You don't look a bit like the dirty Jews. Anyway, Tuvel isn't a Jew name. Say you're not a dirty Jew and I'll be your friend."

I looked at her for a few minutes. She was pretty and always surrounded by friends. I would have liked to be included in her group.

"Say you're not a Jew!" Annie repeated.

I turned away.

"Come on," she said to her friends. "Who needs a stinkin' Jew?"

They walked to the other end of the schoolyard, calling back again and again, "Dirty Jew . . . Dirty Jew . . . Dirty Jew . . ."

Since I still had no friends I studied harder, finding school both exciting and interesting. I finished the third grade with high marks and continued to do well in the fourth grade as we studied such difficult subjects as algebra and German. Romanian history was equally hard; there were hundreds of lesser kings who fought many big wars and we were required to know which king went with which war. We also studied the history of every other nation in the world, especially the United States. I learned about the Mississippi River, about the huge cities and the towns, about how the people worked hard to make it a good country, but I also read *Uncle Tom's Cabin* and cried over it. The United States sounded like a place one might wish to visit. As for me, I would be happy to live in Transylvania forever.

Especially exciting about that year was the contest in the spring. Each year every school in Transylvania was required to send the fourth-grader with the best grades to the provincial capital, Tirgu-Mures, for a chance to win a scholarship to the gymnasium in Bucharest. I was immensely interested, for at the end of the fourth grade every student had to decide between advancing to the gymnasium in the city or staying in the village school for three more years. If you wanted a basic education, you remained in the village school to obtain the equivalent of a high school degree; our schools were very difficult and one could learn there in seven years what a child learns today in twelve. If you wanted to obtain a college education, however, you left home at the end of the fourth grade and attended the gymnasium. No one in our family had ever done so. My older brothers were very content to complete the seven grades and then work in a mill like our father or in some other business. My older sisters thought only of marriage and children. Perhaps Berta would have entered a scholarly profession had she lived in another time, but she did not.

I knew that my father would not approve. *Well,* I decided, *if I do obtain the scholarship perhaps he will change his mind and let me go. I'll worry about that later.*

Finally the morning came when the teacher, Mr. Tepes, was to announce who was eligible for the contest. I ran to school as fast as I could. It seemed that Mr. Tepes smiled especially at me. *Perhaps he's feeling sorry for me,* I thought, *and that's why he's being friendly.* After he had rung the bell for order, Mr. Tepes said, "I have decided who will enter the contest at Tirgu-Mures. Seren," he said, looking at me. "No other student's grades even came close to yours. You will go." My heart almost jumped out of my chest. "See me after classes, Seren," he continued, and then we began our lessons.

Slowly the rest of the school day passed and then Mr. Tepes and I sat down together after the other children had gone home. He explained to me how this was only his second year of teaching and how he wanted his students to excel. By choosing me, he felt, our school would have a very good chance of obtaining the honor of one of its students winning the scholarship.

"Now, we will hope for two things," he continued. "One, you will try as hard in the contest as you do here in school. And two, you will look so much like a little Romanian girl with your blond hair and blue eyes, especially since you will be wearing the national costume, that no one will even think to ask you about your nationality. You see, the scholarship has never been given to a Jewish student." He paused, smiling at me. "I know you'll do well."

I went home on wings! I could not wait to tell my mother. She became very excited when I explained everything about the contest and began immediately to wash and press the costume. My father, as always, was more reserved. His attitude was: Let her go through with this foolishness and when it is over and she has not won, she will forget about the business of going away to school.

ON THE DAY OF THE CONTEST MR. TEPES AND HIS wife came to our house early in the morning to take me to Tirgu-Mures. My mother had risen before dawn to fix me a hot breakfast, but I could not eat. I was not worried about the contest; I was fairly certain that I would do well. Still, it was an important day and I wanted to make sure that I was as prepared as possible.

"Let me take a look at you," my mother said as I twirled around the kitchen with a little flourish, the short, embroidered black aprons at the front and back of my skirt whirling out around me. The bright blue and red flowers embroidered all along the neck and sleeves of my white blouse were my favorite part of the outfit. On every national holiday I wore this costume and marched in a parade with the other schoolchildren. I felt honored that I could wear my costume today while the others could not.

"Ah . . ." my mother said with a smile. "You look wonderful!" Then she kissed me good-bye and Mr. Tepes and his wife and I walked to the train station.

The contest lasted for three days and consisted of written examinations in math, Romanian history, world geography, religion, reading, and the language one had studied, either French or German. I worked quickly through all of the algebra problems first, checked my answers, and then sat back to look around the room. The other contestants, mostly peasant boys, were still working, heads down, pencils scribbling furiously, eyes squinting. I wondered how they had learned anything when they missed so much school during planting and harvest times.

At the end of the first day one of the examiners told each of us in which home we would spend the night. When he read my name and the name of the local family I would stay with, Mr. Tepes ran up to me and whispered, "No, you will stay here with my wife. I'm afraid you will forget and let slip that you're Jewish." I nodded yes, even though I did not see where we would sleep.

That night we stretched out on the hard benches. Mrs. Tepes did not seem very comfortable, but in the morning she amused herself by arranging my long hair first one way and then another. She was our embroidery teacher in school and had often combed my hair when the lesson was completed. Blond, wavy hair was uncommon in our area, so I often attracted attention.

One day followed another, and we were told that the winner would be notified as soon as all the tests were scored. There was nothing to do but return home. Every day I ran to school and asked Mr. Tepes before the first class, "Did you find out who won the contest?" and every day he answered, "No, but I'll tell you as soon as I do." A second week went by but now I did not ask every day, only every other day. Finally, I decided that I had not won and so I would forget about the contest altogether.

Then one day, after we had settled into our seats, Mr. Tepes said, "I have just received word about the winner of the fourth grade contest held last month."

I looked up. *One of the peasant boys must have won it after all,* I thought.

"The winner is very lucky," he continued. "She will be able to attend the gymnasium with paid tuition and board."

So it is a girl! I thought. I could remember only two other girls at the contest and wondered which one was the winner.

"She has brought a great deal of honor to our school," the teacher said. "The winner is none other than our very own Seren!"

The class started clapping while I sat there with cheeks blazing. *Can it be possible? What will my father say? Surely he will be as happy for me.*

As soon as I arrived home I ran to my mother in the garden and told her the good news. While she was still hugging me, I asked, "Will Father let me go? I want to so much!"

"Well, why don't you ask him after he has had supper and is in a good mood," she answered. "He always feels better with his stomach full."

That night I picked at my food, waiting for the meal to end. Finally, my father put down his knife and fork and sat quietly with his hands folded and resting on the table. I looked at my mother. She nodded.

"Father," I began softly.

"Speak up!" he answered. "What is it?"

"I won the contest at Tirgu-Mures. I have been given a full scholarship at the gymnasium."

"What?" he exploded. "You are not going to take it! Going to the city for a contest is one thing. Leaving home to live in Bucharest is another. You will not go!"

My heart sank. So it had all been for nothing. Then my mother said gently, "It's a great opportunity for Seren. She's a very intelligent child and has always done well in school."

"Then she already knows everything she needs to know!" he shouted. "If she's so smart she should quit school altogether. An education is wasted on a girl. Let a boy take her place. She can stay home and learn what she really needs to know—how to make a decent meal. I'm sure that's something she doesn't know, does she?"

"She'll learn those things in time," my mother answered, even though she knew that while I loved to eat I could not even make tea.

"Even if she did go, how would she eat?" my father continued. "There won't be any kosher food. If we had another name besides Tuvel they would have known that she's Jewish and wouldn't have given her the scholarship in the first place. I suppose they can't take it back now, but they certainly will not see to it that she's given kosher food. No, she can't go. I will not discuss it again!"

I returned to school, utterly discouraged. During the few remaining weeks of that year and all during the next fall, I tried to put my heart back into my studies. Each day we went over material that I had taught myself months ago, having read every book I could find. Finally, as the year drew to a close, I decided that there was nothing more that this school could teach me and that I deserved to attend the gymnasium. I had won the scholarship. I would go.

My announcement was met with great anger by my father. He told me that not only would I be defiling my body by eating the nonkosher food at the school but I would be very disappointed if, by some miracle, I did manage to graduate. Since the scholarship was for training to become a teacher, and teachers were state employees, they could be sent wherever the government chose. The few Jewish students who had graduated from the program had been sent to the most remote village schools that could be found. "Who knows what happens to them!" my father said repeatedly. He did not change my mind. I simply knew that I had to learn, to become as educated as possible.

So, in the late fall of 1931, when I was thirteen years old, I walked alone to the train station one morning. I had already said good-bye to my mother while she was busy preparing breakfast for my father. "Come home as often as you can," she told me over and over.

"I will," I promised her.

"If she does *you* can talk to her," my father said to my mother from his place at the table. "I will have nothing more to do with her!"

MY FIRST LOOK AT THE GYMNASIUM FILLED ME WITH great hope. It was a large building with separate rooms for each class and different teachers for each subject; the girls' and boys' dormitories were nearby. I was given a clean room to myself and told when meals would be served in the cafeteria. I knew I would not starve. I was sure I could survive on my own; I felt a new strength inside.

The next day when classes began I received the first disappointment: I was the sole Jewish girl in the entire school. The one other Jewish student was a boy who did not even acknowledge my presence. I probably would have no friends.

My second disappointment came during religion class. For the other classes we had regular teachers like Mr. Tepes, but religion was taught by an elderly priest. Every day he told us how all Jews were thieves and murderers. He would point to a passage in the Bible and say, "Now this is when the Jews killed Jesus!" He knew that the one boy and I were Jewish, but he did not change his lectures because of us; he would have said the same things had we not been there. I sat there in the front row listening to him week after week, wondering how much longer I could endure it.

One day, two months later, the priest began his class by saying, "I want all of you to be very careful tonight! Passover begins tomorrow and we all know that the evil Jews use Gentile blood to make their matzos. Whatever you do, do not go near any Jews tonight. They will kill you!"

Suddenly I was standing up. Then I was grabbing the inkwell from my desk. I watched myself fling it at the priest. It thudded against the board, and ink splattered all across it and then onto the priest's robe in long, black, quite satisfying splashes. I turned, walked out of the classroom and out of the school into the next stage of my life.

Part Two

A sewing society of Romanian Jewish girls, 1936.
(From the archives of the YIVO Institute for Jewish Research.)

Four

I KNEW THAT I WOULD NEVER RETURN TO THE school. In my dormitory room, I gathered my clothes together, hurriedly threw them into a suitcase, and walked to the center of Bucharest. Going back home never entered my mind. The village school had no more to offer me and I could not bear the thought of drinking tea and embroidering linens while waiting for the perfect young man to come along and ask me to marry him. I felt peculiarly exhilarated. Here I was in the capital city of Romania, in "Little Paris," a large city with wide, cobbled streets set in the middle of a lake-studded plain, and I was on my own.

The idea of becoming a dressmaker's apprentice took form in my mind as I began walking down the central streets. I had always loved to make things out of cloth. I wandered first up the street of the cap-makers, Sepcari, and then down Blanari, the street of the furriers. Through the windows I could see the well-dressed customers who frequented them talking animatedly with the owners. My older sisters had talked about how fashionable Bucharest was, and now I was actually seeing elegant ladies ordering their winter coats, their black limousines waiting at the curbs.

Turning the corner and coming onto Strada Domneascu, I saw what must be one of the largest dressmaking salons in the city. It was the middle of the day and apprentices were streaming out the doors, the girls looked to be about thirteen or fourteen years old. They were probably hurrying home for the noon meal. I counted ten of them and knew I had come to the right salon—one large enough to take on another apprentice. While the young men in the cities were expected to continue their education, most young women engaged themselves as apprentices in one trade or another. In small villages this was not so, as working was considered unsuitable for young ladies. None of my older sisters had left home to work, nor had I heard of any other girl from my village doing so. *I will be the first!* I decided.

The owner of the salon, a tall, large-framed woman who towered over me, must have spotted me immediately for who I was, a naive and foolish young girl, for she walked up to me and asked, "Have you come to engage yourself as an apprentice in *my* salon?"

"Yes, if you can use me," I said, with a catch in my voice that surprised me.

"Have you run away from home?" she asked then, looking at the suitcase sitting on the floor beside me.

"No," I answered. "My parents know that I'm here. I'm from the village of Lunca de Mijloc."

"How hard can you work?" she asked.

"Very hard," I answered. "I have been sewing since I was four."

"Well, an apprentice does not even pick up a needle during the first year!" she said. "If I take you on, you will receive room and board with me in exchange for whatever work I need done around the shop or upstairs where I live. This will include sweeping and scrubbing the floors, delivering garments throughout the city, waiting on the seamstresses, running errands, and any other jobs I might need done. During the second year you will begin to work on the garments. At the end of that year, if you pass the examination, you will acquire a license. Only at that point will you start receiving pay. Are you willing to do this? I can only use good workers."

"Yes," I answered quickly, before I could change my mind.

"Fine. I want you to sign an apprenticeship contract. This is recognized by the government and is an official document. Do not commit yourself if you are not positive you can last two years."

"I am sure," I said, and signed the contract carefully.

"Come upstairs," she said. "I'll show you the room you will have. There is one other girl who is from a village and lives above the shop with me. Then we'll have something to eat, come back down, and get to work."

The rest of the day passed quickly. The other new apprentices and I all worked in the back room with the beginning seamstresses. They, of course, enjoyed telling us what to do, as they had only recently graduated from being first-year apprentices themselves. I spent most of the afternoon sweeping the floor, but I did not mind. Bits and pieces of colored fabrics—blue silks, soft, gray flannels, bright plaids—lightly littered the floor, and I kept thinking, *In a year I will be allowed to work with these fine materials too!*

I came to enjoy working at the salon very much. The other girls were friendly and while our employer, the owner, was demanding, she was a good businesswoman and as fair as any other salon owner. We had no fixed hours. If it was a busy time of year, as in the beginning of spring, when all of the clientele were demanding that their summer dresses be finished by May, we worked from six-thirty or seven o'clock in the morning until late in the evening. As I got to know the streets of Bucharest, I was sent out more and more to buy notions or to deliver a finished dress. The first time I carried a beautiful gown to the door of a very expensive home, I thought, *How nice to walk through such fashionable streets.* When the lady of the house came to the door she smiled and said, *"Merci."* Most of the upper class spoke French, I came to learn. As I turned to go she held out her hand and placed several coins into mine. A tip! I was to have money of my own even before my apprenticeship was over.

As my tips accumulated I learned how pleasurable it is to make money of one's own and then to spend it as one pleases. Dress in Bucharest was very formal in 1931; a young woman never went without gloves, a hat, and proper shoes. The first things I purchased were a beret like the ones all the other girls wore, fine leather gloves, and a pair of pumps with straps and thin, high heels. Later I bought a bright red dress with a wide collar and narrow detachable sleeves that buttoned on like gloves under the regular sleeves. As I grew older, I wore that dress many times to dances and dinners. Once, years later, I had my photograph taken while wearing it. I loved that dress.

BEFORE I REALIZED IT, SPRING HAD SLIPPED AWAY. Working at the salon was in some ways like being in school; we could have the whole summer free if we wanted it, since business was slack during these months: most of the clients spent the summer in resorts somewhere in the Carpathian Mountains. I wanted to go home, of course, as all my older sisters and brothers brought their families and visited all summer long. My mother and father still believed that I was at the gymnasium. I would visit them as if I were on summer vacation like all the other students.

When I arrived home after the long trip, Miksha and Ernie, Herman's sons, ran up to meet me as I climbed down from the train.

I quickly fell into the daily joys of working in the garden beside my mother, picking tomatoes and beans and peas, and listening in the kitchen to the babble of Herman and Tamara, Louise and Bela, Rose and her husband, Eugene; and Berta and her husband, Morris, all trying to talk at once while the children ran in and out among them. Each one asked me about my studies in the manner of all relatives. "How's school?" Eugene might ask, noticing me sitting nearby.

"Fine," I would answer.

"Are you learning everything?"

"Yes."

"Well, that's good!"

When the next relative came home we went through the same routine. Otherwise school was forgotten. My father normally would have asked to see my report card, but since I had disobeyed him by leaving home, he showed no interest in me whatsoever.

Too soon summer was over and I began making plans to return to

Bucharest. While my father had not said more than a word or two to me all the while I was home, he now took a sudden interest in me again.

"You are home. Stay home!" he said one evening after supper.

"I'm sorry, Father. I can't," I answered.

"Are you too good for us then? Is that it? You have been to the gymnasium, so now you can't live with us anymore. Isn't that right?"

I did not know how to answer him. I was not even in school. If I had been I certainly would never have considered myself superior to my father, who could speak seven languages, but I did not know how to tell him that.

"'Sharper than a serpent's tooth is an ungrateful child,'" he said then, very softly. I almost ran to him and told him everything, but I knew I would be losing my chance to learn and to be on my own if I did. I turned, walked out of the room with a heavy heart, and went to my room to pack.

WHEN I RETURNED TO THE SALON I TOOK UP MY DU-ties once again. By now I recognized most of the clients and enjoyed watching them being measured for a new dress. My favorite ones were those from the court of King Carol II, the son of King Ferdinand. Carol II had been next in line after Ferdinand, but several years earlier he had fallen in love with a half-Jewish woman, Madame Lupescu, and renounced the throne to be with her. Carol's son had taken his place. In 1930, however, Carol had returned, deposed his son with the support of the National Peasant Party, and proclaimed himself king.

We were called to the palace for a fitting quite frequently. Perhaps Queen Mother Mary needed an elegant dress for an elaborate state dinner or Elizabeth, the king's sister, desired a new gown for a ball. Then the owner of the shop would gather up the latest designs from Paris as well as boxes of silks, laces, and ribbons, and she and I would go to the royal palace. It was my job to carry the boxes.

On arrival at the palace we were ushered into a room reserved for sewing. There I laid out all the fabrics in glossy piles on the floor and hung up the sample dresses and gowns. Mary and Elizabeth would each choose a style, then the fabric from which it would be made, and finally climb up on stools to be measured and pinned. I was also in charge of the pins, making sure they were plentiful and nearby when needed. Then we went back to the salon, the royal family satisfied that no other women would appear at a state function with dresses as lovely as theirs. The salon followed a strict code of fashion: Each gown must be unique. Every customer was thus assured the attention which was given to her simply because she wore a gown different from all the other new gowns.

The fall and winter went by peacefully and quickly, and soon my first year of apprenticeship was at an end. The other girls and I began sewing under the watchful eyes of the licensed seamstresses. At first we were not given the dresses of the most exclusive clients like the royal family or the wives of foreign diplomats, but we did advance our skills little by little. I discovered that I could sew quite easily and soon felt so confident that I decided to make matching dresses for my mother and me.

On a weekend when I went home for a visit I took along a length of brown-and-white-checked flannel. I told my mother that I was learning to sew at school, which was the truth but not in the way she thought, and asked her to climb up on a stool so I could pin the fabric around her.

"I feel quite fortunate," she said with a little laugh. "My daughter is going to make a dress for me!" My heart seemed to constrict a little in my chest; I loved my mother so.

"I'm going to make one for me too," I said. "Then we'll have mother-and-daughter dresses."

"How nice!" my mother said. "What are they wearing now in Bucharest? Do you ever see any fashionable ladies?"

"Oh, yes, once in a while," I answered. "Some of the women love to wear draped dresses. They come up in a sweep from the hem to the shoulder and are very beautiful. I saw Princess Elizabeth in a dress like that."

"Oh, you've seen her? Was she visiting the gymnasium?

"I'm not sure where I saw her. You should see all the tiny waists!" I quickly went on. "Many of the girls wear dresses with padded shoulders that slim down to a very small waist. They are so thin!" I thought of how my employer often called me into her dressing room to lace her corset. I had to put my knee in her back and pull as hard as I could to draw the laces of her thick corset together. The memory of my struggle with the hooks made me laugh aloud.

"Are you laughing at me?" my mother asked.

"No, no," I said. "I was thinking of the stiff corsets some women must wear."

"Well, I am small, thank goodness," said my mother. "How could I wear such a girdle and still do my cooking and cleaning?"

AS SOON AS I RETURNED TO BUCHAREST, I BEGAN sewing on our dresses in the evenings. I began with my mother's dress, as I wanted to give it to her when I returned home in June. Everything went well until I started the sleeves. They were pleated at the top, and I simply could not make the pleats correctly. I tried again and again, pushing the sleeves higher each time, until finally they fit into the armholes. When I had sewed them in, I realized that the change in the sleeves had made the shoulders much smaller than they should have been—only several inches across in all. *Perhaps it will be all right,* I thought, and quickly finished the dress and my own as well.

The other apprentices and I finished our spring orders, business waned once again, and I was free. I had the summer all planned: I would stay with my parents for a month and then visit Meyer and Lottie, who had married during the past year and were living in Galati.

As soon as I arrived home I unpacked my suitcase and showed the matching dresses to my mother. She was very pleased and decided to try on hers immediately, even though she was in the middle of making challah for Shabbat. As soon as she came back into the kitchen I saw how badly the shoulders fit. *The dress is a complete failure,* I thought. *How foolish of me to think I could sew!*

"It's beautiful!" my mother said, turning around in a little twirl. "I love the checks. Oh, but I've dusted flour all over the skirt." She began brushing it off impatiently. I started to help, brushing her off in the back, when she turned to hug me. "Thank you, Seren," she said. "I'll wear the dress to temple tomorrow."

She did wear the dress the next day, mistakes and all, and many times after that. I never loved her more than when I saw her in that dress with the narrow little shoulders and the high, flapping sleeves.

IN THAT SPRING OF 1933, IMMEDIATELY AFTER MY FIF-teenth birthday, I finished my two-year apprenticeship, passed an examination, and became a licensed dressmaker. At last I began to receive a regular salary and could move out of my employer's house and into a room of my own. I found one with a pleasant Gentile family but I did not stay there a great deal, only in the early mornings before work and in the evenings. At the salon I made a number of friends and these girls invited me into their homes on the weekends.

It was awesome to have such freedom, to come and go as I liked, to be able to buy things with my salary. I began to think of what presents I would like to bring home to my parents and decided on a lace shawl for my mother and a blue silk tie for my father. While I had told my mother about working in the salon after I made the dress for her, my father still thought I was enrolled at the gymnasium. Now that I was making a salary and living by myself I felt it was time to tell him as well. I would give him the tie and say, "Father, I bought this for you with money I earned myself!" Hopefully, the gift would detract from the disgrace of having a daughter of his leave home to work rather than to marry.

The plan failed completely. When I made my little speech and gave my father the gift he opened it, glanced at the tie folded neatly in the tissue paper, and set the box down again without saying a word. He did not even raise his eyes to mine. Then he went outside, slamming the door behind him. The box was left lying on the table like a foolish trifle.

A week later my father came into the yard to see if we were ready to leave on a trip to visit Herman and Tamara. He was wearing the tie. The rich, blue fabric against his white shirt brought out the color of his eyes, deep like a summer sky. "You look very handsome today," my mother said, brushing a speck of lint from his shoulder. He said nothing, as always when anyone complimented him, but he looked quickly at me to see if I had noticed. I looked back, smiling. After that he wore the tie often.

The following year my parents moved again to what would be our last home. It was there that my father was arrested, there that my mother was forced to abandon everything forever. Perhaps it would have been easier to leave a place not so beautiful, not so green and lush, that sometimes, when I lay down among the tall grasses beside the spring and watched the clouds drift, like transparent shadows, across the tree-lined ridge, I thought that the Garden of Eden could not have been fairer.

The village was Valea Uzului, in the valley of the Uz, spread along the banks of a river so wide and clear that one could see all the smooth stones at the bottom of the riverbed. High up in the Carpathian Mountains above the village, twenty-four kilometers high, a wealthy Jewish baron had found a medieval castle. This baron had formerly lived in Germany but fled in 1930 when it was becoming apparent that anti-Semitism was increasing. He built a lumber mill high up on the mountain above the village, converted the castle into a home, and created a paradise for himself. At that time he felt secure, as did most Romanian Jews, who could not believe that what was happening so far away in Germany could ever affect them here. While I had seen the new Iron Guard party parading through the streets of Bucharest, this remote village seemed safe to me as well.

The baron offered my father a job in 1934 as manager of the mill. My family was overjoyed. One by one, most of the other mills in Transylvania were closing down, still suffering the effects of the depression, and my father's old job could have been lost at any time. This new mill was very modern and large, employing approximately fifteen hundred men, but it had very few families. Most of its employees were single men who worked at the mill for two or three years, saved their money, and then went back to their homes.

I could not wait to visit my parents' new home. My mother had described all of the modern equipment at the mill—huge electric saws that whirred all day long. "We have not told anyone here that you are working as a dressmaker," she also wrote. "Could you please your father in this one thing and not tell anyone? Your job is a great source of embarrassment to him. I know that he is very old-fashioned about women working, but this is the way he is. He feels it is his responsibility to provide for his family."

Ah, Father, I thought. *I will not betray you.*

That summer I took the train north from Bucharest and then west to Valea Uzului on the far western edge of the Carpathians. Once at the village, I changed trains, boarding a small lumber train that ran from there up to the mill and back again. The steam engine slowly chugged up the steep grade, curving round the slender pines gracing the mountainside and reaching up high above us. After several miles we came into a clearing and there was the castle, towering above the forests exactly like one in a fairy tale, exquisite gardens of flowers and shrubs growing all around it. Rounding a curve, we came upon another delight—a tiny wooden hunting chapel almost hidden beneath the trees. I knew I would come back to see everything again and again, and I did, especially the chapel. All along the inside walls were the most beautiful paintings I have ever seen. Their brilliant colors glowed when I sat staring at them on quiet afternoons, the sun filtering through the narrow windows in long shafts. If I ever have the courage to go back to Romania, it is that chapel I would most like to see again—the deep ruby reds, the cobalt blues, the light streaming through the stillness.

Five

MY SEVENTEENTH YEAR WAS FILLED WITH JOY. BY now I had acquired a large circle of friends. Some were seamstresses too, others were young Jewish men and women who worked in other trades. In the evenings we met on the streets outside the shops. Often, we went as a large group to a nearby restaurant.

On Saturdays our group of friends spent the entire day together, meeting downtown and then attending the theater or literary discussions in the afternoons. In the evenings we'd dine at a restaurant with a garden and a dance floor. In warm weather we sat outside by the rushing fountains nestled among the lavender and purple petunias and bright pink geraniums. The music from inside drifted out into the balmy air, mingling with the gushing sounds of the fountains. We added to the noise with our own babbling, quibbling over whether the broiled meats were better at this restaurant or at the one we had been to on the previous Saturday night. My favorite dish was shaped like a hot dog but made out of ground beef and broiled at the end of a prong. I looked forward to Saturday night so I could order it once again. In the colder months we moved inside the restaurants but otherwise it was the same—chattering like a flock of starlings, eating the delicious meals together, dancing first with one partner and then with another until the restaurant closed for the night and reluctantly we went out into the streets and back to our homes.

IN THE EARLY SPRING OF 1935 I BEGAN TO FEEL THAT this way of life was all being threatened, that everything would come crashing down around our heads.

Every day at noon as I left the salon, I saw the Iron Guard strutting down the middle of the streets, their high black boots stamping on the cobblestones. The men wore dark green shirts and brown trousers, drab and dull as gunmetal, but on the sleeve of each arm, raised straight out at a peculiar angle, a band of red caught my eye. It was a brilliant red, blood red, and was marked in the center by a blue hooked cross turned on its side in the middle of a circle of yellow. The same hooked cross stood out on the rippling flags carried by some of the marchers. *What does it mean?* I wondered. The years I had spent in the village schools where a cross served as a backdrop for attacks on the Jews made me feel very uneasy.

Others in my group began to feel equally uncomfortable. During our literary meetings on Saturday afternoons we would forget to discuss the book and shared our growing sense of uneasiness. One Saturday, Rivkele, one of the girls, burst into the room. "I barely made it!" she gasped. Her eyes were wide with fear, her lips drawn tightly together. Deep marks stood out on her face—red stripes running from the bridge of her nose to her neck.

"What happened?" one of the group asked.

"I was on my way here," she began. "When I got to Capcari Street the Iron Guard was marching down it. I was late, so instead of waiting until they were past I ran in front of them. But I ran as fast as I could! I didn't even think they would notice me. When I got to the other side of the street I was suddenly grabbed from behind. A man in a uniform pinned me against the side of the building." Her voice broke and she began to cry, sobbing loudly for a few minutes.

"He shouted at me, 'Swine! Jew swine! The time is up for filth like you.' Then he slapped me across my face and threw me to the ground. When he left he spat on me. He spat on me!" She began to cry again. Several of the other girls went to comfort her, taking her to a couch in the next room where she could lie down.

"They are spreading all over Romania. I've heard of them marching in other cities. They always bear the same symbol—the swastika," said Abram.

"Is that what it's called, the blue hooked cross?" I asked.

"Yes," Abram answered. "It almost looks like their emblems."

"And what are they?" Ben asked.

"The crucifix and the pistol. Now do you believe me?"

"I do," said Edna, one of my girlfriends from the Russian sector of Bucharest. "I've been frightened for some time. My sister and I have applied for passports to emigrate to Palestine."

"To Palestine!" I exclaimed. "I've never known anyone who was actually going there. Is it really a beautiful land of milk and honey?"

"Well, I don't know," she answered. "I do know that we won't live a life of luxury once we're there. If we're lucky enough to receive the passports, we'll be sent to a training center somewhere in Romania for six weeks where we'll be taught how to farm. Everything is operated by a Zionist organization." She paused, laughing. "Can you imagine me as a farm girl?"

"Why farming?" asked one of the other girls.

"They have the land," Edna answered, "even though Palestine is under the English mandate. The people there don't have much of anything, but they are allowed to farm. They need young people who can make the land produce."

"When do you think you'll go?" I asked.

"As soon as the passports come," she answered. "I hope my sister really wants to go. She's been walking around all dreamy-eyed ever since she met this young man named Hiram. You'd think she'd never seen a man before!"

"I think you're being very wise," Abram said. "If my mother wasn't so old I would apply for a passport too. I can't leave my mother, but I would love to go to Palestine."

———

EMIGRATING SEEMED THE ONLY SENSIBLE THING TO do, especially since I kept hearing about what was happening in Germany. Ever since Hitler became chancellor, rumors had come drifting like acrid smoke on a winter wind—rumors of endless columns of brown-shirted men with the same swastika on their sleeves, of mobs of people cheering them on through the streets, of the flickering lights of thousands of torches at mass rallies. The shouts of *Deutschland erwache! Jude verrecke!* carried out into the cold night air across the fields and forests of Germany, across the plains of Hungary and into the very heart of Romania. What if the words "Germany awake! Jew perish!" came to mean "Europe awake! Jew perish!"

Several months later I found Edna waiting for me after work one evening. Her face was flushed, her eyes bright and sparkling. "They've come!" she said hurriedly. "The passports have come . . . the ones from Palestine. My sister has become engaged and doesn't want to go. Can you imagine? So I want you to come with me. Will you? Please say you'll come!"

I stared at her for a minute or two. "You're asking me to come with you?" I said. "You'll let me have your sister's passport?"

"Yes!" she cried. "Will you come?"

"I'd love to come," I answered. "Yes, I'll come! I'll come!"

"I'm so glad," Edna answered. "It will be wonderful—a whole new life."

That night I went over the entire conversation again in my mind and realized the full implications of my decision. If I left Romania I could never return; those were the conditions of the program set up by the Zionist organization. Since Palestine was under the English mandate, very few passports were given. If I took one I would be expected to remain in Palestine forever. I would never again see the Carpathians jutting up into the sky, the clouds moving across them in great white sweeps, never again hear the stream trickling down the slope in the tall green grasses near our home in Valea Uzului. I would never see my family again. My mother's face flashed into my mind. Could I bear to leave her?

The following weekend I went home to tell my parents about my opportunity to emigrate. I barely had the words spoken when my father shouted, "No! No! I forbid it."

"But Father, I haven't even explained—"

"I said no!" he interrupted. "It's bad enough that you insist on defying me by working in Bucharest. Now you want to run away to Palestine."

"Could I at least tell you why I want to go?" I asked.

"You can tell me. But I will not change my mind!"

I thought about all the things I could tell him—the daily marches by the Iron Guard, the Jewish shops I had seen with the word "Jew" smeared across them in red paint one week and a week later boarded up and closed, confiscated by non-Jewish people, the increasing fear that my friends and I felt as we walked through the city. But I was afraid that he would say that life was always more violent in the city and this was my punishment for leaving home. Instead, I began relating what I had heard about Germany from a friend who had recently returned from there.

"It's become almost unbearable for the Jewish people in Germany," I said. "Many of them are leaving the country as fast as they can. A man by the name of Hitler has been declared Führer. He could be very dangerous for all Jewish people."

"In Germany?" scoffed my father. "What does that have to do with us?"

"Little by little Hitler has taken away almost everything from the Jews living there. They can no longer work as teachers, doctors, lawyers, or even artists—even if they have only one Jewish grandparent and are otherwise of Gentile blood. He's even passed a law stating that no German citizen can marry anyone with the slightest trace of Jewish blood. He thinks us to be less than human. 'Vermin' he calls us, 'spoilers of the race.' Jews are segregated from Gentiles on buses, on trains, forbidden on the streets after sunset. Signs are appearing everywhere saying, 'Jews not wanted here.' A friend of mine was visiting there and couldn't find a restaurant or hotel that would allow him inside. He was humiliated! He came back home within a few days."

"Well, that should teach him to stay home," my father answered. "But why be concerned about what is happening so far away? Surely someone will come to the aid of the Jews there. You don't have to worry about it."

"No one has come to help them so far. No one does a thing. Hitler can do whatever he likes and he is never even questioned about it. Who has ever come to the aid of the Jews? No one will save us. We must save ourselves. That is why I want to go to Palestine now that I have the chance."

"You're too anxious. We're still safe here in Romania. This isn't Germany."

"But the same things are beginning to happen in Bucharest," I said. "Last week a young man I know named Levi was going home from his job in a woolen mill. He was doing absolutely nothing wrong, simply sitting quietly on the bus. A man wearing the uniform of the Iron Guard asked to see Levi's identification papers. When he saw the word 'Jew' on the papers, he grabbed Levi and shouted, 'Don't you know that a rotten Jew never sits when there are Gentiles standing? No filthy Jew rides on this bus!' When the bus stopped at the corner Levi was pulled off and thrown onto the sidewalk. Several uniformed men kicked him until he lost consciousness. Luckily someone who knew him saw him there in a spreading pool of blood and took him home. Levi is still very ill. He bleeds and bleeds. The doctor cannot stop the bleeding."

"Well, he's to be pitied," said my father. "But Jews have always been beaten. Remember the times the politicians came to our village of Fulehaza and stirred up the peasants? Those meetings always provoked an attack on one Jewish man or another. Arbitrary persecution is nothing new. I still see no reason why you should run off to Palestine. I've heard enough. You will not go! Do not mention the subject again!"

I looked at my mother. She was sitting in her chair by the table pretending to be busy with some needlework, her fingers lifelessly moving up and down. She had said very little to me ever since I burst into the kitchen with my announcement of the passport. Now she must have felt my gaze upon her, for she suddenly looked up, her eyes meeting mine. Liquid and shiny, they blinked rapidly five or six times, stopped, and then blinked again. She did not allow herself to cry, but the battle was over. I had lost. I could ignore my father this time as I had when I left home for the gymnasium. I could not, however, deny the pain in my mother's eyes. Giving up my hopes for a new, free life in Palestine, I returned to Bucharest once more.

Six

I PASSED THE NEXT FOUR YEARS POURING ALL OF MY
energy into dressmaking. A number of clients came to value my judgment.
It was very flattering to have a fashionable woman choose a style and then
call me from the work area in the back to see if I approved of her selection.
I discovered that I was able to fit a woman who could not wear a ready-made
dress without alteration. This skill brought me not only pride in my work
but added income: if I successfully altered either a dress from the Paris collection or one from the salon's stock, I was tipped generously.

By now I had earned a two-week paid vacation. I would take this first
and then continue to relax throughout June, July, and August. Despite the
growing threats to our freedom, Jews were still allowed to travel throughout Romania.

My good friend Rachel, who was also a seamstress at the salon, lived in
Bucharest with her family. I often spent weekends at her house, sitting
down to the Sabbath meal with her family, feeling like I was at home. In the
late spring she and I would both request the summer off from work, with-

draw our savings from the bank, pack a suitcase, and walk to the train station in Bucharest.

The trains were quite inexpensive and we would board any one and ride until we arrived at a town or village that looked interesting. In Transylvania most of the cities have stations with lattice arcades and vines trailing down gracefully to the sidewalks, forming an archway of greenery. When we saw one of these that was particularly thick and lush we looked at each other. One of us would ask, "Here?" and the other answer, "Yes!" Quickly we would jump off the train and stroll beneath the vines, arm in arm. In the evening we found a hostel for the night and perhaps the next night too—if we found the village to be pleasant. If not, we boarded the train in the morning and set forth again, willing to go wherever the train took us.

We traveled like this for weeks at a time, sometimes living on nothing but plums, bread, and cheese. There were no dining cars on the train and we could not afford to eat in expensive restaurants, but there were always peddlers selling fruit and juice in the stations. While the train was still settled, quietly rumbling in the station, we leaned out of the windows and stretched our arms to the vendor holding plum-filled cones made of rolled-up newspaper. Sometimes the cones were filled instead with apples or fresh, hard pears. We experienced at these times such simple delights—biting into a tart, crisp apple, leaning against the cool window, watching the hills and villages roll by, confident that wherever it was that we were going, it would be fine.

Then when Rachel and I had our fill of the vagabond life, she would go back to her home in Bucharest and I to mine in Valea Uzului to accompany my mother and father on their vacation. While we were all home my father could never take advantage of his paid vacation; taking us all to a resort would have cost much more than he could afford. Now that my older sisters and brothers were all married, he could finally enjoy his vacations. Even my younger brothers no longer lived at home. Shlomo had met a young woman from a city a thousand kilometers from Valea Uzului and married her in that distant city, my mother having been the only one of our family able to attend the wedding. Eliezer had visited me several times in Bucharest but was now in the Romanian army. This left only Esther and Zipporah at home.

As I had money of my own now, my father invited me to come along with my mother and him to a resort while Esther and Zipporah stayed home to tend the house. After all the years of being one of the small children who were mostly ignored and then the only daughter who was labeled disobedient, I could not believe that I was singled out for the honor of sharing my parents' vacation. We spent hours soaking in the mineral baths. I jabbered about my work, my friends, my travels. My mother laughed often as I entertained her with stories hour after hour. Then she would suddenly flick her hand across the warm water, splashing my face. I tried to splash her back but just like that she was up, out of the water and safely on the grass. "I'm not so old. See!" she would call.

Sometimes in the late afternoon while my mother was chatting with a friend she had made at the spring, my father and I walked together. Often it had rained earlier in the day, the rain falling and falling all afternoon in quiet drummings. Then the clouds would break apart abruptly and the sun would appear, bouncing off the sparkling drops of water still clinging to the leaves. The world seemed freshly created at these times, the smells of earth and rain mingling with the lightness, a scud of clouds billowing across the water-blue sky.

As my father and I walked, he told me things that I do not think he ever mentioned to any of my sisters and brothers—how it was at his parents' home, what he liked to do as a boy, how he felt about his responsibilities. "Some people do not take being a parent seriously," he said one day. "There is nothing more important than keeping a family together. I have always tried to do that above all else. Even the mill does not mean as much to me as my family." So my father and I grew to enjoy each other's company under the radiant skies of Romania. I treasure almost more than anything the memory of those walks with my tall, fair father.

AT THE END OF 1937, IT BECAME APPARENT THAT THE relative calm of the last few years was ending. In the December elections the National Liberal Party, one of the moderate groups that Carol had managed to control, was defeated. The way was open now for the powerful right-wing groups to come into power. Frightened by this possibility, Carol dissolved parliament. He proclaimed a royal dictatorship in April 1938 and tried to suppress the Iron Guard. But its members responded by increasing their marches and attacks.

One day, Rachel and I met two friends after work and went to a nearby restaurant. Our lives were different now. My friends and I were circumspect and met only in small, quiet places where we would not attract attention. As we sat down that night the conversation began with a familiar theme: the outrageousness of the latest rumors. "Have you heard?" asked Simon, Rachel's companion. "They've broken into all the Jewish shops in Germany—smashed the windows with their guns."

"No," Rachel said. "I cannot believe it."

"It's true! Entire shops were destroyed. Soldiers set fire to the synagogues. The rabbis ran through the streets but they could not stop them."

As he said the words I could see the bearded rabbis in their long robes stumbling over the sharp shards of glass lying all over the streets, the menorahs and scrolls flung into the muddy gutters. It could not be true. I could not imagine the destruction of temples. The small buildings at my father's mills where we had worshipped; those synagogues had never been harmed. "Maybe this is just another rumor started by the Iron Guard to frighten us," I said.

"It happened!" exclaimed Simon. "Jews were pulled out of their homes, books piled into heaps and burned all night long."

"But why would the Germans do this? What reason did they give?" asked Rachel.

"Some poor Jew who couldn't stand the persecution any longer killed the German legation secretary in Paris. He couldn't have done anything worse. The Nazis used it as an excuse to rampage through the Jewish sections of city after city."

"I still don't believe it," I said. "No human beings would do this to other human beings. Maybe things like this happened hundreds of years ago, but not anymore. We are civilized. We have radios and telephones." Even as I said the words, I did not believe them. My instincts had told me to leave for Palestine over three years ago.

THEN ONE SPRING DAY IN 1939, RACHEL DID NOT come to the salon to work. The next day she was still absent. I told myself that she was ill and would come back soon, but as the days went by and she did not return I could stand it no longer and ran to her home after work one evening. No one was there. The house was locked, silent, one broken chair left on its side in the dining room. I went from window to window, trying to find a sign that her family was simply away on a visit—a note on the back door, a suitcase not needed at the last minute. I went back to my room alone. I never saw Rachel again.

That summer I went directly home. Rachel was gone. I did not feel like traveling without her. The journey from Bucharest to my home in the mountains high above the quiet valley floor seemed more and more like waking from a nightmare into a fairy tale dream. Even a fairy tale has hungry wolves, however, and while such creatures were beginning to prowl across Europe, my family continued to blind themselves to everything. When I walked listlessly through the house, missing Rachel almost more than I could bear, my mother suggested that perhaps it was time I quit my job in Bucharest and stayed home with them, where it was safer.

"But how long will it be safe here?" I asked her. "On my way home from Bucharest I can ride through seven villages in a row and not find one single Jewish family. I've stopped at all of them at various times and asked the stationmaster, 'Is there a Jewish family living here?' knowing they would let me spend an hour or two with them between trains. In every one of those seven villages the stationmaster has looked at me suspiciously and said, 'No, the only Jews nearby are at the lumber mill.'"

"Yes, I know," answered my mother. "If I had not been so busy taking care of all of you I would have been quite lonely with so few other Jewish families nearby. But we have always been unharmed. Even that time when we thought the students were coming and you were almost boiled alive, we were left entirely alone. It was just a rumor. I can still see you falling across the doorsill!" She began to laugh, hugging me close. "Oh, Seren, why don't you stay home with us now?"

"I have to go back," I answered. "My job is waiting for me. It is too much to give up."

"Well, I can't convince you," my mother said. "You have always been my little bird with wings that won't be clipped. But remember that we'll always be here. You can come home whenever you like if you change your mind."

In late August of 1939, I went back to Bucharest with that thought. Then on September 1, Germany invaded Poland. A few days later the streets were full of Polish army officers and their families. They had run from the advancing German army, coming however they could—in cars, trucks, and tanks, on motorbikes and bicycles. Entire households were stuffed into trunks, tied to the roofs of cars, thrown into the back ends of trucks, balanced precariously on handlebars, heaped into tiny wheelbarrows wobbling over the cobblestones. One afternoon a tiny girl brushed against me as she stumbled along, clinging to her mother's coat with one hand and rubbing tears from her eyes with the other. She looked exhausted from walking. *At least I do not have children,* I thought. I was twenty-one by now and I had no husband or babies to worry about. *If I can continue to take care of myself,* I decided, *I will be doing well.*

That night, however, when I came back to my room, the image of the child who had stumbled into me suddenly appeared in my mind. A great sense of sorrow overwhelmed me and I fell across my bed. All night long I cried—for the child, for all children, for mothers and fathers in time of war, for Rachel, for myself.

ALL THROUGH THAT WINTER OF 1939 AND THE SPRING of 1940 war seemed imminent for us too. The great powers of Hitler's Germany on the west and Stalin's Russia on the east and north appeared waiting to cut down Romania at any moment, especially now that they were allied and Romania only a trifle between them.

My friends continued to disappear. One week Abram was arguing with us and the next week not a trace of him could be found. Simon disappeared next and then two of my girlfriends from the salon. I never knew whether they had fled the city during the night and were safe, or had been arrested by the Iron Guard and were huddled in a jail cell.

In June Romania began to disintegrate. Russia demanded both Bessarabia, the northeast corner of Romania, and Bucovina, a little sliver of land on the northern border, and received both. This blow was quickly followed in August by the loss of three fifths of Transylvania to Hungary. My worst fears had come true: the war had reached our home in Valea Uzului. My family was no longer living on Romanian soil. The village of Valea Uzului remained with Romania; the mill up on the mountain above the village was on land that became part of Hungary, the new border running between the village and the mill. My family was caught between two nations that resented each other bitterly. Romania felt that her land had been stolen outright by both Russia and Hungary; Hungary felt that she was simply regaining territory lost during World War I.

The Jews were used as the scapegoat for all of this resentment. Three months after Romania lost Bessarabia to Russia, I walked to the neighborhood in Bucharest where several of my friends lived. This whole area of the city had been settled by Jewish people coming from Bessarabia and was called the Russian sector, as Bessarabia had adjoined Russia before it was annexed. I was particularly anxious to see these friends, who were sisters, as they were the only ones I had left in the entire city. *Perhaps they'll have news of acquaintances who've disappeared,* I thought, *and we can comfort and encourage each other.* As I strode through the late-September afternoon these thoughts filled me with hope and I noticed for the first time the brilliant reds and oranges of the turning leaves. I could even smell the strong odor of burning and found pleasure in imagining someone tidying a yard as if everything were not falling apart. If a man or woman was burning leaves, then perhaps life was still somewhat normal.

As soon as I drew close to the Russian sector, I knew I could not have been more wrong. It was not leaves that were burning; whole houses had been flaming and were still smoking. Blackened buildings stood in outline against the sky wherever I looked, in all directions, empty shells quietly sifting into ash in the still twilight. A sense of emptiness washed over me. No one was walking home after working in the city all day, no one was opening a door in welcome, no one was dishing supper into bowls. I walked hurriedly on to where my friends lived, hoping that their house had been spared. We told ourselves things like this throughout the war: someone else has felt pain and horror but somehow it will not touch me or anyone who knows me. The mind tries to protect itself again and again.

When I reached the spot where their home should have been, only a pile of burned boards and a soot-darkened chimney remained. I stood there for a long time, until suddenly I felt very cold. Realizing that it was rapidly growing dark, I turned away and began running, saying to myself over and over, all the way back, *Let them be safe! Let them be safe! Let them be safe!*

Every day after that I would think, *Am I crazy for staying here? Should I go home?* Then I would answer myself: *Home would be no better. There is nowhere to go that is safe.* I remained in Bucharest, taking each day as it came. Romania had by now lost a third territory: southern Dobruja.

Then one day a girl at the salon told me, "The Iron Guard has begun arresting all of the prominent Jewish people in Bucharest."

"Are you sure?" I asked.

"Yes. My father works for the Jewish Federation. Yesterday soldiers with swastikas on their arms came into the room where they were having a meeting and grabbed all the officers of the Federation. Luckily, my father is only a clerk so they left him alone. But he's frightened. He didn't want me to come to work today but I talked him into it. 'Nobody cares about me,' I told him."

"I can't believe it," I said.

"My father had heard of others who were also arrested—Mr. Bergblatt, the president of that huge department store downtown, and Mr. Stein, the manufacturer. He thinks the Iron Guard may also be arresting some prominent doctors and lawyers. Aren't you glad that you are just a little seamstress? No one will want us. We aren't important enough."

"How can you say that no one will want us?" I asked. "Rachel is gone. Most of the other girls are gone. You and I are practically the only ones left in the salon. I don't know where any of my friends are."

"Oh, they must have done something wrong that we didn't know about! But we have done nothing. We're nobodies. They have no reason to arrest us, so they won't."

I could not share her optimism. All of my friends had been cautious, law-abiding people. I knew that any Jewish person could be singled out for persecution without a reason. I had been beaten by classmates for no reason, humiliated by teachers repeatedly for no reason, lost my best friend for no reason. I was terrified.

The following morning I boarded a streetcar for work, rapidly climbing up the steps to the car. As soon as I was seated I began to glance at the other passengers, positive that someone was watching me. Cringing further into the corner of the seat, I wished that I could disappear into its fabric. Although my light hair and blue eyes gave me the appearance of a Gentile, I realized that the government knew that I was Jewish. Maybe they could even come across my papers today and tonight I would hear a knock on the door, a loud demand, and be pulled from my bed and shoved into a prison cell.

As I was imagining this—the cruel faces of the soldiers, the cold, dark cell—a woman sitting in the front of the streetcar began to scream. The other passengers and I quickly twisted in our seats, trying to see exactly who was screaming and why. Was she being attacked? Arrested? Then the man in front of me said in a soft voice overcome with horror, "Oh, my God." He pointed to the window. I looked out but saw at first only trees and benches. We were passing a small park called the Square of June 8. Then I saw it— a sign nailed to two stakes and proclaiming in large, red letters: "Kosher Meat for Sale." Behind it, suspended on huge thick steel butcher's hooks, were the bodies of men, Jewish men, hanging lopsidedly, their heads drooping to one side, arms falling limp beside their thighs. An early snow from the night before clung to their dark wool coats, to their legs dangling apart in the still, cold air, to the useless shoes pointing downward to the earth.

I recognized several of the men as the leaders of the Jewish Federation, while others looked like doctors or businessmen. Then, as quickly as it had materialized, the scene was gone. The streetcar had passed by and was soon one block away, two blocks away from the park. I sank back into my seat and closed my eyes, unable to believe what I had just viewed from my window. I kept seeing the dead men. There must have been twenty of them fastened there in a row. Behind my eyelids they still swung back and forth, impaled on the sharp hooks.

Suddenly I felt as if I would vomit. Bolting from the streetcar as soon as it came to a stop, I began to run, running as fast as I could, running blind.

$\mathcal{S}$even

$\mathcal{T}$HE THOUGHT OF REMAINING IN BUCHAREST EVEN one more day was unbearable. I had to get out. Home was where I wanted to be more than anywhere. In her last letter Mama had written:

> Dear Seren, my child,
>
> Won't you please change your mind and come home to us once more? It's lonely here. We're completely cut off from the village now that the border has been changed. Your two sisters and I spend most of our time inside the house while your father keeps busy shipping out the last loads of lumber.
>
> I'm so worried about your brother Eliezer. Herman heard a rumor that Eliezer has deserted the army. One night some soldiers from the Iron Guard came into his dormitory and started removing Jewish men. They took them outside to shoot them one by one. Eliezer crept out the back door and ran away before they got to him. No one knows where he is. I'm afraid that he will be killed.

Many young Jewish men are building a road across the mountains. The Iron Guard took them out of Budapest and put them into a group they call the labor force. Maybe Eliezer will be placed in one of these groups . . . if he isn't shot first, God forbid.

The weather has turned very cold. At night the wolves from the forest come right up to our bedroom windows looking for food. I'm so frightened when I see their eyes glowing at me in the darkness.

I'll ask just one more time and then I'll close. Please come home to us. We all send our love.

Mama

I did not know exactly how I would get there, as some of the trains were no longer running, nor did I know if I would be able to cross the border at the village once I arrived. But, one way or another, I would reach my mother and father, my sisters, the love that was waiting to enfold me, welcome me home.

Abandoning the idea of traveling with suitcases, I pulled out my knapsack, which would allow me to walk for long distances if necessary. As I was going through my drawers, my landlady knocked softly. I jumped, positive that she had been listening on the other side of the door. Kicking the knapsack under the bed, I said in a voice that I tried to make as calm as possible, "Come in."

She opened the door slowly, as if she knew that she was intruding, and crossed over to the bed, where she sat down. For a long while she said nothing, looking at her folded hands. Then she began, "I've wanted to tell you something for some time, but I didn't know how to say it. I . . ." She paused for a few seconds and then continued. "The things that have been happening to the Jewish people are horrible, horrible. I am so ashamed." She stopped again. Finally she raised her eyes to look at me. "I worry about you. If it were up to me, none of this would be happening."

"I'm leaving," I said. "Tonight. I was packing as you knocked." I opened a drawer as if to convince her and saw my wool sweater the color of wheat. It was as thick and soft as the down I had once lain on high in the hayloft in Fulehaza. "Would you like to have this sweater?" I asked. "It would take up too much room in my knapsack."

"Will you be all right? What will you do?" she asked, ignoring the sweater.

"I'm taking the train home tonight."

"That's too dangerous!" she answered quickly. "My son Nicolai, the one in the army, came home last night. He can stay for only a day. Oh, how I hate this war! Anyway, he came on the train from Brasov and he said that the Iron Guard is patrolling all the trains. They are looking for any Jewish people."

"But I have to get home!"

She looked directly into my eyes then, as if seeing me for the first time. "I have an idea," she said. "Nicolai has to report back by midnight. He can go with you, at least while you board the train. With your blond hair and fair complexion, you could easily pass for his sister."

"Will he do it? He doesn't know me. I don't think he has ever seen me for more than a few minutes."

"Of course he will do it!" she answered. "Since when can a son refuse his mother? I think he would do it anyway, even if I didn't ask him. He did not choose to be in this war. He is a good person . . . loving, kind, like his brother." She looked down at the floor for a minute or two without saying anything.

Taking the wheat-colored sweater and placing it in her arms, I said, "I would be very grateful if your son would go with me to the train."

Finally she said, "Do you remember when my other son, Pietru, married last year? I went to the wedding in a village on the Russian border and was gone for a week."

"Yes, I remember."

"He married a Jewish girl. Her name is Anna. She is a beautiful girl with thick hair that flows down her back in black waves. They are expecting a baby in six months." Her voice broke. "I'm so frightened for them," she continued. "They've gone into hiding near Anna's home village. I wanted them to stay with me but, 'No, no,' Pietru said. 'The Iron Guard will not search outside the villages.' I can't even visit them! My first grand-child . . ."

"I'm sorry," I said. Then I remembered that I must finish packing. "Please take anything else I leave," I told her.

"I'll put everything away for you. When the war is over you can come back and stay with us. You've been a good boarder. We'll get to know each other better then."

"Yes," I answered. "I'll come back when the war is over."

THAT EVENING, AS SOON AS IT WAS DARK, NICOLAI and I set out for the depot. He walked briskly beside me in his uniform, say-ing nothing after he warned: "Remember. You are my sister and you are go-ing to visit our grandmother, who is ill. Do not say anything. Act normal." When he said it I thought, *But what is normal? I have forgotten what it is like not to be afraid.*

At the depot, Nicolai purchased my ticket and placed my knapsack in a corner of the rear car next to the other baggage. "Follow me," he said as he rapidly climbed up the steps to a passenger car and strutted down the aisle.

Suddenly he stopped. I could not believe it. He had marched all the way to the other end of the car, past all the civilian passengers, to a seat holding two officers of the Romanian army. Looking to my right, I saw an elderly woman sitting with a large basket on her lap; she looked kind and I was very tempted to ease down in the empty seat beside her. Then I heard Nicolai say to one of the officers, "This is my sister. She is on her way to care for our grandmother, who is quite ill. Could you look after her? She has never trav-eled alone before." Nicolai took me by the arm and gently pulled me for-ward.

The officer stood up immediately. "Of course!" he replied. "She can sit here between us. Is she traveling far?"

"To Valea Uzului."

"Ah, so far. Well, she will be fine sitting here. It's a good thing you brought her to us. Who knows what might happen as long as they let those damn Jews ride the trains. The sooner they get rid of all of them, the better!"

"Yes, precisely," Nicolai answered. Then he turned to me. "Have a good trip and say hello to Grandmother. Tell her I sent my hopes for a quick recovery." With that he saluted the officers, turned on his heel, and quickly paced down the aisle.

In less than a minute Nicolai was at the other end of the car. I sat down, drawing my arms tightly against my chest and away from the uniformed shoulders on both sides of me. The two men ignored me completely, the officer on my left lost in reading and the one on my right, the one who had spoken to Nicolai, putting his head back on the seat and closing his eyes. I sighed, greatly relieved, for I was sure that I would be revealed for who I was if questioned about anything. *If I can simply sit here while the long hours crawl by,* I thought, *everything might be all right.*

The train had barely pulled out of the station when I saw, out of the corner of my eye, a number of men in the dark green shirts and brown trousers of the Iron Guard come pounding down the station platform. Four of them reached the steps to our car, vaulted up them, and rushed to the other end of the car. *They've come to get me!* I thought, my heart beating rapidly. *Someone recognized me while Nicolai and I were on our way here. They reported me! Maybe Nicolai reported me!*

My hands broke out in a sweat so cold that they felt icy, frozen, and I longed to bury them inside my coat, but I was afraid that the slightest movement would draw attention to me. The soldiers were striding down the aisle, now two on each side of the rows of seats, shouting in harsh voices, "Show me your identification!" All of the passengers held out their cards, their eyes pleading: *Let me be all right.*

Through the first half of the car the identification was the proper one; the passengers were Gentile. Then one of the soldiers, stopping beside a very old man clutching a bundle, grabbed the old man's card and stared at it. A few seconds later, he grasped the man by the collar of his coat and yanked him out of his seat.

The blanket-covered bundle flew open and five or six photograph albums spilled onto the floor. Close to my feet I saw a black-and-white photograph of a young boy standing barefoot on a path in the woods. He was wearing a jacket, breeches, and a little cap pushed back on his head. He was looking straight at the camera, smiling, his eyes slightly lowered. As I was considering reaching and picking up the photograph for the old man, the Iron Guard soldier yelled, "Filthy scum! Filthy Jew scum!" Then he shoved the old man in front of him, forcing him to walk over the spilled photographs. A minute later we heard the door at the end of the car open, the wind rush in, and then a scream, beginning in a high whine and then suddenly dropping in tone, trailing behind the train for a few seconds until it was lost in the roaring dark.

The Romanian army officer on my right spoke for the first time. "These Iron Guard men are a little too coarse for me. You would think they could find some better way of getting rid of the Jews! The rest of us should not have to be exposed to this kind of thing. What are our women to think? This is not something they should have to see." He looked quickly at me, and I began to shake violently. I could not tell whether I was on the verge of vomiting or fainting. *Stay calm. Stay calm,* I ordered myself, hugging my body with my folded arms and closing my eyes. I could hear the Iron Guard soldiers returning from the exit. There was no one left to show the identification card except me and the Romanian soldiers sitting beside me. *I will wait until they ask,* I decided. *I will sit here perfectly still until they ask.*

Then the soldiers marched by again. They were not going to ask me! I realized in an instant that they had assumed I was with the Romanian officers and obviously not Jewish.

During the rest of the night I sat there trembling. I knew that different soldiers from the Iron Guard could board the train at any of the depots along the way and I would have to go through the same agony all over again. I could not even get off the train at an earlier station, as Nicolai had told the officers that I was going all the way to Valea Uzului. I counted off the stations, one by one. *See if you can make it from here to Ploiesti,* I told myself. *Do not think about the rest of the trip. Just think about getting to Ploiesti.* Once the train was in Ploiesti I willed myself to endure until Moinesti. Finally, toward morning, we pulled into the station at Valea Uzului.

The faintest traces of light were appearing on the horizon as I descended the steps to the platform. I wanted to fall down on the ground by the station and rest until the terror subsided, but I was not at my home, I still would have to ride the small lumber train up into the mountains to the mill. I picked up my knapsack, walked to the locked door of the station, and sank down in the cold darkness to wait.

Finally I heard the lumber train rumbling toward the station. I jumped up quickly, stamping my feet, my toes numb and lifeless after sitting so long in the cold. As soon as the train stopped I began to climb into the cab of the engine where I always rode. The engineer, not the one who had always been there but a new one, stepped in front of me as I was climbing up the last step.

"Hey! Where do you think you're going?" he yelled.

I could not think of what to say for a minute. Finally I stammered. "To the m-mill."

"No you're not. No one is allowed to cross the border. Guards are posted all along it."

"But I live there! I mean, my family lives there. My father is the manager of the mill."

"The mill is shutting down. Now get off this train!"

"I rode this train before—every time I came home for a visit."

"Hey, Gregor," the engineer yelled to a man loading boxes onto a car, "do you recognize her? She says she lives at the mill."

The man stared at me for a long minute. His clothes were covered with grease and his hair was slick with dirt and oil. A thin mustache trailed down both sides of his mouth. "Naw," he answered. "I never seen her. But I'll take her home with me. Come on over here, why don't you?" he called to me.

My stomach lurched. Turning around abruptly, I ran away from the men, who were laughing at me as I fled. Quickly I reached the edge of the forest, which began at the bottom of the mountain and reached up above me for as far as I could see. Somewhere between here and the mill was the border, but I had no idea of exactly where. I decided that I knew these woods better than any border guards; all I would have to do was avoid them. I would hike up the mountain until I came to the road that the owner of the mill had built for his car and follow it home.

I began to climb, grateful that I had worn sturdy walking shoes and had only the knapsack on my back. I picked my way among the ferns and ivy growing lush on the forest floor. For the first hour tall pines surrounded me on every side. I walked through beds of soft, dry needles that swished lightly with each footstep.

It would have been easier to follow the train tracks, but as the train could not go up the steep grades, the tracks curved back and forth in long switchbacks. I chose instead a more direct route—almost straight up the steep side, which was by now growing more rugged. Huge outcroppings of rock jutted from the mountain, ending abruptly in cliffs falling down to lower valleys. After climbing up one of these, my breath coming in short gasps as I dug into the niches with my fingers, I crawled away from the edge and rested against a slab of granite. Looking down, I saw the whole village spread below me on the valley floor. Smoke from the peasant huts drifted up into the clear air. Two black hawks circled in low glides, crossing each other's arcs.

I began to feel that I was the only person up on the quiet mountain. Then I heard crashing sounds in the distance. I hid behind a large tree. A group of men, thirty or thirty-five in all, were approaching. They were wearing yellow armbands bearing the Star of David and were accompanied by soldiers. *This must be the labor force,* I decided, for the men all carried shovels, picks, and axes. They walked by quickly, their feet crackling through the branches.

Hours passed without my seeing any other person. I crossed a level plain and then climbed another ridge, my legs numb with fatigue. I longed to be home, sitting by the fire, drinking a cup of my mother's hot tea.

By the middle of the afternoon I reached a thick fence of barbed wire. It was the border, I realized, but there were no guards. Following the fence, I came across a gate held closed by a simple latch. *Suppose this is a trick!* I thought. *Maybe the guards are hiding in the woods and will seize me once I open the gate and cross to the other side!* I looked in every direction, but I could see no one. Very carefully I opened the latch, stepped through the gate, and closed it behind me.

I hurried on, soon reaching the small road leading to the mill. Just ahead, I knew, was the castle where the owner lived and beyond that the beautiful gardens of flowers and strawberries, the mill, our house. By the time darkness was beginning I finally saw the outline of the mill buildings through the trees. Scrambling up the last stretch of road, I reached my house at last. My mother was turning to go inside when she heard my footsteps and saw me collapsing on the front steps.

"Seren! Oh, Seren! Where have you come from?"

I lay there gasping, unable to catch my breath. "Have you come through the woods?" I nodded my head. She ran to me then. "The wolves!" she said. "The woods are full of wolves. They're starving. They might have attacked you!"

"Oh, I forgot about the wolves," I answered. "I completely forgot."

"You forgot?" she said, bursting into laughter. "You forgot?" She drew me to her, her head bobbing up and down on my shoulder. We remained like that for a long while, arms around each other, laughing into the fading autumn light.

Part Three

Seren, Esther, and Alfred in Romania. Seren was probably about eighteen when this picture was taken.

Eight

THAT EVENING MY MOTHER AND FATHER AND I SAT AT the supper table far into the evening, taking pleasure in the simple delight of being in each other's presence once again. There were only the three of us, since Esther and Zipporah were staying with friends overnight. My mother and my father, my mother and my father—I looked from one to the other. I could not get enough of gazing at them.

My mother's face continually broke into smiles. She was still a young woman, lightly jumping up from the table to get another loaf of bread that was warming in the oven, a fresh pot of tea. Twenty-five years of marriage had aged her very little. The young bride my father had brought home to mother all his children, to give him more, looked at him still. He sat quietly, softly stroking his goatee from time to time, but his hand trembled slightly and his eyes were full, shining. I reached over and stroked his arm, as strong and firm as the arm of a young man, and asked, "How are you, Father?"

"I am well," he answered. He was. Although my father was sixty-seven by now, he looked twenty years younger; his hair was full, the light color of it masking any gray that may have dared to appear, and he walked with the determined gait of a man in full possession of all his capacities.

"You tried to board the lumber train?" my father asked.

"Yes, like I always have."

"But you would have been arrested!" he said. "That train stops at the border every time it goes back and forth between Valea Uzului and the mill. It is searched by the border guards. They would have thought you were a spy."

"But how could I be a spy? I was only trying to get home."

"Anyone trying to cross the border is a spy to the Hungarians. No one can go from one side to the other. We have been completely cut off from Valea Uzului and from all the rest of Romania since the border was put between the village and the mill."

"Then we can see no one?" I asked.

"No one. My family can no longer come to their own home. Meyer and Lottie, Louise and Bela, Berta and Morris, Herman and Tamara . . . the children. Who knows when we will see them again?" he asked.

"The war will end sometime," my mother said, going to him. "Surely the border will be opened then. We will all be together again. Now, let's go to bed. A good night's rest will do us good and the world will look better tomorrow."

The world did not look any better the next morning, nor would it for a very long time. We did not gather together as one family ever again. While Esther, Zipporah, and I were given one more year with both our mother and father, the portion of the family living in what was left to Romania was gone from them and from us, forever.

Even the members of the family living on our side of the border were kept from us. All of the Jewish people living in the villages in the part of Transylvania that was now Hungary were ordered to move into designated cities. A permit to live in the city had to be secured, and once there, you could not leave for any reason. Herman, Tamara, and their three sons, and Eugene, Rose, and their five children all moved out of the neighboring village into the city of Reghinal-Sasesc; Eugene and Rose had moved out of

Brasov when the depression caused Eugene to lose his job at the bank, and Herman had found work for him at his mill. We still received mail from all of them, as well as from Shlomo and his wife, but it gave us little comfort. The letters were heavily censored, leaving us feeling more alone than ever.

While I welcomed the peacefulness of the quiet days and nights after the turmoil of life in Bucharest, I soon realized how long a day can be when there is nothing to look forward to: no job, no entertainment, no friends to visit. Even the men at the mill were gone. When the Hungarians occupied our part of Transylvania, any Gentile who was living in the newly acquired area automatically became a Hungarian citizen within a few days after the occupation. Since the young workers at the mill were from many different countries besides Romania, most of them escaped to their homelands before the border was closed. Only a few older Jewish men who had families living with them remained at the mill, for if one was Jewish, there was no homeland to which one might flee. We did not become Hungarian citizens as did the other Romanians living in Transylvania. Neither nation wanted us, Romania or Hungary, so we were regarded as aliens. Suddenly, we were a people without a country.

Time slowed to a melancholy crawl. For about six months my father continued to go to the mill every day as the last orders of lumber were loaded onto the train and shipped. Some days when I could not stand for one minute more the long, silent afternoons inside our house, the idleness driving me to distraction, I wandered over to the mill yard. The big saws sat cold and quiet. The air was still. Everywhere I looked, there was nothing to see but the leveled, empty spaces where the piles of lumber used to stand.

Zipporah, Esther, and I spent our days and evenings attempting to comfort our mother and father as well as we could. At the same time, we could not help feeling that they should be happy to have the three of us there. Then one day we were given a godsend: the labor force came to work nearby. The same men that I had seen passing through on my climb up the mountain last October were now brought back to build a road around the mountains. Zipporah, of course, was the first to notice them. One day in the early part of April she came dashing up to the house from the small road by the mill.

"You will never believe it!" she said.

"What? Is it so wonderful?" I asked.

"The labor force is building a road all around the mountain—around and around and around." She whirled in the late afternoon light, catching the fading sun on her dark hair, turning until she had to stop from dizziness. "All these men are going to be close to our house for months! It is two hundred kilometers around the mountains. A man told me so."

"What man?"

"Oh, just a man . . . a very handsome man. I invited him to supper."

"Just like that?"

"Just like that."

"Can he come? Will the Hungarian gendarmes allow him to leave the camp?" I asked.

"He assured me that he could come. What will I wear? I don't have a thing to wear . . . Could I wear your blue blouse? Oh, I must fix my hair!" She ran off to her room quickly before I could say no to her request.

That evening the young man appeared at our door. He brought along several other men from the labor force as well. I noticed that Zipporah had grown even prettier. Her hair was very long and carefully brushed five or six times a day so that it was always glistening, and her face had lost its childishness. She moved like a tall, lean dancer, quick and light on her feet, and was so vivacious that all the young men, each and every one, found her to be fascinating. Once in an hour's time one of the men might remember to say to me, politely, "It sure was a cold winter, wasn't it?" Before I had a chance to reply his eyes were back on Zipporah and I was completely forgotten again.

Still, the men were company for us. My mother looked forward to the evenings as much as we did, for now she had a good reason to resume baking an extra cake or pie. My father engaged first one and then another man in conversation about life in Budapest, where all the men had lived before the war. I also enjoyed talking to several of them about their families, their work, their holidays before the war. Those visits carried us into summer on a warm, balmy wind.

Then they moved on to a different part of Transylvania to build another road for the army. We were left alone again. Our resources began to diminish. While the mill was operating my father made enough money to support us, but now we had no source of income. The pantry which my mother had stocked as usual in the fall tided us over through the spring and then we planted the garden again, but there was never an abundance of food as before.

On Shavuot we brought in the flowers, the plum branches and apple blossoms, but they gave us little cheer. Despite the new green shoots of life sprouting everywhere, the world seemed to grow more and more gray. Summer passed in the same manner with no change and when Yom Kippur came around in the fall our hopes were even fewer. Another long, dark winter stretched before us. We might as well have been adrift on an ice floe in a lonely arctic sea.

ONE VERY EARLY MORNING IN OCTOBER OF 1941, everything changed. A loud knocking banged against the front door. It continued insistently as everyone huddled under the covers, reluctant to jump out onto the cold floors. In another minute the sounds of my father's heavy footsteps could be heard from below as he hurried to the door, and then voices came from outside. I ran to the window to look out, but the glass was so laced with frost crystals that I could not see. As I was about to crawl back into bed again, I heard my father call up the stairs, "Seren! Seren! Come down here. Seren!" My heart seemed to stop. Surely the loud knocking on the door could have nothing to do with me.

I pulled on a dress, shoes and stockings, and a warm sweater quickly, not even stopping to brush my hair, and ran down the steps. There, just inside the door, stood two tall, heavyset men wearing the dark green uniforms and black hats with ostrich feathers swirling up high of the Hungarian gendarmerie. A rifle with a bayonet jutting out past the barrel of the gun was pointed at my father. I gasped. Another bayonet's sharp blade was quickly turned on me. My mother and sisters were walking down the stairs when one of the men asked, "Which one is Seren?"

"This one, here," said my father, pointing to me.

"How old are the other girls?"

"They are still children, as you can see." With her hair down and in her nightgown, Zipporah did look very young, and Esther looked not more than twelve.

"Seren's coming with us, then. I want the two of you outside. Now!"

The two gendarmes brought the bayonets almost to our throats. My father and I ran to get our coats and scarves, putting them on as fast as we could. I followed my father out of the door. The men came directly after, ordering us to march ahead of them to the middle of the mill yard. We were joined by five other Jewish men who lived near the mill and three of their daughters.

As soon as the ten of us were accounted for, the Hungarian gendarmes shouted: "Start walking!" We formed a line, the men at the front and the daughters behind, a gendarme across from each of us, gun raised, bayonet stretched out at an angle toward our chests. I could scarcely breathe. I knew that my mother and sisters must be standing at the edge of the mill yard to see what was happening to us, but I did not dare to look back at them. Was this what happened in Bucharest to my friend Rachel, I wondered, to be taken away without even a chance to say good-bye?

We walked on, one behind the other, for mile after mile, down the road recently finished by the labor force. Gusts of wind whipped open my coat, tore the scarf from my head. The only sounds were the wind whistling down and the tramping of our feet.

The road wound up, down, and around the mountain. Every few miles we passed a thatched-roof hut belonging to a peasant family, but there was no one to see, no one to wonder where we were going. Lunchtime came and went as we walked.

Finally, when the sky was already dark and I could see the eyes of an animal glowing from deep within the forest, we were ordered to halt at the edge of a small farm. A lantern glowed softly in one window of the hut; I pictured the warm kitchen, the fire going, a kettle of simmering hot soup. Two of the gendarmes banged on the door with their rifles and soon the peasant and his wife appeared. "Open your barn!" one of the soldiers ordered. The old farmer came outside in his shirtsleeves and pants, shuffled to the barn and slid the door open.

"Get inside! All of you!" the gendarmes told us. We walked in quickly, grouping in the aisle between the cow stalls and the feed trough. Then the gendarmes turned to the farmer. "What have you got to eat in that hovel?" he demanded.

"A little bread . . . some milk," the man answered. He was poorly dressed, his shoes held together with twine. "Not much, I'm afraid."

"Bring it out here! We'll be spending the night in your barn. And see if you can come up with something more decent for breakfast!"

The farmer and his wife returned with the food and we were each given a small piece of bread and a cup of tea after the soldiers had taken what they wanted. Once the food was passed out we heard the clicking of a bolt pulled across the outside of the barn door. We were locked inside, the gendarmes standing guard all around the barn. We could hear them pacing back and forth in the darkness.

The men talked in quiet whispers, then searched for a place to sleep that was not matted with manure. One of them found some clean straw and we spread it around quietly, afraid to make any noise lest we be ordered to sleep outside in the wind. My father beckoned to me and I lay down near him, using my scarf for a pillow.

"Are you all right?" he whispered.

"Yes," I answered.

"Are you too cold?"

"No, just my feet. They're like ice."

"Here," he said, "put them under the straw next to mine." I did so and felt a little warmer.

"Where do you think they're taking us?" I asked.

"I'm not sure. Perhaps to a work camp. Perhaps nowhere. It has something to do with our living near the border, I think." He paused. "Maybe we will find out what happened to Eliezer now." Again he paused, sighing. Then: "Get some rest, Seren. We will need it for tomorrow."

I closed my eyes, wondering for a moment how my mother could sleep after her husband and daughter had been taken away too. Then I gave in to exhaustion, sleeping soundly amid the straw and the cattle nuzzling in their stalls.

The next morning we were awakened when it was barely light by the voices of the guards.

"Outside! Outside!" the gendarmes yelled. We gathered in front of the barn, where we were given a piece of bread with cheese and a cup of hot water tasting slightly like coffee. After we were each given a turn in the farmer's outhouse, we were again lined up and began marching down the road.

That day passed the same as the one before. We slept in another barn that evening and were fed again by a farmer. Every day after that we tramped along the road around the Carpathians jutting up into the cold, gray October sky. One of the girls, Ruth, developed large blisters, as she had not worn good hiking shoes. She hobbled as she walked, tears silently running down her face.

Finally, after a week, we came down out of the mountains and reached the outskirts of the new capital of the province, Miercurea-Cuic. We had walked two hundred kilometers. We followed the road into the middle of the city, relieved that we seemed to be nearing the end of our long days in the biting wind but also fearful of where they were leading us.

"Halt!" one of the gendarmes yelled. He came to an abrupt stop, his plume trembling. We were directly in front of a three-story building made of thick gray bricks darkened with moisture and age.

We stood there for two long hours, the gendarmes guarding us all the while. Sometimes a man would pass by on the sidewalk, but no one ever looked up; each person kept on walking, eyes down, hurrying by us as fast as he could.

Finally, a gendarme came out of the building and shouted, "Move! Inside!" We entered a long, dark hallway smelling of mold and dampness. It was a prison. The men were shoved into a large cell. Then the door was locked and the other girls and I were ordered to move forward to another door at the other end of the corridor. It was opened and we were roughly pushed inside. The bolt was locked with a clang that echoed in the stillness.

Nine

ARLY THE NEXT MORNING WHEN WE WERE STILL asleep, a gendarme we had not seen before came to the room where Ruth, the other two girls—Mozelle and Leah—and I were huddled together on mats on the floor. "Ruth Bergman!" he shouted. She stood up, trembling, drawing her shoulders together against the cold. Ruth was the tallest of the four of us, but as she stood she seemed to shrink, hiding like a child inside her long coat, her hands disappearing within the dark brown folds of the sleeves.

The guard stared at her for a moment, silently, his eyes narrowed, glanced down at us watching him, and then looked again at Ruth. "You are wanted," he said to her, and opened the door to the room. She followed him out. The door was locked. We heard them walking back down the corridor, past the room where our fathers were, past the corner, to a place we could not even imagine.

An hour later they returned. Ruth's face was red, swollen, her eyes liquid with tears. She did not look at us or come to us but went instead to the other side of the room and slumped down into a corner, hiding her face in her hands. "Leah Handler!" the guard shouted. "You are next." Leah clutched at Mozelle's arm; the two of them were friends and had walked one in front of the other all the way here. "You better go," Mozelle whispered to her, so she went, pressing one hand hard against her mouth. Again the door was locked.

I went to Ruth, who was crying softly. "Did they hurt you?" I asked.

She shook her head back and forth without lifting it from her arms.

"Did they hurt your father?"

This time she did not answer me. I suddenly feared that her father and all our fathers were harmed.

"Did they?" I asked again.

"I don't know. I didn't see him." She began to weep with deep, wrenching sobs. I could think of nothing to do, of nothing to say to her. Then the guards returned with Leah. It was my turn now; I knew it even before he said my name.

I followed him down the corridor as the others had done, glancing quickly at the room where our fathers were as I went past, but I could see no one; the door was closed and the opening covered. We came to a room with a small, wooden desk placed to one side and one metal chair standing in the middle of the room. There was nothing else—no other chairs, no cabinets, no lamps. Even the top of the desk was bare. The guard ordered me to sit on the solitary chair and then closed the door, leaving me alone. For what seemed like a very long time I sat there waiting. Then the door opened swiftly and two gendarmes strutted in, slamming the door, and faced me, one on each side of the chair.

"What is your name?" demanded the gendarme to my right.

"Seren Tuvel."

"Where do you live?"

"Valea Uzului."

"Wrong! Where do you live?"

I looked up at him. This soldier was a member of the Hungarian gendarmes, as were the men who had arrested us. He already knew where I lived; his unit had brought us here.

"Valea Uzului," I said again, this time a little louder.

"Where exactly do you live?"

"Near Valea Uzului . . . at the mill up in the mountains."

"You live near the border. Isn't that right?"

"Yes."

"In fact, you live almost on the border."

"Yes."

"You have lived there for a number of years."

"Yes."

"You are an alien, not a Hungarian citizen."

The second gendarme, who had up to this point been silent, suddenly lunged forward and shouted in my face, "You are a spy!"

I sat there stunned. A spy . . . but for whom? I had never been out of the country.

"Admit it! You are a spy."

"I am not a spy," I said softly, my eyes lowered.

"Admit it!"

"I am not a spy." Raising my head, I looked at him directly. "I don't know what you mean."

"You are a filthy Jew . . . a rotten communist Jew! A traitor!" continued the second soldier.

"You know exactly what we mean! You are a collaborator. You do not live on the border for nothing!" the first gendarme shouted. "You will sign a paper admitting to this."

I looked from one to the other and then down again at my hands clenched tightly together in my lap. I could think of no response. The interrogation continued for another half hour, the same accusations stated over and over until I grew numb. It began to seem as if I were on the outside of the room somewhere looking in at myself sitting there, head down, eyes closed. Finally the first gendarme yelled, "Look at me!" I raised my eyes to his. "We are not finished with you. You will admit to these crimes! You will be punished!"

He turned and left, the second man following behind. Immediately a guard came and took me back to the other girls. I sank down on the mat, relieved to be back in this room.

As soon as the gendarmes were through interrogating us, the guards clomped to our cell, handed us buckets and mops, and herded us out into the streets. We were taken first to the train station, where the passengers stared at us, a strange group comprising young women carrying pails, brooms, and rags guarded by soldiers with bayonets drawn and pointed. I wanted to crawl under a bench and hide. I, who had walked confidently through the streets of Bucharest to the salon, to the dresses waiting for me to sew them into creation, proud of my ability to please my clients, now went as a scrubwoman . . . as a criminal.

The four of us were directed to the women's rest room in the station and told to scrub out the toilets and wash the floors. Filthy rags littered the floorboards and cockroaches scuttled out from every corner, scurrying ahead of my feet. The toilet bowls were caked, yellow, grimy; I had to refrain constantly from vomiting into the bowl I was scrubbing.

From the train station we were marched to the government office buildings, where we had to clean more toilets and scrub all of the floors. Everywhere we went the guards followed us, standing as close as possible, watching every swish of the mop, push of the bucket. Finally at dusk, when all of the toilets and floors were clean, we were taken back to our cell, locked inside, and given our first meal of the day—a bowl of broth and a small chunk of bread.

The next morning each of us was again taken out individually and interrogated in the small room, asked the same questions, told to admit to the same things. In the afternoon the procedure was also identical; we were forced to clean more toilets and floors. As this routine continued for the next three days, I realized, little by little, that the Hungarians did not feel as free to persecute us as the Iron Guard had. While the Iron Guard arrested and murdered Jews without a moment's hesitation, for no cause, the gendarmes of Hungary felt the need to have a reason to arrest us, as there were many intermarriages in Hungary, especially in Budapest, and even the premier had a Jewish daughter-in-law. The daily interrogations were meant to force us to admit to treason, a just reason for persecution.

Finally, after five days, the guards did not come to us with pails and mops after the interrogation. It was Sunday and the offices would not be open for us to clean. In the afternoon we were led out into the walled court-yard of the prison for an hour. There I saw my father for the first time since we arrived, sitting in the sun with the other men, his back to me. As soon as I looked into his face I could see the difference in him; strands of white were beginning to appear in his beard and hair and he sat bent over, his shoulders hunched together. He smiled when he saw me.

"Seren," he said.

"Hello, Father. How are you?" I asked anxiously.

"I'm . . . all right. And you?"

"I'm fine."

I sat down beside him and we gazed into each other's eyes for a few mo-ments. "Are you sure you're all right?" he asked.

"Yes, I'm sure." The guards were there as always, walking back and forth with their rifles.

"They have accused—" I whispered.

"Yes, I know," he whispered back, before I could finish the sentence.

"Have you been to the train station too?"

"No, on the streets, scrubbing," he answered.

We sat there together for the rest of the hour, hand in hand, each dreaming our separate dreams of home, of Esther and Zipporah, of my mother. Then we were taken back to our cells again.

Another week went by, the days merging together as we went from the interrogation room to the train station to the government buildings and back again to our cell. Every day I was asked the questions, over and over. Every day I was told to confess to the crime of spying. Although I would not admit to anything I had not done, I could not understand how one signed something invisible; no paper was ever shown to me.

One morning as I was crouched in the metal interrogation chair, trying to comprehend exactly what it was I had allegedly done, I glimpsed a movement out of the corner of my eye and then, before I had a chance to flinch, a sudden explosion smashed against the side of my face. I had never felt such intense pain. My whole body contracted into my head as the stabs of pain expanded, overwhelming all other sensations. Then I felt a warm wetness trickling down my cheek and I touched it tentatively. There was red on my hand—blood.

Another wave of shock hit, this time in my shoulder. A loud roaring broke through the stinging every few seconds and finally I realized that the men were still shouting at me. Then my long hair was grabbed by one of the men, wound around his fist and pulled, yanked so hard that I felt as if my scalp would tear away from my head. Finally he let go and I collapsed on the floor. Kicking me in the side with the toe of his boot, the soldier yelled, "Get out! Get out!" I stumbled back to our cell.

That afternoon we were again shoved into the streets. While the men and women on the sidewalks had grown used to seeing us by now, for we had been coming and going like guarded criminals for almost two weeks, they looked at me this time as if I had suddenly appeared from nowhere. A man dressed in the manner of a businessman, all in black, approached me and stopped momentarily as he saw my swollen, bruised cheek. As he continued on by me I felt a sudden stickiness on my cheek, a slime. As I wiped the spit from my face a group of schoolchildren walked by, laughing and chattering. The drawn bayonets fascinated them and one or two ran back to look at us again. An old man shuffled by then, spat out, "Dirty, rotten Jews. Get out of my way!" One of the boys immediately kicked Mozelle in the leg, and when she cried out he glanced at the guard, who looked away. The boy kicked her again and then ran off, chanting, "Dirty Jew . . . dirty Jew . . . dirty Jew."

Finally it was Sunday again and I could see my father. The beatings had continued all week, always including pulling my hair, until finally one day the skin behind my ears cracked and blood ran down my neck. Now I saw my father sitting on a bench next to Reuben Handler, talking quietly. I could not believe it was my father; his hair and beard had turned entirely white and he sat hunched over, bent down like an old grandfather. I stared at him for a few moments. Then I walked up to him, smiled, sat down beside him and clutched his hand in both of mine.

"It's a nice day," I said.

"Yes," he answered softly.

"The sun feels warm."

"It does."

"I'm so happy to see you again."

"Thank you." He paused, looking into my eyes. The strong blue color of his irises, as clear as the sky above the mountains after a rain, seemed to have been washed away, leaving his eyes pale, faded. "How are you, Seren?" he asked.

"Oh, all right. I always get along." I did not mention the change in his appearance, the withering. So we sat, his hand in mine, taking comfort in simply being with each other for as long as we were allowed.

The next morning when I was taken in for questioning, a different officer was there, wearing a uniform unlike those of the gendarmes. His was more like those worn by the Iron Guard: tall, black boots with the trousers stiffly tucked inside; a black belt over a brown military jacket; a dark, slanted cap bearing an eagle and the same symbol, the red swastika. He spoke to the other men in German, saying, "Leave me alone! I will take care of her." They closed the door and immediately he began to yell at me in German. I had studied the language in school and could understand the meaning of the words themselves, but still could make no sense of what I was being asked to admit.

"You are a spy. Admit it! Now!" he demanded.

I sat there, trying to think of what to say.

"Admit it!" he shouted again, striking me on the shoulder.

"I don't know when I was a spy. I don't know what to admit," I said quietly.

"Don't play those games with me! This is an officer of the Third Reich who is speaking to you. I won't stand for all of those lies you have been telling the stupid Hungarian officers. Do you understand?"

Again he paused, waiting for me to answer. Then he struck me again. "Do you understand?"

"Yes," I said.

"Good. I have been warned about you. You are the worst of this whole stinking lot! Not only have you lived on the border, not only have you been a spy for our Russian communist enemies, but you have crossed the border.

You entered Hungary illegally over a year ago. You came from Bucharest as a spy and stole across the border. You are in league with the capitalistic, communistic devils who are trying to take over the world with their god-less atheism. There is nothing worse than an evil Jew, a Christ-killer, who has turned his back on his country as well as on God!" He went on and on, shouting the same things over and over, pacing back and forth in front of me for more than an hour. I tried not to listen but I heard all of the words; they rang in my head like hammers and I could not stop them.

Finally the haranguing stopped, the pacing stopped. I looked up. He fell on me, striking my face with both fists, slamming into my eyes, my cheeks and jaw, cursing each time he struck. I tried to cover my face with my arms but he flung them away, pinned them behind me with one hand while he continued to pound with the other. Then I blacked out, the words "You will be shot. Shot!" fading away into a long, dark tunnel that had no end.

I woke up on the floor of a black room, the pain so intense that I could not lift my head. I knew that I was not in the cell with the other girls, but I did not know where I was or what time it was or if it was still the same day. Sleep must have overtaken me again; light was struggling into the tiny cell through a small window high up on one wall. When I raised my head the room began to whirl and a pounding beat against my temples. Again I sank into sleep.

The next time I awoke the crashing inside my head had subsided some-what and I could sit up without feeling as if I would collapse again, but one eye would not open. Struggling to the window, I looked out with the other eye. The courtyard was spread out before me, snow softly falling on the benches where my father and I had sat together. I was in the basement of the prison. Hanging on to the walls of the room, I made my way around the cell, finding a mat on the floor, a toilet, a sink, and a small metal mirror. I looked into the mirror. A lump of swollen flesh looked back at me, every-thing red, mashed, one eye a mass of broken blood vessels, the other com-pletely swollen shut. Tears welled up behind my eyes but they did not fall.

For two weeks I was locked in that cell, a guard bringing food every night, shoving it at me without a word. I kept track of the days, of the light coming and fading in the window, of the snow drifting down without a sound, and slept and was afraid, terrified that I would never get out of that cell, that I would never see my mother, my father again.

Then one afternoon I heard creaking sounds in the courtyard. A hand pump not far from my window was making the sound as I watched Mr. Bergman push it up and down. The other men were shambling across the courtyard to the pump, slowly removing their shirts as they came. Evidently it was Sunday and the prisoners were being allowed to wash themselves. Then my father walked by my window. His back was bloated, bruised, striped with cuts running the entire length, from his neck to his waist. Streaks of dried blood ran along each festering slash. He walked even more bent than the last time I had seen him and his face was thin, the cheeks sunken into hollows. "Oh, Father," I whispered, tears running like rain down my cheeks.

The next morning a guard opened my cell door and ordered me to follow him. *Either I will be beaten again, now that my face is almost healed, or I will be shot,* I thought. But I was taken back to our cell and told that we were all being taken to a prison in Budapest. First, however, the other girls and I were to go back to our homes, pack up our families and move them somewhere, anywhere we could find, but they could not remain living near the border.

"Oh, Seren," Mozelle said, as soon as the guard had left us for a minute, "we thought maybe you were dead."

"I'm alive!" I said, laughing at first but then stopping when my cheek began to hurt again.

"Why do we have to go back by ourselves?" she asked. "Why can't our fathers go too?"

"Haven't you seen them?" I asked her. "They don't want anyone to see how our fathers have been beaten."

"But where will we move our families?" Leah asked. "Where can they go? We have no permits to settle anywhere."

"We'll have to see," I said. "We'll just have to see . . ."

The four of us began the long trip back to Valea Uzului accompanied by the same gendarmes who had taken us away from our homes a month before. It was by now the end of November and bitterly cold. We had fourteen days to return home, find a place for our families to live, and come back to the prison at Miercurea-Cuic. If we were not back at the end of the time limit, a warrant would be put out for our arrests, and when found, we would be shot. We hurried along, stopping again at farms in the evenings to eat and sleep, and by the end of the fifth day we were only a few miles from Valea Uzului. At the last peasant farm the gendarmes commandeered a horse and wagon to use in moving our families. Then we were at the mill and the gendarmes left us, but not before reiterating once more the length of time we had left and what would happen should we fail to return.

As soon as they were out of sight I ran to the house and opened the door. My mother was standing at the stove, stirring a pot absentmindedly. She looked up, startled at the noise of the door opening and closing. "You!" she exclaimed. She ran to me and held me very tightly. Then she asked, "Where is your father? Is he all right? Where is he?"

"He's in prison . . . in Miercurea-Cuic," I answered. "I've been there too."

"Is he all right?"

"He is . . ."

"Is he all right? Tell me!"

"He could not come. They wouldn't let him. But he's all right—hurt a little, but all right."

She began to cry, pulling me close to her again. I could not tell her about the beatings, about my father becoming a haggard old man almost overnight. She probably sensed it, however, for she cried in my arms for a long while. Then she straightened and said, "How long can you stay? Are you free now?"

"I can stay for only a little while. I have to be back again by the end of next week."

"Then why did they let you go?"

"To help you move. We can't live here anymore."

"Oh, no! Not that too!" My mother looked around her kitchen, at the familiar black kettles sitting on the stove, at the long table where we had all gathered on many joyful holidays. "But where can we go?" she asked. "We have nowhere to go!"

"Well, we will have to get a permit somewhere. Maybe we can get one in Reghinal-Sasesc. Herman and Tamara and Eugene and Rose all live there. It would not be so bad if you could live with them."

"No, no . . . it would not be so bad. But my house . . . Is it because we live so near the border?"

"That is what they have said."

"Oh, Seren, do you think we will ever be allowed to come back here again? Have you heard anything about the war?"

"One day I overheard the guards talking. They said there were plans to resettle all the Jews, to take us to the island of Madagascar. Maybe we will all be sent there eventually. Maybe we will all be together again after the war."

"Yes, perhaps. But still . . . Well, we can only hope for the best. There is nothing else we can do. We better tell Esther and Zipporah and begin to pack."

The next morning we led the horse and wagon from house to house, loading only a trunk or two and a basket at each stop, for there were six families to move.

Finally we were ready to begin the long journey through the mountains. Our plan was to walk with the horse and wagon to the town of Miercurea-Cuic to see the men in prison. From there the different families would go wherever they could.

We set out early one afternoon. On the seat of the wagon were Ira Bergman's wife and two small daughters, the reins grasped tightly in Mrs. Bergman's hands as the horse walked at a slow, clopping gait; behind her old Mr. Stern sat bundled in a large wooden chair while the frail wife of Samuel Mosheh reclined on a pile of quilts. Behind them were the black trunks, the wicker baskets, bundles tied with string, and finally, a little nest made of pillow and blankets for the small children who would begin to cry after struggling along for a few miles and want to ride, pretending they were still at home in their warm beds.

As we started away from the house and mill, my mother kept glancing back, taking a few steps forward and then stopping, looking back once more until there was nothing to see but the road stretching behind into the forests.

The journey was hard, slow; we had to stop often to rest, to quiet a crying child, to find water and food. We had brought along what little money we had available to us, the money our fathers once had in the Romanian banks lost to us forever. We bought food and the privilege of staying in barns overnight. When the money was gone we exchanged old family jewelry for these necessities. Before we left my mother had given me her emerald ring, which I wore on a chain under my dress. She carried all of the other jewelry my father had given her in a silk bag. At one farm a silver chain was traded for food, at another a gold ring.

Snow fell off and on through the cold November days, the wind gusting the flakes into drifts the horse could not struggle through. We helped him along, the women pulling from the sides and the other girls and I pushing from behind until we were through one drift and up against another. We pushed and rested, rested and pushed, the small children climbing up on the wagon to nap and then down again to walk for a way, holding their mothers' hands. Zipporah trudged along beside one girl and then another, chatting all the while. The trip was harder on Esther, who was the youngest of the family, who had always been allowed to remain a favored child, to sleep until very late in the morning, to do little work in the house, and who now had to sleep in a cold stable and do without even a cup of tea. But Esther had a sweetness that Zipporah did not, and her sweet smile, her uncomplaining ways made me love her more than ever.

Finally we arrived at Miercurea-Cuic and hurriedly walked through the streets my father and the other men were forced to wash each day. The women all hoped to see their husbands once again, but when we arrived at the prison we were told that not only was this impossible but if we did not find a place to settle immediately we would be arrested and imprisoned. There was nothing left to do but board the train to Reghinal-Sasesc, hoping that Herman or Eugene would be able to secure permits for us. The other families went to different cities, to other relatives, all longing for the same thing—a bed, a stove, a simple room where no one would say, "You are not wanted here!"

When the train stopped at the station, I left my mother and sisters at the depot and rushed through the streets asking people I met if they knew the whereabouts of Herman; he, if anyone, would be known in the city as he was always a friend to everyone and everyone a friend to him. One of the first persons I asked directed me to the exact apartment number in the building where he lived. We reached his building quickly. It was an old brick building surrounded by many others all looking the same. We climbed the stairs to the apartment and then hesitated before the door.

"Maybe this isn't the right apartment," Esther said. "We might be arrested if we disturb someone."

"We have to take the chance and knock," I answered. "I don't know what else to do."

Then my mother said, "Listen! Listen!" Above the clanging of the streetcars going by, above the chattering of the birds on the roof, could be heard the strums of a guitar and a clear, rich voice lifting up into the air, higher and higher.

"It's Tamara!" Zipporah cried.

"Yes, it's Tamara," my mother said, and smiled for the first time since we had left home.

THERE WERE STILL MANY DIFFICULTIES TO OVERCOME, however; not only did my mother and sisters have no assurance that they could remain with Herman and Tamara or with Rose and Eugene, but there was almost nowhere for them even to sit down if we did, by some miracle, secure the permits. Herman and Tamara lived with their three near-grown sons, Miksha, Ernie, and Joseph, in one room with a small kitchen. Eugene and Rose, who lived in the same building, had even less space with their five children: Emma, who was fifteen; Alfred, fourteen; Magda, thirteen; and two little girls. The seven of them all slept in one room, ate in one room, sewed and swept and read and played—all in the one room.

It was decided that my mother would stay with Rose and Eugene to help with the children, Zipporah with Herman and Tamara, and Esther would be sent to Shlomo in Satu-Mare. Thus, each family would be adding only one more person.

That evening Herman came back from the mill outside the city where he and Eugene had managed to secure work. He was cheerful, boisterous, welcoming us as if he had a palace with many rooms to offer instead of the small corner of one room.

"I will be able to get permits for you and Zipporah," he told my mother. "Don't worry. We will all be fine!" He was tall and fair, straight as a pine tree, and I felt such sorrow remembering how our father had been the same.

The very next day Herman came home with the permits, as he promised. I'll never know how he accomplished it, for the police supposedly were not giving out any more to Jews. In the morning, Esther and I went back to the station and I waited with her for the train to Satu-Mare.

"What if Shlomo and his wife don't want me to come?" she asked.

"How can they not want you? You are family! Besides, Shlomo and Zipporah never got along. They are both fireballs. But he has always liked you. Who doesn't?" I teased, reaching up to stroke her cheek, for she was much taller than I was.

She smiled, tentatively. "Will you write to me?"

"Of course."

She waved to me out of the open train window. As I rode a different train back to my father, to prison, that image stayed with me—her hand slowly moving back and forth until it was only a light speck against the long black train receding further and further into the distance.

Ten

THREE DAYS AFTER I LEFT MY MOTHER AND ZIPPORAH in Reghinal-Sasesc, my father and I and the other eight people who were arrested with us were taken from the prison and put on a train to Budapest. It was, by now, early December. A penetrating, bitter wind seeped in through the cracks around the windows. Although we fought against it, stamping our feet to keep the blood circulating, moving stiff fingers inside our gloves, pulling our coats tighter, trying to sink into the warmth of the wool, nothing helped. Not even the seats, small, hard benches with no coverings, gave comfort.

Having taken the trains many times back and forth between Bucharest and home, I expected the discomfort and brought along a pillow for my father. I knew that he would be too tall to curl up on the bench like the others did.

"Here, Father," I said. "I brought this for you."

He opened his eyes and looked at me intently, asking silently, *Have you seen the wounds on my back that I've tried so hard to keep hidden from you?*

"I want you to be comfortable," I quickly said. "I don't need a pillow."

"Thank you, Seren," he said, his eyes still looking into mine. Then he lay back, whispered, his white hair falling against his face, "I'm getting old . . . so old . . ."

I clasped one of his hands in mine and sat quietly, staring out into the passing fields.

For eight days we traveled through Transylvania. Each afternoon or early evening the train pulled into the outskirts of another city, slowed, eased into the station. It made no different except that the name of each new city meant that we were being taken further and further away from the rest of our families without knowing when we would see them again. Every time we reached a new city we were handed over to the local police, who kept us either for a few hours or overnight in the city jail.

The ten of us did not speak among ourselves; there were other, Gentile passengers, and each of us was lost in thought, too afraid to voice the fears that kept running through our heads in time to the rhythms of the clacking rails beneath the train. Once or twice I tried to say a few words to Nehamias, the doctor, who had been kind to me whenever I was home for a visit. Now he sat alone, his wife and small children left behind. Often he sat quite still, staring at his hands. I had looked at them in quick glances when I thought he would not notice. They were dark red and mottled with shiny purple splotches, the fingers twisted in stiff knots.

One day he suddenly began to speak to me as if I had appeared to him in a dream. "Did you know that each country has its favorite method of torture?" he asked, his voice quiet, the words coming out slowly, carefully.

I looked at him, knowing that he must have suffered as much as my father had.

"The Chinese once used the water torture, the French the rack. Do you know what the Hungarians do that is unique?" he asked.

I shook my head.

"They place an egg in boiling water, leaving it in until it has absorbed as much heat as possible. Then they quickly flip it out into a man's hand. They close his hand over it and hold it closed while the heat burns into the flesh in one, long sear. When the egg has cooled they replace it in the boiling water and repeat the process on the other hand. Once the hands are so badly burned that they will no longer open, they place the steaming egg under the soft flesh of the armpit."

He stopped abruptly, and closed his eyes. The restless hands trembled in his sleep.

ON THE EIGHTH DAY AFTER LEAVING MIERCUREA-Cuic, the train reached the old border between Hungary and Transylvania. The gendarmes handed us over to the Hungarian police who would take us the rest of the way to Budapest. While the other girls and I had previously stayed together in one big room, this time each of us was put in a separate room. I did not understand what was happening, the reason for this isolation, yet in the back of my mind I knew that the gendarmes would not leave until morning. I had sensed their eyes on the other girls and me during the long days and nights on the train. Not adventurous like the younger men who had rushed off to join the German army, these men were old and fat. They repulsed me.

During the night I neither got undressed nor went to sleep, sitting on my bed hour after hour, listening. Finally, long after midnight, I heard heavy footsteps coming toward my door and a key chain rattling with each approaching step. Quickly I ran to the window and checked it, finding it unlocked. I opened it, climbed up on the sill and jumped down the two stories, landing on my feet but then losing my balance and toppling over on the cement, scraping my leg. Looking around hurriedly, I saw that I was very close to a coal chute leading to the basement of the building. I slid down the chute onto a pile of coal, the air musty and pitch-black, absolutely unable to see anything, not hearing anything except the galloping of my heart. Finally, realizing that no one was coming after me, I curled up on the coal and went to sleep.

In the morning the new guards came looking for me and found me there, smudged and chilly. The gendarmes were gone. I do not know what happened to Ruth, Mozelle, and Leah during the night; I never asked them and they did not tell me. While none of us could prevent suffering, each of us could at least save the others from the added burden of another's sorrow. We gave by denying our own needs to share pain.

WE SOON DISCOVERED THAT WHILE WE HAD THOUGHT the first part of the trip was insufferable, the remaining part would be even more difficult. While the Transylvanians had not respected us, and tried to avoid any close contact, they did not seem to hate us. This was not so with the Hungarians.

We were seated in a compartment at the front of the train in a car that had no toilet. When one of us had to use the toilet all ten of us had to go along. The guards marched us through the entire length of the train past all the other passengers to the toilet on the last car. As we walked by them each one did something to us: one kicked at our legs, one spat at our faces, one punched our backs, and still another called out, "Dirty Jews! Filthy, rotten Jews!"

It was so with each car, all the way to the end of the train and back, day after day, until my legs were bruised, my face slimy from the spit.

One of the worst of the tormentors was an enormous Hungarian woman who was in the last days of pregnancy, her belly greatly swollen and bulging from her coat. Every time we passed her she held up her two small children, one in each arm. The little girl spat at us and the boy flailed his feet into each passing arm. Their mother urged them on, crying, "Vermin! Vermin! Vermin!"

The train inched across the vast plains of Hungary, great desertlike stretches of nothing but snow and sky for as far as one could see. On the thirteenth night we again stayed on the train as it continued on through the long, lonely stretches of countryside. In the evening one of the men had to use the toilet; he had restrained himself all day, as we all had to save ourselves from the tormenting trip through the train, but he could wait no longer. In the first two cars we were kicked and abused as usual, but in the third car, no one paid attention to us. The passengers were all huddled around the pregnant woman, who was wailing and thrashing, her voice moaning loudly above the roar of the train. An old woman was wiping her brow, another quieting her children.

A short while after we returned to our compartment, one of the Hungarian policemen came up to us and asked, "Which one of you is the doctor?"

"There's no doctor here," Nehamias said softly.

"Don't lie to me! It says on my papers that one of you swine is a doctor. Now which one is it?"

"I was a doctor once," continued Nehamias, "but no more. I am no more . . ." He held up his hands briefly and then let them fall into his lap.

"Well, see if you can do something, pig! That woman's having her kid. She's yelling her damn head off. See if you can shut her up!" With that he grabbed Nehamias by the back of his jacket and shoved him out of the compartment and down the aisle.

We sat there for several quiet hours, each lost in thought as the wheels rolled relentlessly on through the darkness. Finally Nehamias came back and sank onto the bench. He said nothing for a long time, staring out into the blackness.

"She's dead," he finally announced to no one in particular. "She died. The baby too. There was nothing I could do."

He lapsed back into silence and, finally, into sleep. His hands flew to his face once, twice, and then were still.

Eleven

THE NEXT MORNING WE ARRIVED IN BUDAPEST. AS soon as the train came to a full stop, we were ordered to get out and line up at the far end of the station. Our bodies were half turned to wood from the days of sitting on the hard seats, and walking was painful.

After several hours we came to a high fence of barbed wire, and beyond, a grouping of buildings barely visible in the dreary, gray light of late December. Shivering in the sleet blowing at us on a strong north wind, we stood at the gate to this prison, which we would later come to know as Kistarcha, for an hour, two, until finally we were led to our new cells, one for the men and another for the other girls and me.

Again we were interrogated, accused of being spies, threatened. This time, however, it seemed to be merely a formality, for at the end of the second day a Hungarian guard came to us and said, "Get out! We don't want you here, you filthy pigs. Get out!"

"We are free?" I asked.

"Can't you hear? I said to get out, didn't I?"

"Oh, I can't wait to see my father. He will be so happy that we can go back to Transylvania," Mozelle cried.

"Who said anything about the men?" the guard asked. "They're staying. This is a men's prison. We don't allow Jew whores. Get out! Get out! Get out!"

He came at us with his gun raised. Quickly we put on our coats, running to the door with only a button or two fastened and our scarves trailing behind us. Once outside we ran until we were at the gate, the soldier chasing after us, and rushed through it and out into the countryside, the fields barren and brown under a light coating of snow.

Mozelle began to cry. "What are we going to do?" she sobbed. "We are in the middle of nowhere, so far from home. We don't even have a home. What are we going to do?"

"We could go to our mothers if we had some money," said Leah. "But how can we? We have nothing. And if we stay here the Hungarian soldiers will arrest us again."

"My mother gave me an emerald ring," I said, pulling it out from under my dress where it hung on a chain. "Let's walk back to Budapest. I'll sell it there and we'll all have enough money to buy train tickets."

That is what we did. I sold the ring and we boarded the train once more, riding the long, long miles in reverse, wondering if we would ever see our fathers again.

When I arrived I went immediately to Herman and Tamara's room.

"Seren, you're back!" Tamara said. "How wonderful! Have they let you go?"

"Yes, but not my father."

"Oh, I'm so sorry . . . but at least you're here. You can stay with us too. We'll have a nice time together! I've invited some friends over tonight to sing with me. You'll like them!"

"No. No. I am going to find a separate place for Mother, Zipporah, and me. You hardly have enough room for yourselves here."

"We want you to stay! The more people there are around, the better I like it! It makes me forget about the war," she answered.

"I simply can't impose on you. We have some jewelry left. We'll sell a few pieces and I'll find a place with the money I get for them."

"But what will you do when that money runs out?"

"I'll find work. Surely someone will hire me. I acquired a lot of experience in Bucharest," I said.

"No one is hiring anyone! Herman and Eugene are lucky that they have found work at the mill. All of the Jewish women who might have once hired you to sew for them are now afraid to spend any money. No one knows what will happen. They're holding on to their money if they still have any, and all of the Jewish shops are closed." She smiled at me and pulled out her guitar. "Please stay with us. I'll sing for you. Zipporah comes and goes so much that she is little company."

"Thank you for asking me, but I can't," I answered.

"At least stay until you find a place, then."

"All right."

"Good! Now listen to this new song a friend taught me."

She sang a song about spring and the blossoming flowers, sang until I had almost forgotten that my father was in prison, our home gone, Eliezer perhaps dead, and the rest of the family broken apart and scattered.

EARLY THE NEXT MORNING I BEGAN TRUDGING UP and down the streets of Reghinal-Sasesc, looking for a room to rent. For days I continued to look, inquiring wherever I went, but no one had even heard of a vacancy. Finally, one morning when I was walking along a street of old family dwellings, thinking that perhaps someone had recently decided to rent out a room, I saw an elderly Jewish woman tacking a notice to her door. I walked up to her and asked, "May I see the room?"

She glanced at me, frightened. "Why would you want to rent from me?" she asked, her eyes darting from my hair to my face and back again.

"It's all right," I said, realizing that she had mistaken me for a Gentile. "I'm also Jewish. I need a room for my mother and sister and me."

"Come on, then," she said quickly, and turned to go inside.

I followed her into the very small wooden house. She led me to the second of two rooms and opened the door. "Here it is," she said. Hurriedly, I entered. Peeling green paint hung from the ceiling, from the walls, curled along the windowsills, revealing a deep gray underpaint. A small window on the far wall was broken in one corner and stuffed with a dusty brown gunnysack. The room itself was bare; not a chair or rug or even a bed stood on the worn floor.

"Doesn't it come with furniture?" I asked.

"No, I don't have any. And I have no money to buy some. But you can use the kitchen," she said. I remembered seeing an icebox, an old iron stove, and a table with two small chairs at one end of the other room. "My daughter lives next door and I eat my meals with her."

It would have to do, I decided, and gave the woman enough money for the first month's rent.

"Thank you," she said. "I'm a widow. It's become very hard for me to get along. This will help out some." Timidly she smiled at me and closed the door.

The next day I came back with two benches that Rose and Eugene were not using and some weathered boards that Herman found at the mill. Placing the boards across the benches, I made a bed and covered it with straw-filled sacks. Tamara had given me some pillows, and Rose some sheets. Once I swept the floor, I was ready to move my mother and Zipporah out of their crowded places.

That evening we came back with our few clothes—an extra dress each and several pairs of stockings. Zipporah took one quick look at the room. "You don't expect me to stay in this, do you?" she asked. "It's a hovel!"

"It's not so bad," my mother said.

"Not bad? There isn't even any furniture! I'm going back to Herman and Tamara's," she yelled, and started walking toward the door.

"I looked and looked! There isn't anything else!" I shouted. "You shouldn't stay with Herman any longer. We've imposed on them long enough!"

"I'll ask him," she answered. "He won't mind. He's my brother!"

"He wouldn't say no even if he did mind. He's too tenderhearted."

"But he doesn't mind. I'm not staying here!" She marched to a box in the corner and sat down.

Too exhausted to answer, I crawled into the makeshift bed. My mother, who had given up arguing with Zipporah long ago, followed me. Zipporah remained on the box, arms folded across her chest, saying over and over, "I'm not staying . . . I'm not staying." Finally, after several hours, she lay across the bottom of the bed and fell asleep.

In the morning Zipporah left for Herman's one-room apartment, my mother busied herself in the kitchen, and I set out to find work. I decided to look first in the salons, which were small and not at all luxurious like those in Bucharest where I had worked, but I was not looking for elegance. Many of the shops were closed, the word *"Juden"* written across the door in large red letters. On one salon a notice was posted: *"Wer beim Juden kauft ist ein Volksverräter"* (Whoever buys from a Jew is a traitor to his people). The street where most of the Jewish shops had been was deserted, strewn with broken chairs and tables, broken boards. Shattered windows were scattered over the cobblestones, the persistent clacking of an unhinged shutter rising above the howling of the cold wind.

That night my mother and I had nothing to eat for supper. We sat over tea, warming our hands on the hot cups. "I will find work," I told my mother. "It takes time."

"I know you will," she answered. "A little fasting never hurt anyone."

"Herman and Rose have so little. I don't want to ask them for food. If they give it to us they will be taking it away from Miksha, Ernie, and Joseph."

"I know. I know . . . But we'll be all right. I've never seen you give up on anything once you decide you want it," she said, laughing, squeezing my cheek.

The next day I went from door to door, asking if there was any sewing that I might do, receiving the same no over and over. Then, late in the day, I came to a house set back from the street on top of a hill. Below the house spread a wide yard with two wooden sheds on one side. A tall, thin old man came to the door. "Well?" he said in an impatient tone.

"I'm looking for work," I answered. "I'm a seamstress . . . a good one!" I smiled at him as if my heart were not racing, my palms perspiring.

"Can you make men's shirts?" he asked.

"Of course," I said, even though I had never in my life sewn anything for a man.

"I have a commission to make shirts for the army and I do need someone. But I can't pay you very much. In fact, the pay is almost nothing . . . two forints per shirt."

"I'll take the job," I answered.

Early the next morning my new employer brought out bolts of dark material and two sewing machines, instructing me to follow him to the bottom of the hill to one of the small shacks I had noticed the day before. "This isn't fit to live in," he said, "or I would have rented it out. But you can sew here, can't you?"

"Yes, certainly," I answered quickly.

"Here's the shirt you're to make and you have the cloth. There's some thread up in the house. I'll bring it down to you."

"Fine."

He left me with the treadle machines, a dusty, cold shed, piles of cloth, and a shirt for which I had no pattern. I did not even have a worktable. Looking around, I found two sawhorses and an old tabletop in the corner, and there, after a little dusting, was my cutting board. Setting up a machine on another old table, I began to unravel the seams of the shirt. Once I had it all apart, I had my pattern. When my employer brought down the thread, I was cutting, he was pleased, and by the end of the day I had completed several shirts.

A week later I came home to our room to find Esther sitting at the table with my mother. A few days before, Shlomo had been arrested by the Hungarian police and taken away. My mother was heartbroken. "Shlomo, Shlomo," she cried to herself. "First it was Eliezer and then your father and now, you. When will it end?"

"What happened to his wife and baby?" I asked. "Surely they were not taken too?"

"They have moved in with her parents," Esther answered. "I didn't want to stay with them. They have barely enough to eat themselves. So I came back here."

"I'm glad you came back to us," I said. "We've all missed you. And we have our own room now. You can stay here, and you can even work. I have a job and my employer could use another seamstress."

"But I don't know how to be a seamstress. I've never sewn one seam!" she cried.

"It's not so hard. Will you try?" I asked.

"I would like to work with you . . . if you think I can do it."

"Wonderful! You'll learn quickly. I'm a good teacher," I laughed, hugging her. At least I had my little sister back again.

The next day I took Esther to work with me and taught her how to cut out the shirts; she cut and I sewed. She learned so quickly that my employer asked me if I could find another girl to work and I thought of Emma, Rose's eldest daughter. She was fifteen, two years younger than Esther, and glad to have the chance of earning money to help her family. Very soon the three of us were working together. Every night we had enough money to buy a few groceries for our dinner, sometimes nothing more than a potato or two, but we did not go hungry.

We worked throughout the winter of 1942. I managed to pay our rent on time every month. We would have been relatively content, if one could call it that, had it not been for the knowledge that our father was still in prison without any hope of release and continuing to deteriorate. In the beginning, in December of 1941, he wrote clear, logical letters asking about the family or telling about the condition of the other men with him. After a month he began to seem confused, asking about events that had happened long ago. "Have you heard from Herman?" he wrote. "Tell him I forbid him to desert the army again." Another time he asked me to speak with the foreman at the mill about shipping a load of lumber to Bulgaria. Each time I received a letter I was afraid to open it, afraid that it would not be from the man I knew to be my father, but from someone living in a reality of his own creation. At the end of January my fears materialized: we received a letter from the prison authorities stating that my father had suffered a nervous breakdown and had been sent to the mental institution in Budapest.

ZIPPORAH TOOK TIME OUT FROM HER DAILY GATH-erings with her friends to visit us. I often sewed on work I had brought home with me while chatting with my mother. On this particular afternoon Zipporah came bursting into the kitchen, her face flushed from the cold, a bright red scarf thrown over one shoulder.

"Mama!" she yelled. "Where are you? I want you to meet someone!"

My mother came running from our room, where she had been resting. "I'm here! Who is it?"

"You'll see. Just wait a minute." She dashed outside and came back almost immediately, pulling along a young man who was so tall he had to duck when he came in through the door.

"Mama, this is Samuel Stein," she said, smiling up at him.

"I am very pleased to meet you," my mother said.

Samuel held out his hand and took my mother's in his. "I can see who Zipporah can thank for her beauty," he said.

"Oh, such a flatterer, Zipporah! Where did you have the good fortune of meeting him?" my mother asked.

"At Herman and Tamara's. Samuel's brother Joshua is a friend of Herman's," she answered. "Isn't Samuel handsome?"

He was. Even I, who usually had no patience or time for Zipporah's friends, had to admit that he was quite attractive. His hair was dark, curling softly about his face, his back broad, body lean and muscular.

"And who are you?" he asked suddenly, turning to me.

"Oh, this is my sister Seren," Zipporah said. "My older sister."

He held out his hand. "Another beauty! Your hair is wonderful! I have always loved long, golden hair. And whom do you take after?" he asked me.

I looked up at him, not sure if he was sincere. "Our father, I guess."

"How lucky you girls are—both so lovely!" he said.

"Well, we're on our way to see another friend," Zipporah said quickly. "Your house was on the way so we stopped in. Good-bye, Mama.

I'll see you again soon." They were out the door and gone in half a minute.

"That Zipporah!" My mother laughed. "She has a good time no matter what!"

LATE THE NEXT AFTERNOON, ESTHER, EMMA, AND I finished our sewing for the day and came out into the early-evening light, climbing the hill to our employer's house to deliver the shirts we had completed.

"Ah, what a day!" Emma said. "How many shirts did we cut out today, anyway?"

"Seventeen," Esther answered.

"Seventeen! No wonder my hand feels like it is ready to fall off."

"Look!" said Esther. "A man is coming up the hill after us. Isn't he Zipporah's friend Samuel?"

"Yes, I believe he is," I said. "I wonder why he's here. You don't think something has happened to Zipporah, do you?" I ran back down to him. "Where's Zipporah? Is she all right?"

"She is fine," he answered. "She's at Herman's."

"Oh, I thought perhaps she was arrested and you came to tell us," I said.

"No, she's fine. I came to see you," he answered.

"Me?"

"Yes. Are you so surprised?"

"Why have you come to see me?"

"Why shouldn't I?"

"You are Zipporah's friend."

"Can't I be your friend too?"

"I suppose."

"Good! May I see you home?"

"I suppose."

"Do you also suppose that you could accompany me along the riverbank tomorrow evening. I want you to see the lights shining on the water."

"Well . . . if you are here after work, I suppose."

He laughed, a rich laugh coming from deep within his chest.

SAMUEL WAS BACK THE NEXT NIGHT AND THE NIGHT after that and all the rest of the nights during that week. We walked along the river, along the quiet streets, along the fields at the edge of the city stretching out under the distant stars. The thought of having someone intelligent and pleasant to talk with at the end of the day made the work go even faster.

The days began to grow warmer, the lilacs to bloom. The three of us worked throughout the balmy days. Often on Saturday evenings everyone went to Herman and Tamara's, where spring blossomed indoors in the laughing songs of Tamara. She invited to their room one woman she met in the market, another she saw across the courtyard. Herman brought home men from the mill. Together they filled the room with people until we were almost sitting in each other's laps. Then Tamara was happy. Then she sang until her voice was hoarse and it was late in the evening and we were all yawning and falling asleep.

On one of these evenings Tamara came up to me during a pause from her singing. She was wearing a jacket I had sewn for her several years ago. Made of beige and brown plaid wool, it hung a little looser on her now than it had when we all had enough to eat. But the tailored cut of the jacket, the slight flaring about the hips, still flattered her full figure.

"You still wear that jacket?" I asked.

"Of course! I love it, especially since you made it for me. Oh," she went on, squeezing my hand in both of hers, "I have something exciting to tell you!"

"What?" I asked.

"Samuel is in love with you. He wants to marry you!"

"This is exciting?"

"Yes! He is so handsome, so fine. Don't you agree?"

"He is pleasant," I answered.

"Pleasant?"

"Pleasant."

"But he wants to marry you! Is that all you can say?"

"Why did he tell you this? Why didn't he tell me?" I asked.

"He says that you are always talking of work, work, and nothing but work! He didn't know whether you really cared about him or not. So he asked me what I thought you would say if he asked you to marry him. I said that any girl would be very lucky to have him for a husband."

"Not this girl. I have no time to even think about getting married!"

"No time? How can you not have time to get married? You're already twenty-four years old, if you'll forgive me for saying so. Many girls younger than you have been married for years. I was practically a child when I married your brother."

"I realize that. But I have to work! Who will feed my mother if I can't? I will not ask you and Herman to help us. You have too little to share. And why should you? I am perfectly capable of working. I enjoy working."

"This is all fine, but how can you turn down a good man like Samuel? Besides, if you marry him he can provide for you and your mother."

"I can't depend on that! Look what happened to my father, to Shlomo, to many other men."

"Well, it might not happen to Samuel. He might not be arrested and taken away."

"But then again, he might. I just don't feel like becoming engaged. It's the last thing on my mind! The war is growing, we have very little to eat, and my father is far away in prison. I worry about him more and more each day . . . I simply can't become engaged to Samuel or to anyone now."

Tamara had been listening with an impatient expression on her face, one hand on her hip. Now she picked up her guitar and half turned away from me. "Well, there's no talking to you!" she said. With quick, determined steps she walked back to her friends on the other side of the room. For the rest of the evening she ignored me.

THE ATTEMPTS TO PERSUADE ME TO MARRY SAMUEL did not cease, however. They were renewed with great enthusiasm the next time I saw Tamara. She also enlisted the aid of everyone we knew in Reghinal-Sasesc: Herman, Rose, Eugene, my cousins, my mother, Samuel's brother. I could go nowhere without someone singsonging in a sweet, condescending voice, "Samuel is such a fine, young man," or someone else saying, "He's a good man, that Samuel!"

Zipporah, however, was far from pleased at losing Samuel as one of her boyfriends and glared at me while the others were encouraging me to become his fiancée. One Sunday afternoon as my mother and I were sitting quietly together, she mending one of Esther's dresses and I sewing on some shirts I had brought home from work, Zipporah suddenly opened the door from the outside and came into the kitchen, alone.

"Hello, Mama," she said quickly, her voice tight, contained.

Before our mother could answer, Zipporah turned to me, her dark eyes narrowed. "I want you to stop seeing Samuel!" she said, still standing by the door. "I mean it, Seren!" With a quick toss of her head she swung her long, black hair behind one shoulder like a young bay mare. Looking directly into my eyes again, she asked, "Do you understand?"

"Samuel has been coming to see me," I answered. "I haven't been going to—"

"He's mine!" she interrupted. "He was mine long before he even saw you! I will not let you take him away from me."

"Zipporah, I never intended to take him away from you. He was just there one day when I finished working. He asked if he could see me home. Can I help it if he enjoys my company more than yours? Besides, look at all the men you stole from me at the mill dances. When I asked you not to, you said, 'I'll do whatever I like.'"

"You heard her, Mama!" Zipporah shouted. "You see how mean she is to me!"

"Zipporah, Zipporah . . ." my mother answered, sighing deeply. "You have so many friends. Samuel wants to marry your sister. He talks of nothing else to me. Couldn't you be happy for her?"

"Happy for her?" Zipporah asked. "When she steals my boyfriend right from under my nose? I knew you would take sides with Seren! She's always been your favorite just because she wants to work all day like an old washerwoman and I want to have a little fun once in a while. Well, see if I care! I'll find a man ten times better than Samuel. You wait and see!"

She turned and rushed into the street, slamming the door behind her. For a few seconds my mother and I listened to the sounds of the door reverberating in the cold, still air. Then I burst out, "I can't stand her sometimes! Who does she think she is—coming in here and ordering me around! And the way she talks to you is outrageous!"

My mother sat silent, staring at the needle she held between her thumb and finger, sliding it in and out of the cloth without pulling it through. "She doesn't hurt my feelings," she finally said. "She is how she is. She's Zipporah . . ."

AT WORK, ESTHER AND EMMA BEGAN TO TALK CONstantly of Budapest as rumors of deportation steadily grew stronger. We knew we would not be allowed to remain in Reghinal-Sasesc much longer and feared we would be resettled in another country. The only hope of remaining in Hungary was to escape to Budapest, whose Jewish population was large and intermingled with the rest of the population. Jews made up the majority of the middle class and were almost indispensable to the economy; they were still free to live where they pleased and could come and go as they liked.

One day Esther came to me and said, "All of my friends have gone to Budapest. Couldn't we go too?"

"But what about our work?" I answered. "I can't leave this job. I don't know if I'll get another one."

"Well, could Emma and I go then?" she asked.

"Do you really want to go?"

She hesitated, looking down at her hands for a long moment. Finally she looked at me again. "Yes," she answered softly. "It's not that I want to leave you and Mama. You know that, don't you? I'm so frightened living here! I would feel safer in Budapest."

"Let's see if we can scrape together some money then," I answered. "I've been saving for a train ticket to visit Father. But if you live in Budapest you can see him all the time. I'll stay with Mama."

It was decided: Esther and Emma would leave as soon as possible. When Rose heard of their plans she was reluctant at first to let Emma leave, for she was still a young girl of fifteen. However, Rose knew that Emma would be safer in Budapest, so she gave in and the tickets were purchased.

On a warm April afternoon, a Saturday, we all gathered at Rose and Eugene's tiny room to say good-bye to the two of them. Rose stood looking at her daughter for a long time without letting the tears welling in her eyes fall. Finally she said, "Eugene, could you take a picture of them before they go? It's almost time to leave for the station."

Eugene found the little camera they still owned buried inside one of the boxes packed in the corner of the room. He ushered us all outside into the late-afternoon light slanting across the rooftops, across the streets. "Come on, you two!" he ordered in a pretend-stern voice. "Over by this wall. Now!"

"You too," Esther called to me. "Come and be in the picture with us. You're wearing my favorite dress!"

I stood between them, my sister and my cousin, our arms around each other's waists. *How can I give them up?* I thought.

Herman and Tamara's tall, gangly sons, Miksha, Ernie, and Joseph, were all there, pointing at us and laughing to each other. "The three little tailors . . ." Joseph called out.

"The three giant lumberjacks . . ." Emma called back.

"Silence!" Eugene ordered.

The photograph was taken, the gathering ended. Emma and Esther took the train to Budapest.

A week later, Esther sent a letter with the good news that a woman who owned a small lingerie business had hired them to sew for her. "It's much better here," she wrote. "There are so many intermarriages that almost everyone is part Jewish. I wish you could come too."

While I considered the possibility of joining them, I could not bear to leave my mother alone in our tiny room. The thought of being free of

Tamara's continued attempts to convince me to marry Samuel, however, was nearly enough to persuade me to leave Reghinal-Sasesc. "How can you let him go?" she asked me over and over, interspersing this question with, "Why don't you listen to your sister-in-law who is older and wiser than you?" and, "Don't you want a little happiness for yourself?"

Finally, she had a new approach: "Seren," she said one day, "I have another reason, the best reason, why you should marry Samuel."

We were sitting together, I sewing and she strumming on her guitar.

"Don't you want to hear the reason?" she asked.

"No," I answered, continuing to sew.

"You're impossible! I'll tell you anyway. Herman, who is friends with the police, as you know, has it on good authority that all single women will be arrested soon. The government is setting up a labor force for Jewish women like they have now for Jewish men. But the labor force will only be for single women, not married ones. How can you refuse to get married now?"

"I don't want to get married!" I answered. "Why can't I make you understand such a simple idea? Besides, I wouldn't marry anyone just to get out of something."

"Seren," she said then, stopping her strumming and taking me by the shoulders, "you know that I won't let you have any peace until you agree to marry Samuel. I only want the best for you. I want to see you married."

Deep within me I knew that as stubborn as I was, she was even more persistent; she would not let the matter rest until I gave in. The bickering was wearing me out. "All right," I said. "You win. I'll marry Samuel."

"Oh! Oh!" she exclaimed, jumping up and down, hugging me, twirling me around and around the tiny kitchen. "I'm so happy for you! I can't wait to tell Herman!"

The very next night Samuel was waiting for me after work, his face shining with joy. "Herman has told me the wonderful news, dear Seren," he said softly. "You have made me overflow with happiness." His eyes were filling with tears.

"Oh, well . . ." I stammered, at a complete loss for words.

"I've brought you something," he whispered. He reached into his pocket, pulled out a wide, gold band and slipped it on my finger. "There," he said with a deep sigh. "Now we're officially engaged. I can't wait to get married! How soon can the wedding be, my beautiful Seren?"

"Oh, not for a long time," I answered quickly.

"But why?" he asked, his face crumbling.

"It's not that I don't want to marry you," I answered. "You're a good man, a decent man . . ."

"And you are a treasure!"

"But I'm very busy now. I have a job and I must take care of my mother . . . These things take time."

"Of course. But I won't let you take too long!"

"Yes . . . well . . . I've had a very long day. I think I'll go to bed early tonight." We were still standing at the foot of the hill below my employer's house.

"If you must," he answered, coming closer. "I'll walk you home."

I began to walk very quickly, running at times, almost leaving Samuel far behind. At last I reached our door. "Good night," I called back to Samuel—who was gasping down the sidewalk a few yards behind me—and escaped inside. Feigning a headache, I hurriedly undressed and climbed into bed before my mother could see the ring. As I pulled the covers over my head, burrowing deep down beneath them, I wondered, *What in the world have I let myself in for now?*

Twelve

ONE WEEK LATER MY EMPLOYER RAN OUT OF SHIRT material and could not obtain any more; I was dismissed. Immediately I began to consider joining Esther and Emma in Budapest, but the thought of leaving my mother alone still made me hesitate. Finally, after I had been without work for a week, spending every day looking for another position without any success, I decided that I had to look for employment in Budapest. As my mother and I sat together one evening after supper, I told her of my decision.

She looked directly into my eyes, covering one of my hands with both of hers. "I've been expecting you to go," she said.

"I'll be with Esther and Emma," I answered quickly, relieved that she was not distressed at my leaving.

"I'd like that. I worry about Esther. Rose talks constantly about Emma. The girls are so young. I'd feel better if you were with them."

"I'll look after them."

"Yes, I know," she said, smiling, stroking my cheek with her fingertips. "I can always count on you."

A fullness gathered in my eyes and throat. I looked quickly away. The fullness persisted, even as I jumped up to grab a wet cloth from the sink and wipe away a small spot I had found on the table. Finally the feeling was gone, and I sat down.

"As soon as I've saved some money I'll send for you," I said. "We can all live together again like we did here."

"Oh, I don't know if I would want to leave," she said, looking down at the dampness still clinging to the table.

"Why not? It's safer in Budapest, and you would be with us."

"But Rose and Eugene and the children are here. Rose brings the children by several afternoons a week. The baby calls me Nana now . . . Oh, I told you that yesterday, didn't I? And Tamara invites me to their room for tea even though she already has many friends there. It isn't that I don't want to be with you and Esther, you understand. You do know that, don't you?"

"Yes," I answered, looking away again.

"We always had such a houseful! Remember all the holidays? There was so much work. All that food to prepare! But I wouldn't change one minute of it . . ." She gazed off into space for a long while.

"I don't think I could live in a big city with all those strangers," she finally continued. "I'm a simple person from a small village. I miss our home . . . the trees, the stream, the flowers in the valleys. The violets! How I loved to see them poke through the snow . . . all the lavender petals springing up in the sunlight. Do you remember?"

"Yes, of course I remember. I miss it all so much I can hardly bear it at times. But we have no money. We can't go back to our home and we can't impose on Herman or Rose and their families. When I find work in Budapest I'll send you part of my wages so you can keep this room. It isn't at all like home, but at least it's yours."

"What would I do without you, Seren?" she said, taking my hand again. "Will you also visit your father for me? I know you will visit him, but will you tell him that I think of him every day?"

"I'll send you train fare," I answered. "Then you can come and see him too."

She looked at me, her face paling. For a few minutes she sat very quietly, staring into space again. Finally she looked up. "You will think I'm heartless," she said, "but I couldn't. I just couldn't bear to see him." Again she looked down and was silent. "Do you remember the neighbor we had in Lunca de Mijloc who fainted every time he saw a specialist in Bucharest?" she asked then. "He was so afraid of what the physician would see when he examined him that he lost consciousness as soon as he entered the doctor's office. That's how I would be if I went to see your father—terrified of what I would see."

"I'll visit him, Mama. I'll be near him. It's all right."

"No, it's not all right. I'm humiliated to be so weak."

Her eyes filled with tears. She walked quickly to the bed, pulled down the covers, and began to undress. I sat at the table for a while longer, watching my mother as she pulled off her blue-checked dress, one of the two dresses she owned, and stood in her white slip, barefoot, staring out of the broken window at the blackness. For a moment she looked like a young girl, slight, her hair unrolled and falling down her back in dark waves. Then she shuddered, winding her arms tightly around herself, her hands clasping her bare shoulders. Letting her arms fall, she crawled into bed, turned over onto her side, her back toward me, and was still.

TWO DAYS LATER I RODE THE TRAIN TO BUDAPEST. Emma had written that the shop where she and Esther worked was located only a short distance from the railroad station on a street named Sziget-utca, Island Street, running from the station to the shores of the Danube. The river separated the twin cities, Buda and Pest, the salon being on the Pest side. I began walking down Sziget-utca past apartment buildings stretching up above me in the early-afternoon light in muted shades of gray and brown, past fountains and statues of tall men on horseback. Rain had fallen earlier in the day and a faint white mist still hung above the damp sidewalks, reaching up and around the five- and six-story buildings.

After a few blocks I came to 5-7 Sziget-utca and was surprised at how beautiful the building was, standing elegantly amid a row of brick buildings. I could imagine within it fine, polished parquet floors, gleaming stair railings, sparkling crystal light fixtures similar to those I had seen in the upper-class homes in Bucharest.

On the first floor was the lingerie salon, just as Emma had described it, with a large window facing the street. Looking in, I saw Emma bending over a sewing machine and Esther carrying a pile of fabric to the back of the room. I rapped on the window. Emma jumped up, startled, and ran to the door. "Seren!" she cried. "Oh, Seren, you've come!"

Esther came running and then fell against me, hugging me to her. Both of them began talking at once, telling me about their new life in Budapest. Everything was more than satisfactory: the wages were sufficient, the work was not difficult, and their employer was an agreeable, middle-aged woman who lived on the second floor of the building with her elderly mother.

"She knows very little about sewing, so she can't be too fussy with us," said Esther. "But she's a good businesswoman and sells lingerie to a number of different stores. There's always work. It will be just like it was in Reghinal-Sasesc when the three of us work together again."

"Who's the girl beside you?" I asked then. A small, childlike girl with short black hair and dark eyes was looking at me with a faint smile on her lips. Down her top lip ran a red mark in a line a little to one side of her mouth so that her lips came together in a slightly irregular way when she smiled.

"Oh, this is Ellen!" Emma answered. "She's from the border near Czechoslovakia. She was sent here by the Jewish Congress to be an apprentice."

"I'm pleased to meet you," I said, taking her hand in mine.

"Thank you," she answered in Hungarian, her voice low and soft.

"You look so young to be far from home," I said. "How old are you?"

"Fourteen. There were rumors . . . We were afraid . . . Someone said we would be taken to a ghetto far away," she answered, stopping often as if she could not find the right words. "Mama wanted me to leave while I still could. She hopes that . . . someday I will go to Palestine and I will send for her . . . I had to leave her." Her voice broke and she looked down at her hands twisted tightly together.

"You'll be fine here," I said, patting her on the shoulder. "I left home at thirteen and I'm still around. Esther and Emma can't get rid of me!"

"Don't be silly!" Esther exclaimed. "We can't wait for you to begin working with us again."

"Show me what you do," I answered.

"Look!" Esther said, pulling me to her sewing machine. "First I take a long strip of cloth, make two straps and sew them onto the back panel of the brassiere. Emma adds the front section and Ellen finishes the garment with hooks and eyes."

"You do the same thing over and over all day long?" I asked.

"Yes."

"You never complete a whole garment?"

"No."

"I want no part of it! I would not be able to stand it. I'm a dressmaker, not a machine!"

"You get used to it," Esther said.

"No, never! I have to have variety. I'll stay with the two of you, but I'll find my own work."

At that moment another girl came into the room carrying a large stack of boxes that extended from her arms to the top of her head. "Rozi!" Esther said. "My sister's here! Put down your boxes so you can meet her."

The girl struggled with the boxes, trying to shift them all to one arm and hip. A small, oval face, a thick pair of glasses almost covering it completely, bobbed in and out from behind the boxes, smiled quickly at me, dissolved into surprised dismay when the boxes fell to the floor and scattered about her feet. "Oh . . . Oh . . ." she moaned. "It will take me forever to pick these up again."

"We'll help you in a minute," Esther said impatiently. "Now meet my sister Seren."

The girl, Rozi, was Gentile, slight, barely five feet tall, and pleasant-looking, a cap of dark blond curls framing her face and the enormous glasses. "I'm so glad you've come too," she said, smiling at me. "Mother will want you to stay with us—with Esther and Emma and me."

"Her mother has been so kind to us," Esther said. "Her name is Mrs. Balogh, but we call her Aunt Terry."

"The three of us are together all the time," Emma broke in, her face flushed and excited. "Won't you please consider working here too, Seren? At least try it."

"We'll see more than enough of each other," I said, laughing.

In the early evening we set out for the small apartment, two bedrooms and a kitchen, that was to be home for six of us: Mr. and Mrs. Balogh, Rozi, Emma, Esther, and me. The apartment was located in an old, square brick building with a steepled roof in the rolling hills of Buda. As it was on the other side of the Danube, we crossed the river on a bridge towering above us in massive arches and guarded on each side of the entrance by great stone lions with mouths open in a roar. Bucharest had been a fair city before the war started, the Paris of Romania, but Budapest was still untouched and even fairer.

When we reached the apartment, Rozi's mother came to the door to greet us. She was a sparse-looking woman, her face long and thin, black hair pulled into a bun at the nape of her neck, her cotton dress faded and frayed. She dusted her hands on the high apron covering most of her dress. "I was just making biscuits," she said. "Please excuse the flour all over the kitchen."

I glanced quickly around. A red oilcloth, the threads showing all around the edges, covered a wooden table. Four white chairs with mended backs were neatly tucked beneath the table. There was no other furniture except the built-in sink and a small gas stove.

Mrs. Balogh held out her hand. "You're Seren, aren't you?" she asked. "Esther said you were coming. But I wouldn't have known you were sisters. You don't look anything alike." She blushed quickly. "Oh, I shouldn't have said that. I just met you."

"It's all right," I answered. "Esther takes after my mother's brothers—tall and thin, with their features. I'm short like my mother but fair like our father."

"Well, that explains it," she laughed. "Have the girls told you about the room? It's pretty small, I'm afraid. The four of you will just fit in the two double beds I have in there. But you can use the kitchen for cooking when you get back from work at night. I'll be through by then, though you might have to put up with Rozi's fiancé. He's here almost every night and they sit in the kitchen and talk for hours!" She paused, smoothing back her hair with one rough hand. "Laszlo's a nice young man, though," she continued. "Even Papa can find no fault with him, can he, Rozi?"

"No, even Papa likes Laszlo," Rozi answered, smiling.

"Now . . ." Mrs. Balogh continued. "The sink is here by the stove. If you want to do your laundry here, that's fine. Up there we have racks. See them?"

I looked up. High above us metal racks clustered like bare branches against the white ceiling.

"When you want to dry your clothes you pull on this rope by the sink and the racks come down. After you fill them you pull the racks to the ceiling again, where the warm air dries them. Now," she continued, "I'll just finish my biscuits and in a half hour or so the kitchen is all yours. And by the way—I'm Aunt Terry."

Within an hour I had put my clothes in a drawer Rozi agreed to share with me, helped Esther and Emma cook supper, and tested my half of the bed. I almost felt at home.

THE NEXT MORNING I WENT TO THE OFFICES OF THE Jewish Federation to inquire about a seamstress position. Although there were no salons that were still open, a Jewish matron, Mrs. Kolman, had asked for someone to do sewing in her home.

"I feel I must warn you, however," the clerk at the Federation said, "we've already sent four or five other seamstresses to Mrs. Kolman's home. Each has come back at the end of one day and absolutely refused to return."

"Why is that?" I asked. "Does this Mrs. Kolman bite?"

The clerk laughed. "I guess in a way she does. She is so particular that no one can sew well enough for her. She is a very demanding woman!"

"I have sewn for the royal family in Bucharest!" I answered. "If I can sew for them I can sew for Mrs. Kolman."

The clerk smiled, drawing his lips down on one side of his mouth in a sardonic way.

In a few minutes I was on my way to Mrs. Kolman's house, riding the streetcar to the edge of the city. The house was large and surrounded by pink and red roses hanging lavishly over low rock walls. A lush, freshly cut lawn rolled away below the house in waves. *The Jewish people here still live as if there were no war,* I thought as I rang the bell, *nor even a rumor of war . . .*

A tall, middle-aged woman wearing a long dressing gown of blue silk opened the door. "Yes?" she asked in a brusque tone.

"I'm from the Jewish Federation," I answered. "My name is Seren Tuvel. I'm a seamstress."

"Are you?" she answered, emphasizing the first syllable. "Come along then." She turned away from me and began walking down a long hallway.

I followed her to the back of the house past a large dining room, an enormous sitting room, and several other, small rooms all having gleaming parquet floors. When we reached the sewing room I saw a young girl on her hands and knees, polishing the floor with a thick cloth.

"Kathryn!" Mrs. Kolman exclaimed as soon as we entered the room. "Do you call this floor clean? It's disgraceful! The entire room will have to be washed again and then repolished. I'm terribly disappointed in you. Leave the room and attend to the silverware!"

I looked quickly at the floor again; it shone just as brightly as the other floors. For a minute I considered turning around and walking quickly back past all the other floors and out the door. Then, before I could leave, Mrs. Kolman turned to me and said, "You don't know how desperate I've been. I need so many new things and no one the Federation has sent to me seems able to sew a simple seam without making a mistake. I do hope you will not disappoint me too. You can sew, can't you?"

"Yes, of course," I answered. "I worked in one of the finest salons in Bucharest."

"I see," she answered in an unbelieving tone. "Let me show you what I want." She held up a length of soft, light wool, draping it across her chest.

"It's lovely," I said, genuinely pleased to see such fine material again. "That shade of beige suits you well."

"Doesn't it?" she answered. "I thought so too. I'm extremely anxious for a dress out of this cloth. It took my husband months to secure it on the black market. The dress must be perfect! This is the style I want," she continued, handing me a magazine photograph of a woman wearing a long dress with a high neckline and a peplum around the hips. "My daughter and her husband live here with us. Both of them have very prominent positions in a bread factory on the edge of Budapest. They like to entertain important clients here in our house. So you see how important it is for me to have clothes suitable for these occasions. You must also understand that I can't have someone cutting this cloth who doesn't know what she's doing. Since you tell me you can sew, I assume you will be able to measure me and complete the dress to my satisfaction. Am I correct?"

Briefly I glanced at the door. "Yes," I said then. "I'm quite sure that I can please you."

"Fine. Let's get to work. If you do good work I'll pay you well."

After I measured Mrs. Kolman, I cut out the gown and began to sew it together, enjoying the delicate texture of the cloth after all the coarse army shirts. When I had worked for two hours someone knocked on the door. "Yes?" I answered, wondering why I was being disturbed already.

Mrs. Kolman came in. "I've come to see if you would like some lunch," she said, glancing quickly at the pieces of cloth beside me and then back at me.

"That would be very nice," I said.

She left the room and returned in a few minutes carrying a covered tray. "I couldn't find much in the kitchen. The cook is doing the marketing and I barely know where anything is." She pulled the cloth off the tray. Two pieces of fried chicken, a bowl of soup, and several fresh plums gleaming like burgundy wines were placed on the silver tray. The single cold potato Emma, Esther, and I had often shared for lunch appeared in my mind.

"I didn't expect such a fine meal," I said. "You're very kind."

"I feed my help well—if they do the kind of work I expect."

"Would you like to see what I have completed?" I asked, holding up the bodice of the dress.

"Oh . . . if you like," she answered, quickly slipping it on over her blouse. She walked to the mirror on the other side of the room. "It fits perfectly!" she exclaimed. "It's exactly right! You work quickly, don't you?"

"I like to get things done," I answered. "I have no patience for stretching them out forever."

"Well! I'll leave you to your work," Mrs. Kolman said, taking off the section of the dress and handing it to me. "At five o'clock the cook will bring in your dinner. At six-thirty you may leave." With a quick, tight smile, she was gone.

I worked through the afternoon, and when the cook brought in my dinner I decided to wrap it in a cloth and take it home to share with Emma and Esther. Riding the streetcar back to our apartment building, I held the still-warm dinner against my chest.

When I arrived at the apartment Emma was setting the table and Esther was removing our dinner from the stove: three boiled eggs. The end piece of a loaf of bread was placed on a dish in the center of the table.

"Guess what I have here," I said, walking to the table and setting my bundle down.

"Oh, it smells good, whatever it is!" Emma answered.

I unfolded the linen. There before us was a large chunk of roast beef, a dish of dark brown gravy, a substantial serving of tender green beans, and a mound of rice intermingled with herbs and spices. Esther and Emma looked at the food, glanced back at me as if I were someone they had never seen before, looked at the food again. "Can we eat it?" Esther asked in a hushed tone.

"It's not to look at!" I answered, laughing.

We ate it all, dividing it equally among the three of us, and then we ate the eggs and bread as well. It was the first time I had felt satisfied at the end of a meal since my father and I were forced from our home.

————————

I CONTINUED TO TRAVEL BACK AND FORTH TO MRS. Kolman's home. When I had sewn all the dresses and gowns she needed, she recommended me to the owner of the factory where her daughter and son-in-law worked. "The owner isn't Jewish," she told me as I left her house for the factory owner's home. "Just his wife is. Why tell them that you are a Jew? They don't need to know. Your features are more like those of a Gentile. Let them think you are one."

I took her advice and went to work for the factory's owner's wife without mentioning my Jewishness. She, in turn, recommended me to another client. I never went without work, money was sent home regularly to our mother by both Esther and me, and we ate well.

One day I came home to find Samuel sitting on a chair in Aunt Terry's kitchen. "Oh, Seren!" he exclaimed as soon as I came in the door. He grabbed the covered plate from me, set it down quickly on the table, and took me in his arms. "I had to come to Budapest," he said. "I had to see you again!"

My mind went blank. I thought Samuel was safely back in Reghinal-Sasesc where he could not ask me over and over when I would marry him—I had almost forgotten about him, in fact—and here he was, a bear enveloping me with his warm, soft paws.

"Well, that's nice," I finally said, wiggling out of his embrace. "Are you hungry? Sit down! I've brought some food from my employer. It's very good!"

"Now we can get married!" he answered.

"What?"

"We can get married! I'm here. You're here. I'll find a room. We'll get married!"

"Oh, no, not now," I answered quickly. "How can we? I have a good job. I can't take time off to get married. Come on. Do me a favor. Sit down and let me give you a nice hot dinner."

The evening passed quickly as I asked questions about each member of the family. By the time I knew in minute detail what Herman, Tamara, Joseph, Miksha, Ernie, Rose, Eugene, their children, my mother, and anyone else I could think of had done since I left Reghinal-Sasesc, it was time for bed. Samuel left to spend the night with a family next door and all discussion of marriage was postponed indefinitely.

The following day Samuel inquired about lodging in the same apartment building as ours and was directed to a Jewish family with a son, Aaron, of the same age as Samuel. Samuel moved in with the family, found employment in the same firm with Aaron, and would have been content except for two things: the increasing threats of conscription into the labor force and the lack of time the two of us had to spend together. As we both worked long hours we saw each other seldom, even though we lived in the same building. If the weather was warm and we were not totally exhausted by nightfall, we sometimes sat together on the front steps of the building, talking quietly. Often, however, I yawned so long and frequently that Samuel would finally say, "Go to bed, Seren! I would love to see you, but how can I talk to someone who's so bored with my jokes she does nothing but yawn in my face!"

"But I get up at five o'clock!" I would protest. "My client wants her dresses completed by the end of the week. And I can use the money. We didn't even pay our rent this month because Mama's rent was due and Esther and I sent almost all of our money to her. If Aunt Terry wasn't so patient, letting us pay her later, I don't know how we would manage."

"Especially since you won't let me lend you any money! Like I said, go to bed. Good night, my sometime-to-be bride."

Wearily climbing the stairs, we went to our separate apartments. Samuel very likely stayed up talking to Aaron long into the night. As for me, sometimes in the morning I could not remember climbing into bed the night before.

Early one Sunday morning a knock on the kitchen door woke me. When I stumbled to it, Samuel was there with a basket in his arms.

"Good morning, my lovely!" he said. "We're going on a picnic."

"But it's six o'clock! I'm not even dressed! And where in the world can we go on a picnic in the middle of a city?"

"My friends have been up in the mountains above Buda," he answered. "There are lakes at the top with beaches. We can lie on the sand all day and eat and swim. Will you come? Esther and Emma can come too. Two of my friends are waiting for us outside. Say you'll come."

"I'll come! I'll come! Could you at least let me get dressed?"

"Wonderful! I'll wait outside."

We rode the streetcar up into the hills, passing old, beautiful houses built into the side of the mountain, ivy falling about the stones in long, green trailings. We climbed higher, the city below us becoming smaller and smaller, climbed up into the forests. It seemed almost as if I were back at the mill and Esther, Emma, and I had invited some friends on an outing in the trees beside the stream flowing down to Valea Uzului.

"There's the lake!" Samuel shouted when we reached the top of a hill. Below us lay a sparkling turquoise oval in a green clearing.

"Let's race to it!" one of the men shouted.

We all began to run, the men almost flying down the slope, the baskets bumping against their legs all the way down. Esther, Emma, and I were overcome with laughter. In the end we could not even walk, falling against a log and holding our sides, the tears streaming down our faces.

"We better see if there's any food still worth eating," Emma finally said. "It's probably one crumbled mess."

We broke into laughter all over again, but at last could laugh no more and ran down the path to the lake. When we reached the shore the men were standing together, their faces red, veins swelling out from their necks.

"I can't believe it. I simply can't believe it!" Samuel was saying.

"What is it?" I asked. "What's wrong?"

"Look!" He pointed to a sign posted in the middle of the beach. It read: "No Dogs or Jews Allowed."

"Now we're considered the same as dogs!" he said. "What next? What will they decide we are next?"

"Let's go back," I said, frightened. "There are probably gendarmes patrolling the area. They'll arrest us if they find us here."

"I wanted this picnic so much," he said, taking my hand. "I've hardly seen you since I came to Budapest."

"We'll have the picnic," I answered. "We'll eat in our apartment, all of us."

"All right. But it won't be the same."

"No, but nothing is the same . . ."

ONE NIGHT DURING THE FOLLOWING WEEK WHEN I came in from working, I found Zipporah sitting at the table with the girls. "Zipporah!" I said. "When did you come?"

"This morning," she answered, not looking at me. She was holding a red rose in one hand, twirling it around and around, idly watching the red blur.

"Why have you come?" I asked.

She continued to twirl the rose, ignoring my question. I glanced at Esther and Emma, who sat looking down at the floor, Emma tapping her foot up and down on the faded linoleum, Esther holding herself quite still.

"Zipporah," I said, "I asked you a question. Why have you come here?"

"Reghinal-Sasesc became so boring that I thought I would die!'" she answered. "All that's left there are old, dead men!"

"The men are all dead?" I asked. "What happened? Was there a purge? A firebombing? What?"

"Oh, the men are not really dead, but they might as well be. They're so old and frail that they fall into their beds by nine o'clock at night. All the young men left. I had no one to entertain me. I had to get out of there! So I came here. And I'm glad I did. Rozi says there are lots of eligible, young men here."

"So you intend to stay here with us and just have a good time, is that it?" I asked.

"What's wrong with that? Rozi's mother is very nice. She said I could stay here if I didn't mind sharing the room with all of you. She's finding a cot for me right now. And I don't eat very much."

"Zipporah," I interrupted, "we all work here. The girls work at a lingerie salon and I sew at the homes of clients. We work very hard! Esther, Emma, and I share the rent and also the cost of our groceries. Besides that, Esther and I send money home to Mama to pay for her rent and food. Emma does the same to help Rose and Eugene. We simply have no money to spend on you."

"I knew that you wouldn't want me!" she shouted. "Mama encouraged me to leave Reghinal-Sasesc and come here where it's better. She said that you would help me. Was she ever wrong!"

"What did you think?" I demanded. "That we would support you just as Father and Herman always have? I'm afraid not. I'll help you, like Mama said. I'll find a job for you."

"A job? I've never had a job."

"I'm very aware of that." Suddenly I was very tired. It was late and I wanted nothing more than to eat our supper and sink into bed. I leaned against the wall, looking at Zipporah, wondering why she had to come and disrupt our lives. She sat quiet, tense, her back turned to me, tall and straight in the chair.

"What do you think you could do?" Rozi asked then in a bright voice. She had been standing in the doorway to our room, quietly watching us. "I mean . . . have you ever thought about what you might like to do if you did work, Zipporah?"

"Oh, well . . ." Zipporah answered. "I could do almost anything if I really wanted to." She tossed her head, flinging the rose into the center of the table.

"The times are very hard," Rozi continued. "Below us lives a surgeon who's working as a janitor. It's the only work he could find. His wife cleans houses. She used to teach in a university."

"A friend told me that there's an apprentice position open at the hairdressing salon on the next block," Emma said. "It's a nice salon."

"A hairdressing salon!" Zipporah exclaimed. "I'd love to work in a salon! At home I used to comb and arrange my girlfriends' hair for hours. I like to create new styles. Everyone is always quite pleased when I'm through."

"Will you see about the position, Zipporah?" I asked.

"Yes! I just got here this morning. Give me a chance!"

Zipporah moved in, placing the toilet articles she had managed to salvage from our home in Valea Uzului in a line stretching across the length of our dresser. For several days she lay about the apartment, sleeping late, bothering Aunt Terry as she tried to go about her housework, claiming that the trip had exhausted her and she needed to rest. In the evenings, however, she became quite animated, staying up to talk with Rozi and Laszlo until everyone but her was almost asleep in their chairs.

Finally I presented her with an ultimatum: find a job or return to Reghinal-Sasesc. She obtained the apprentice position in the hairdressing salon, where she worked all day standing up. The other girls and I were relieved, thinking that at last we would be able to retire early without having to listen to her loud laughter coming from the kitchen until midnight. Zipporah, however, stayed up as late as before, relating every single incident of her workday to Rozi and Laszlo. Sleeping was something she did only if there was absolutely nothing else to occupy her.

One night as Esther, Emma, and I were lying in our beds, Zipporah's loud laughter rolling over us like ocean waves, pulling us from sleep, Emma whispered, "I've never known anyone who laughed as much as she does." Zipporah was laughing especially long and hard, stopping only to catch her breath.

"Oh, Laszlo," Zipporah finally gasped. "You're so funny! You're wonderful!"

"Do you really think so, Zipporah?" he asked in his low, quiet voice, just loud enough for us to overhear.

"Do I think so? Yes! You're a jewel, Laszlo. An absolute gem! Anytime Rozi tires of you please let me know. I mean it!"

"I think you do," he answered softly. "Oh, of course!" he said louder, jovially. "We're teasing. Only teasing! Rozi and I are engaged! Aren't we teasing, Zipporah?"

Again she laughed, high and trilling this time. "We surely are!"

"I wish Zipporah wouldn't go on like that," Esther said. "I don't think Rozi likes her spending so much time with the two of them. She told me at work today that she wishes Zipporah hadn't come."

"Zipporah is a little bossy, isn't she?" Emma said from her bed. "She told me this morning that she doesn't have enough room in the dresser and I must give her half of my drawer because she has more things than I do."

"Smell this rose . . ." entreated Zipporah's voice from the kitchen. "Roses are so lovely. Don't you think so, Laszlo?"

A long pause followed. I pictured Laszlo looking at the floor, at Zipporah, at the floor again, finally letting his eyes rest on her face, on the smile always radiating from her wide mouth.

"Yes, they are," he said finally.

Then we heard a door open and Aunt Terry's footsteps coming into the kitchen. "I must ask you to leave now, Laszlo," she said. "It's very late. The girls should be in bed. They have to get up quite early. You understand, don't you?"

"Yes, yes, of course," he answered. The sound of his chair scraping against the floor as he rose followed immediately.

"I don't think Aunt Terry likes all these late-night conversations," Esther whispered to me.

"I'm sure she doesn't," I answered. "I've told Zipporah to leave Rozi and Laszlo alone but she won't listen to me."

"She's just being friendly, isn't she?" Esther asked.

"Good night, Laszlo," Zipporah cooed from the other room. "I'll see you tomorrow . . ."

"Who knows what Zipporah is being?" I answered. "Only Zipporah. She does whatever she likes."

TWO WEEKS LATER AUNT TERRY CAME TO OUR ROOM after supper as Esther, Emma, and I were sitting together darning our stockings. Zipporah was out for the evening with a friend from the salon. Aunt Terry entered hesitantly, a thin smile on her lips, her eyes shadowed in wrinkles. "I don't quite know how to say this," she began.

"Do you want us to leave?" I asked. "Has it become too crowded?"

"Oh, no," she answered. "It's crowded, but I don't mind. And I do need the rent money. I don't know how we would get by without it." She stopped talking, tracing a design in the patterned bedspread on our bed with one finger. "It's Zipporah," she said finally, looking up at me.

"What about Zipporah?" I asked.

"Rozi is very upset. Last night Laszlo told her that he's no longer sure they should be engaged. Rozi is convinced that it's because Zipporah flirts with him every chance she gets. I've thought about it all day and I've decided that Zipporah must move out of this apartment. If she doesn't, then I shall have to ask you all to leave."

"But I love it here!" Emma said. "You're very kind to us. Where would we go if we had to leave?"

"I don't want you to go," Aunt Terry continued. "I like you all very much, including Zipporah. But I can't let her continue to live here if she's going to come between Rozi and Laszlo. Rozi is very dear to me. She and Laszlo were very happy before Zipporah came. I can't stand to see her so miserable now. She cries and cries. All night I can hear her sobbing."

"I'll tell Zipporah that she has to leave," I said.

Later that night Zipporah came bursting into the room, the door banging behind her, and threw herself face downward on her cot. "Rozi acts like a spoiled little girl sometimes!" she said. "I can barely stand it! Tonight Laszlo and I were outside practicing a new dance step—I had asked him if he knew it and he said he'd be happy to teach it to me—and Rozi suddenly burst into tears and ran down the street. It was such a childish thing to do! Laszlo and I—"

"Zipporah," I interrupted. "I have something to tell you."

"What?" she asked, looking first at me and then at Esther and Emma.

"Aunt Terry has decided that you can no longer stay with us," I continued.

"What! Why not?" she asked, sitting up. "I thought she liked me."

"You spend too much time with Rozi and Laszlo, just as I've been telling you. Rozi is afraid that Laszlo will fall in love with you."

"That's ridiculous! He likes me—that's all." She stood up, placing her hands on her hips, feet far apart. "I won't go," she declared. "Aunt Terry can't force me to go."

"If you don't go we will all have to leave," I answered. "I want you to go."

"You can't tell me what to do! Just because you're older than I am you think you're better than me. You've thought that ever since we were children. Well, you're not! I'm not leaving!"

"Zipporah, none of us wants to leave here," I said. "It isn't fair to make us go because of you. We all want you to go so we won't have to."

She looked first at Esther and then at Emma, who were sitting in bed pretending to read. "Is that true?' she demanded, glancing from one to the other and back again.

Neither said anything at first. Finally Emma put down her book, climbed out of bed, and went to Zipporah, touching her on the shoulder. "Yes," she said, "but only because I so enjoy living here. I feel at home."

"And what about you, Esther?" Zipporah asked, whirling away from Emma.

"I . . ." Esther began. Suddenly she lay down, pulled the covers over her head, and began to cry, her loud sobs the only sounds in the room.

"All right!" Zipporah shouted. "If that's how you all feel, if no one wants me, I'll go!" She jumped onto her bed, jumped back onto the floor, ran to the light switch, snapped it off, and ran back to her bed, leaving us all in darkness.

In the morning Zipporah arose very early and left before any of us was awake. When we came back in the evening all of her toiletries and clothes were gone; nothing was left of her.

The next day I went to the hairdressing salon to see Zipporah, but she would not speak to me. Another girl told me that Zipporah had moved in with her. Several weeks later when I stopped at the salon again, Zipporah came to me, a radiant smile spreading across her face, and held up her right hand. "Look!" she said. "Aaron and I are engaged!"

"Zipporah!" I answered. "You hardly know him! Samuel lives with him and he has never even mentioned that you and Aaron were friends."

"We've been seeing each other for some time. We just never told anyone. He loves me! He tells me that I am as beautiful as a deep, red rose sparkling with dew. Isn't that the loveliest thing you've ever heard . . ." She held up the hand with the engagement ring and twirled, head tilted back, hair swirling around her like a fan.

"How can you do this? Aaron is a very serious young man. Samuel has told me how he and Aaron sit up late into the night talking, how Aaron often astonishes him with his intelligence. You are just playing with him! Two weeks ago you were flirting with Rozi's fiancée. Now all of a sudden you're engaged to a total stranger. What would Father think if he knew about this? He's in an insane asylum, growing weaker by the day, and you do this!"

Abruptly she stopped turning and looked at me, her eyes growing dark, saying nothing for a long moment. "But Seren," she said then, "you're engaged. Why can't I have a fiancé if you do?"

"I became engaged to Samuel so Tamara would stop pestering me— that's the only reason. I would just as soon not be engaged now."

"And is that fair to Samuel?" she asked.

I looked away, so angry I could not speak.

"You've never liked me," she continued. "We're too different. You want to do nothing but work and work and work some more. I would die if I could never enjoy myself."

"Is becoming engaged for the fun of it your idea of enjoyment?"

"It's not just that! We're in love. We love each other very, very much!"

Tears suddenly clouded her eyes. Turning with a jerk, she ran to the back room of the salon. I walked slowly to the front door and stood there for a minute, a great heaviness settling all around my neck and shoulders. At last I went out into the street, willing my feet toward the nearest streetcar stop.

That night I came back to our room and got into bed before the girls had returned from work, my back aching, arms and shoulders throbbing. I wanted nothing more than to slip into a deep sleep. Sleep would not come, however; no position in the bed was comfortable. My mind repeated again and again the conversation between Zipporah and myself in the salon. *She has no right to compare my engagement to Samuel, an engagement I resisted as long as I could, with her romantic infatuation with Aaron,* I thought. *Of course it isn't fair to let Samuel love me when I don't love him in return, but how little she understands my feelings. How can I love anyone when our father is slowly deteriorating, when all of us might be arrested and imprisoned at any moment?*

Suddenly I remembered a particular evening when Samuel and I had strolled along the river in Reghinal-Sasesc. "I admire you so very much, Seren," he had whispered. "You're always in control of yourself. I'm not like that." My chest heaved as I lay in the bed, deep sobs beginning to well up. I could not stop them. Burrowing down under the covers so no one would hear me, I finally gave in to them and cried until I could cry no more, at last falling into an exhausted sleep.

Later when Esther came into the room and turned on the light to undress, she saw my swollen red eyes. "Aren't you feeling well?" she asked, placing her hand on my forehead. "Are you ill?"

I shook my head, unable to answer her.

"You work too hard!" she said. "You're probably exhausted." For almost an hour she sat beside me, stroking the side of my face, my hair, until at last I sank into sleep again, not waking until morning.

When I returned to the salon several weeks later, Zipporah would not speak to me. Then she changed jobs, moved to another apartment, and broke away from us completely. Once in a while as I was traveling on a streetcar to a client's house, I caught a glimpse of her walking along a street in the city, moving quickly, her long hair flying out behind her in a dark wave. But she would not come near our apartment. Sometimes months went by, and I did not see her even once.

Thirteen

IT WAS WHEN I VISITED MY FATHER THAT THE INSID-iousness of the war became most clear. While Esther worked long, regular hours and could visit our father only on the weekend, I created my own hours and could see him more often. If I was sewing in the home of a client living in the same direction as the mental institution, I would leave work early, stopping to visit my father before I went back to our apartment. Sometimes I would be on my way to work in the morning and would feel a sudden pressure in my chest, a crushing. *My father is alone!* I would think. *I must see him!* I would change streetcars immediately and board one going to the institution.

Almost as soon as I arrived at the dreary stone building, gray and black moss growing thick on the damp, low walls, I wanted to leave again. To reach the Jewish section of the asylum where my father was I had to walk down a long corridor with cells on both sides. In these cells were violently insane men, men who peered at me out of the grates in the doors, rattling the locked doors long and hard as I passed. Often a man would yell in deep moans that filled the empty hallway, bounced off the dark walls, swelled around me as I continued to walk quickly to the other end of the corridor, trembling. A single guard always sat on a chair at the far end, fingering a large ring of keys and watching me as intently as did the men in the cells.

When I reached my father's section an abrupt change in the nature of the patients became evident. There in one cell a man sat bent over, still, head in his hands, hair falling about his face in matted strands. In another cell a man lay rolled up into a ball on his cot, his clothes rags, feet bare and pitiful in their pure whiteness. Like my father, these men could not accept the loss of their homes, of their wives and children, of their integrity and honor. So they slipped into insanity, into memories of the gentle past, into silence.

One day as my father stood up to see me go, having said not more than three words during my entire visit, a movement of his head, a sudden turning to look back over his right shoulder at something I could not see, made me remember the summer vacations when I walked with him along the mountain trails. During these hikes he occasionally wandered off alone to gaze out over the valley falling away below him, glancing back up at the trees spiraling to the sky. I would see his form silhouetted against the bright sunlight—tall, his feet braced firmly against an outcropping of rock, the wind ruffling his hair. *How lucky I am!* I would think then. *My father is a good, handsome man.* Finally his eyes, blue, vibrant with life, would meet mine and we would go on with our walk.

I looked at him now, his head down again, shoulders slumped. Shuffling to the door of his cell in worn slippers, he was pulling a dirty gray blanket tighter around his shoulders.

"Father," I said, wanting to say good-bye. When he did not seem to hear me, I called again, louder. "Father!"

He looked up, his eyes completely empty. He did not know who I was. Touching him briefly on the arm, I turned, walked quickly down the corridor and out of the asylum.

A few months later I went back to Reghinal-Sasesc to spend time with my mother. It was the day before Rosh Hashanah and we sat, the two of us, at the kitchen table. I had not talked about my father; she had not asked. Finally, she said, "How is he?"

"Not well," I answered.

"Is he ill?"

"He has suffered. He's grown . . . confused."

"How does he look?" she asked hesitantly, as if she did not want to know.

"Mama, he's changed . . . He's grown old before my eyes."

She looked at me steadily, her eyes filling, overflowing, the tears running down her cheeks in little streams that she did not check.

She began speaking in a voice that seemed to come from a distant place. "The first time I saw your father—oh, I was such a young girl and I had dreams of a tall stranger coming to my door one day. I had no dowry and I knew that I would probably have to take whatever husband the matchmaker could find for me, even if the poor man was ugly. And then came the news that the matchmaker had found a distinguished man who wanted me for his bride and who was said to be quite good-looking. I thought, *Well, we'll see. Maybe he is and maybe he isn't.* I would become his bride and the mother of seven children—all at once! It was a lot to ask of me, but I was young and healthy and I had always dreamed of a houseful of children. And then the wedding day came and I saw him for the first time. My heart almost stopped beating, he was so handsome and tall. How his hair sparkled in the sun!"

She paused, finally wiping her cheeks with the hem of her apron. Looking at the gold band on her right hand, she continued, "Your father was not an easy man to live with. What he said was the law. I had to obey it . . . but it was his way. He was the head of the family. He always meant well."

That evening after we had washed the dishes and were sitting quietly, there was a loud knock on the door. We both jumped, and I ran to open it. A young boy was standing there holding an envelope. "I have a telegram for Seren Tuvel," he said.

Taking it quickly, I closed the door and sat down again by my mother. "Who's it from?" she asked anxiously.

"I don't know! I hope it isn't from Ellen saying that Esther or Zipporah has been arrested. I should never have left them!"

I tore it open. It read:

Seren,
Father shot by police. Went berserk in air raid. Jewish Federation burial.
Come back soon.

Esther

I handed it to my mother, watching as the color drained from her face. Then she began to shriek and we fell into each other's arms.

Far into the night, far past the dying of the lights on our street, the fading of the last footsteps, past the deepest darkness before the stars begin to fade, I sat up with my mother. "When did you last see him?" she would ask. "What did he say?" An hour later the same questions were asked again, as if she were afraid that she had already begun to forget him and wanted to fix him in her mind forever. One of us would begin to cry and then the other. Suddenly she would laugh at a memory that had come into her mind and then, with a sharp gasp of breath, realize anew that oh, he was dead, and she would never see him again.

When it was almost morning we collapsed into bed, but I could not sleep. Every small rustling startled me. I kept seeing in my mind, the faces of Herman and Rose when I told them of our father's death. Rose burst into tears, drawing her youngest child close, hiding her face in the baby's dress. Herman stood quite still, looking out past the walls of the room to a vision only he saw, the tears running soundlessly down his face and into his beard. A look passed over his face, a resignation. His shoulders slumped; he let his head drop. He and Tamara and their sons and Rose and Eugene and their children returned to our room with us. We sat together through the evening—long moments of silence interrupted only by deep sighs easing down around us. When Rose's baby began to cry they went back to their rooms. My mother and I were left alone.

Now that it was morning again, the sorrow having lodged in a corner of our hearts that would never again be entirely free of pain, we talked quietly. My mother had before her on the table the jewelry, given to her by my father, that we had not sold. Seven or eight long, delicate gold chains trailed across the table, and beside them three silver chains spiraled around a small collection of brooches and rings set with rubies and tiny dots of diamonds.

"I did not realize that you had all of these chains," I said.

"Your father's first wife must have loved them," she answered. "She had so many of them. After she died and he married me, he placed all of them in my jewelry case. I protested but he said, 'Why shouldn't you have them?' I accepted them then, thinking that one day I would pass them on to Berta and Rose and Louise so they would have something of their mother's. Now I don't even know whether Berta and Louise are still . . ." She stopped, took a deep breath, and went on. "Rose has Eugene. He is a very good husband to her. But you, Esther, and Zipporah are alone in Budapest. I worry about you all the time."

"We are fine! We have enough to eat and good jobs."

"Nevertheless, I worry. I want you to take these for the three of you. Maybe sometime you will not have a job and then you can sell a chain or a ring."

"No, no, they are yours," I said. "They are all you have left of Father."

"I want you to take them," she reiterated. "They are not your father. They will not bring him back. Take them."

I could see that she had decided and would not change her mind. I gathered the chains, rings, and brooches together and put them into a cloth case in my handbag.

When the holidays were over I decided to return to Budapest; my sisters were still there, as well as my clients, and I could do nothing more for my mother. It was early evening when my train left, and everyone accompanied me to the station: Rose carrying the baby Estelle in one arm, Eugene holding Elena's plump hand, Magda standing to one side, Tamara and Herman, their sons behind them, and my mother, holding on to Herman's arm so tightly that I wondered if she would fall if she let go.

"Come back soon!" Tamara commanded as she came up to me. "I want you to take this hat," she said, handing me a black turban with cascades of red, yellow, and deep blue ribbons that she had bought long ago in Tirgu-Mures. "It would look wonderful on you in Budapest." She hugged me, enfolding me completely in her arms. Finally my mother left Herman's side and sank against me.

"I won't ask you when you'll be back," she said, kissing me on the forehead.

"I'll be back as soon as I can," I said. "I'll miss you, Mama." Then I hugged her one last time, her small body soft and warm in mine, and climbed into the train. I hurried to a window where I could see them below me on the platform. As the train began to pull away, Rose moved Estelle's hand back and forth, back and forth, and my mother smiled and waved. Suddenly I thought, *I may never see them again!* I had lost my father; anything seemed possible now. I wanted to run off the train, but the engine had begun to pick up speed and in another moment my family was gone from sight.

THE FALL AND WINTER OF 1942 PASSED IN A SULLEN, gray haze that hung over the city, stretching to the very edge of the horizon. I worked, saw Samuel now and then, put food into my mouth, washed my body, slept in the bed next to Esther and Emma—all as if I were asleep and dreaming. My fifteen-year-old nephew Alfred, Emma's sweet little brother, moved to Budapest. He worked with us and we all took great pleasure in watching him tidying up so seriously.

The nights were terrifying. When the sirens began to sound and the explosions seemed so close that my heart contracted into a hard ball inside my chest and I had to bite my lip to keep from screaming, the image of my father suddenly came into my mind. He was running around in circles, banging on the door of his cell, emitting a long, low cry like that of a wounded animal. A shot would sound, stop him dead. *No, no, it couldn't be!* I would think to myself as I bolted up from under the covers. *They only said he went berserk during an air raid so they could kill him. It was not like him to lose control.* Then the bombing would begin again somewhere in the city and I would think, *No one could stand this for long. Perhaps he went berserk. Perhaps he did after all.*

The winter passed. The haze remained. One day in late March Esther came home from work and announced, "Our employer wants Emma, Alfred, and me to move in with her. You may come too."

"Why?" I asked.

"She's heard all Jewish people will soon be forced to leave many areas of the city and made to move in with other Jews—two or three families to one apartment. We'll all have to live in one area of the city. She wants us to move in before she's forced to take in strangers."

"Do you want to move?" I asked.

"It would be very convenient. We could live above the salon. And I like Miss Seidman. She would give us our own room."

"All right. We'll move. I would rather live with her than with just anybody. Who knows where they would put us?"

We left beautiful Buda and moved into a room in Pest above the salon. Esther and Emma thought the convenience well worth the disruption of our lives again and the tearful farewell to Aunt Terry. I continued to travel back and forth to my clients' homes outside the twin cities. Even Alfred was happy, for he could now work longer hours and soon came to enjoy sweeping the floors and doing errands early in the mornings before he began his sewing. He, Ellen, Esther and Emma worked well together and enjoyed each other's company.

While I no longer lived next door to Samuel, I saw him every Sunday as before. He had begun to worry more and more about the increasing threat of all Jewish men being drafted into the labor force. "It will be any day now," he said one Sunday afternoon as we sat on the grass by the Danube. "I'm sure of it. While the thought of being away from you, Seren, is terrifying, what is even more frightening is the way some of my friends are acting."

"What do you mean?" I asked. "They must be so afraid . . ."

"No! That's just it!" he shouted. "If they had any sense at all they would be scared to death! Who knows where they will take us? No, they're not afraid. They're proud! Can you believe it? They think it's patriotic to become part of a labor force. They're going to serve their country! My friend Josiah said to me last night, 'I'm a Hungarian first, a Jew second.'"

"What did you tell him?" I asked.

"What do you think? I told him he was crazy, of course! He just laughed in my face. So I asked him, 'Did you ever stop to think that we Jews will be put in a separate group, that the army will be able to do anything to us that they like?' Do you know what he answered? 'We will be serving our country. There is no higher honor.' At that point I walked away. There was nothing more I could say to him."

TWO WEEKS LATER THE ORDER WAS POSTED: ALL JEW-ish men between the ages of fifteen and fifty were to report in three days to certain locations to be inducted into the labor force. On the night before he was to leave, Samuel came to our room again, as he had for the previous two nights, bringing me the clothes he could not take along and requesting that I keep them for him until he returned.

As he turned to leave that night, Esther, Emma, Ellen, and I all gazing out at him from the doorway to the apartment building, he asked, "Could you come with me to the corner, Seren?"

I took his outstretched hand and we began to walk slowly along Sziget-utca, the stars above us burning through the blackness in sharp glimmer-ings as if there were no ban on lights, no bombings.

"Will you come tomorrow morning?" he asked. "Then I could see you one more time . . ."

"Yes," I answered. "I'll come. I was planning to come."

"Oh, Seren," he said then, stopping and turning to me. "What if I never see you again?" He squeezed my hand so tightly that I wanted to cry out.

"You'll see me!" I said. "I have all your clothes! Do you think I want to carry them around with me forever?"

"But what if . . ." He grabbed me to him and held me as if he would never let go again.

"I have to go back, Samuel," I said finally. "It's very late. I'll see you to-morrow."

He released me very gradually, hesitantly. "Good-bye, Seren," he said then, his voice breaking. Abruptly he turned and walked quickly down the dark street.

Early the next morning I watched the men lining up in the courtyard of the apartment building where Samuel lived, the same building where we had stayed with Mr. and Mrs. Balogh and Rozi. Many of the men were smiling, patting each other on the back, as if they had all been invited to participate in an exciting venture and were congratulating each other on having been included. They were wearing uniforms and strutting briskly up and down the flagstones, completely ignorant of how the yellow Star of David on their armbands marked them.

At first I could not find Samuel, but then I spotted him hovering at the edge of the group, glancing anxiously at the crowd of women who had come to kiss the men good-bye. We were all kept at a distance from the men by members of the National Guard. I stood at the back of the crowd, wondering if Samuel could see me amid all the taller women crowding ahead. Most of these women were as excited as the men.

"I'm so proud of my David," one older woman was saying. "He's always loved his country. Now he has the chance to serve it. He couldn't wait to go!"

"Yes, isn't it wonderful?" a younger woman replied. "My fiancé is exactly the same. He's the one standing next to the steps with the dark, curly hair."

"My, he's very handsome!" the first woman replied.

"Isn't he? He looks so good in that uniform!"

Just then Samuel spotted me and began to frantically wave his hand back and forth. I waved back, attempting to smile. He was a good man, a caring man.

Then the men were ordered to form lines and to begin marching down the street. For a few minutes I lost sight of Samuel as the women began to wave their handkerchiefs back and forth at the passing men, to call out, "Good-bye! Good-bye! Good-bye!" Finally I saw him looking back to see if he could glimpse me one last time amid the sea of handkerchiefs. His face was wet, tears running unabashedly down his cheeks.

"Samuel! Samuel!" I called. He looked again quickly, but then a tall woman moved in front of me, completely blocking my view. By the time I could see anything again, he was gone. The backs of thousands of anonymous men marched further and further away from me. I walked slowly toward the streetcar stop and went to my client's house.

ONE MORNING IN MAY, AS I WAS WORKING AT A HOME on the outskirts of Buda, I heard a loud, hurried knocking and then Esther's voice coming from the living room. Running into the room, I found both Esther and Emma standing there.

"What is it?" I asked.

"The police came!" Esther said. "Emma and I were in the back of the shop packing a shipment when we heard them in the front where Alfred was sweeping."

"They asked for Alfred and me," Emma said, beginning to cry. "I looked at Esther and then we ran out the back door without even thinking . . . We left Alfred." She was by now crying with deep sobs.

"You did what you had to do," I told her. "Now you will have to go away somewhere."

"What do you mean?" Emma asked.

"If you go back they will arrest you."

"What about Alfred? He's my little brother. I've always watched over him."

"You can't help him by going back. I'll try to find out what happened to him. You go with Esther to Samuel's old room. They can hide you temporarily."

When I went back to our room, Alfred and Ellen were gone. The police had taken them both, even though they did not intend to arrest Ellen. I ran to the police station.

"Do you know where I can find Ellen Weise?" I asked the policeman sitting behind the front desk. "She was taken from the lingerie factory on Sziget-utca this afternoon along with a boy."

The policeman was old and had a large, red face with jowls that hung down below his mouth. He stared at me for a long moment without saying anything, his small eyes peering out of the folds of fat beneath them.

"What is it to you?" he asked finally, saying each word slowly, methodically.

"She's my friend," I answered.

Again he stared at me for a few minutes in silence. Then he came toward me until his face was inches from mine and asked, "Why is the whore lying?"

I backed away. "What do you mean?"

"We were sent to arrest a sister and a brother. The sister ran away with another girl, but we got the boy. This Weise whore won't tell us where the girl went. But she knows."

I backed away further, edging toward the door.

"If you know where she is," he continued, "tell her we're not letting Weise go until she turns herself in."

Controlling my pace to keep from breaking into a run, I left and went to Samuel's old room.

"Did you find Alfred?" Emma asked as soon as I came inside.

"The police have him," I answered.

"Oh! And Ellen too?"

"Yes. They are keeping her because they couldn't arrest you," I said.

"I can't let her stay in jail because of me. She has done nothing. I have to go back."

She went back alone, afraid that we would also be arrested if we accompanied her; while I did not "look" Jewish, Esther did. Emma found the police waiting for her inside the lingerie shop. They took her to the police station where they were holding Alfred and Ellen. As soon as she was locked inside a cell they released Ellen, who came back to us at Samuel's room. She was shaking and her thin arms were covered with deep red marks where a policeman had squeezed her flesh with his hand; I could see the outline of his fingers on each arm.

"They kept saying, 'Tell us! Tell us!' and every time they shouted 'Tell' one of them squeezed my arm. But I couldn't tell them where Emma was. Why did she come back? I would never have told where she was."

Ellen's upper lip was quite scarred; she'd been born with a cleft palate. Although she'd had surgery the results were unsatisfactory, and she was always embarrassed by her appearance. Now the line on her upper lip had turned darker and she, sensing this, kept bringing one hand to her mouth to cover it.

"She knew that the police took you in her place," I said. "It's all right. She chose to come back."

"But what will happen to her and Alfred?" Ellen asked.

"I don't know," I answered. "No one knows."

A week later Esther and I obtained permits to visit Emma in the city jail. When I saw her in the cell with five or six other Jewish girls looking out at us fearfully, I thought back to the time, a year and a half ago, when I was in prison with the others from Valea Uzului. While my father and I and those with us had been accused of spying, I could not understand why Emma and Alfred had been singled out for arrest now. We were in Budapest, a long-standing haven for all Jewish people. If Jews were now being arrested here for no reason, we were all lost.

Esther was carrying a kettle of vegetable soup we had cooked for Emma, and handed it to her as soon as we were allowed inside the cell. When Emma put down the kettle Esther hugged her. "Oh, Emma," she said. "How can you stand it?" I had told Esther very little about the time my father and I spent in prison.

"I'm all right," Emma said. "But I'm so glad you brought some soup. They don't give us very much to eat. And they must have a terrible cook. The food has no taste."

"Have they told you why you and Alfred were arrested?" I asked.

"No, they have said nothing. No one even speaks to us . . . Oh, guess who I saw going into the men's section yesterday? Miksha!"

"Miksha! Herman's son?"

"Yes. They must have arrested him at Reghinal-Sasesc and brought him here," she answered.

"Did you see anyone else—Herman or Eugene?" I asked.

"No, only Miksha. I watched again this morning as the men were taken outside to exercise and I saw Alfred and Miksha walking together, but no one else I knew. Miksha walked funny—like his back hurt. I'm glad he's here for Alfred. I know I shouldn't want him in jail and I don't. But since Alfred is only fifteen I'm glad Miksha can look after him here. Do you understand how I feel?"

"Of course," I answered. "You and Miksha were always friends, weren't you?"

"He's my favorite cousin. When we were little we made a fort beside Grandfather's mill . . . your father's mill . . . with some old boards Grandfather let us have. Miksha allowed me to be a general, even though I was a girl." She laughed for a minute and then grew very quiet, looking down at her hands wound around each other tightly. When she raised her eyes to mine they were calm, the dark brown irises large and clear.

"What do you think will happen to us, Seren?" she asked.

While she was talking a realization had jolted me: Miksha had been arrested, brought here, interrogated, beaten, and forced to accuse his cousins, Emma and Alfred, of some crime they had never committed. I had been through the same process; I knew how easily one could be humiliated and broken if there was the slightest weakening of the will. I looked at her. "I know you have done nothing, Emma. Believe in your innocence. That's all I can tell you. Be strong, Emma. Be strong!"

A week later when we came back to visit Emma and Alfred they, as well as Miksha, were gone. No one would tell us where they had been taken.

REMAINING IN BUDAPEST TOOK ON ASPECTS OF LIVing out a play which I had read through and whose outcome I knew, while the other characters went along reading only the lines for each day. While I tried to think of what we might do to escape arrest, where we might go, many of the other Jews living in Budapest laughed at my fears, believing that they were safe. If nothing else, marriage to a Gentile and conversion would save them.

Most of the Jews in the city had converted to Roman Catholicism when they married Gentiles. This practice had begun before the war. It was mainly in the small villages that the Jewish people remained true to their traditions. Other Jews sought Catholicism as a guarantee against persecution, the Christian missionaries constantly encouraging their conversion with promises of safety. According to laws passed in 1938, these attempts were futile. An anti-Jewish law with the title "A Bill for the More Effective Protection of Social and Economic Life" stated that all Jews who had converted after July 31, 1911, were Jews no matter what they professed to believe in or practice. An addition in 1941 was even more limiting: a half-Jew married to a quarter-Jew was a Jew regardless of whether he or she had converted, and a person with a single Jewish grandparent was legally designated a Jew. Many of the people I came to know in Budapest, however, did not believe that these laws would be enforced as long as they had converted and were faithful Gentiles.

One day Mrs. Kolman, who had called me back to her home to sew a summer gown, told me, "You are perfectly safe here. I don't see why you worry so much."

"How can I be perfectly safe here?" I asked. "I can be perfectly safe nowhere as long as Jews continue to be arrested for no reason."

She began to laugh, her silver dessert spoon poised above the plate as we sat over lunch. "No reason! Surely you are joking. No one is arrested without a cause."

"My niece and nephew were."

She shrugged her shoulders. "That is an isolated instance. They must have done something. We are safe here. Both my husband and my son-in-law have been taken into the labor force. But am I worried? Certainly not! They're only doing their duty. Besides, many of the Jewish people, like me, have taken Gentile names. You can look through the entire phone directory and not find more than a few Jewish names. There are so many intermarriages. Premier Horthy himself has a Jewish daughter-in-law. He would not let anything happen to her, would he?"

"She's still legally Jewish. Even he may not be able to help her."

"Nonsense! She's converted!" Mrs. Kolman pushed aside her plate and gazed out of the dining room windows at the lawn turning bright green in the spring sunshine. "That's what you should do—convert," she continued. "I am considering it myself."

"No, I couldn't," I answered. "I was born a Jew."

"But the Church has promised to save all those who do convert."

"If I gave up Judaism and converted to Christianity solely to save myself, what kind of Christian would I be?"

"One who is not in prison."

"I don't think that would save me. I would still be a Jew in the eyes of the Hungarian government as well as in the eyes of the Nazis."

"It can't hurt to try," she went on. "I think I'll discuss it with my daughter's employer, the president of the bread factory. He and my daughter are very close friends. His wife was Jewish, but she converted before they were married and has been a faithful Roman Catholic ever since. Their children do not even know that their mother was Jewish."

During that spring I had come to know Mrs. Stolaki, the wife of the president of the factory; she wanted a new wardrobe and I was recommended to her by Mrs. Kolman. Mrs. Stolaki lived in a large, red brick house on the edge of Budapest with her husband and three children, two girls and a boy, who were fifteen, sixteen, and seventeen years old and attended the gymnasium. Every day during most of June, I rode the streetcar to her house and sat for long hours in her sewing room. She often curled up in an easy chair on the other side of the room from me, an embroidery frame in her hands, and talked about household trivialities. I sensed at these times that she was upset over something, for hours passed while she did not complete a stitch in her frame. Finally one day she said, "My husband is the president of the bread company, you know—the largest one of its kind in the entire city."

"Yes," I said. "I know."

"He has a very important job with many duties, many responsibilities. He is highly regarded in the business world."

She stopped talking and began to pull a strand of floss tight against her hand, winding the deep red threads around her small finger.

"He keeps informed about the war," she finally continued. "He has followed each of the bills concerning the Jews. I am Jewish . . . I mean, I was Jewish. He can't be too careful, you know."

When I came to her house several days later she met me at the door with red eyes, a handkerchief wadded into a ball in one hand. She kept pulling a bit of lace that showed between her thumb and the rest of her hand.

"Are you all right?" I asked.

"Oh, yes . . . but . . . my husband. He has decided . . ." She turned away and walked into the sewing room, closing the door behind us.

"My husband has told the children that I was Jewish before we married. They became very upset. He wants me to leave."

"But where would you go?" I asked.

"That's what I asked him, and he couldn't give me an answer. My parents are dead. This is my home! Why should I leave? Where would I go?"

The next day when I came back to her house I rang the bell but no one came to the door. I rang again, waited, and was turning to leave when a young girl of sixteen or seventeen opened the door. She was dressed in a brown, wool tweed suit and a matching hat with a plumed feather that perched on her blond curls at a slight angle. "Yes?" she asked impatiently.

"I'm the seamstress," I answered. "Seren."

"Have you been working for someone here?"

"Yes, Mrs. Stolaki."

"Well, she's not here. We won't be needing you anymore."

"Where has she gone?"

"If you must know, my brother and sister and I turned her in last night. The police came and took her away."

"You did such a thing? Why?"

"She's a Jew. Isn't that reason enough? All these years and we didn't know it. It was my father who finally told us."

"But she's your mother!"

"She's not my mother any longer! How could a Jew bitch be my mother?"

I quickly turned away to keep from slapping her face and walked down the sidewalk as fast as I could. Shuddering, I boarded the streetcar again and went to the home of another client. A week later I heard of a similar instance. Thereafter many Jews were turned in by their families.

———

NIGHT AFTER NIGHT THE RUSSIANS LIT UP THE SKY with firebombs burning like great orange torches in the blackness. By midsummer 1943 we were spending part of nearly every night in the shelter, crouched in a corner with the other people from our building. As we huddled together the ceiling of the shelter swayed down toward us. The men and women around us began crying out, their eyes fastened on the moving timbers above us, the dust falling in steady streams on our heads. We began rising and falling with the motion of the ceiling up and down, up and down, human waves ebbing and flowing with the roaring dark.

During one of these long nights, as the whole building shook in rumbling convulsions, Esther began to scream—a long, high crying that rose above the thundering bombs.

"Stop, Esther! Stop!" I yelled. "Esther!"

I put my arms around her but she continued to scream. Then I saw the towel that I still had in my hand; we had been washing the dishes when the sirens began.

"Here," I said. "Tear it. Esther, as a favor, tear it."

She looked at me as if I too had gone berserk, her eyes dark and wild, but she took the towel from me and began to tear it into strips. The first strip was slow, methodical, running the length of the towel, the second also, but by the third she was tearing frantically. With one quick wrench the strip was ripped off and thrown onto the floor.

"Slowly, slowly, Esther," I said. "Tear it slowly. Concentrate all of your attention on making the towel last until the bombing ends."

She began to tear again, pulling very cautiously, speeding up when a bomb hit nearby and then slowing down again. When the bombing finally stopped a pile of strips lay about her feet, a ragged edge still held in her hands. Every day after that I brought home scraps of material left over at my clients' homes and kept them under my pillow. When the sirens began to scream I grabbed a scrap for Esther and we ran to the shelter.

EACH NIGHT WHEN THE EXPLOSIONS DIED TO AN OCCA-sional, muted thundering in the distance, we straightened up and waited for the signal so we could go back to our rooms. One night our apartment building was destroyed. We, like many before us, were moved in with another family in the building on the other side of the courtyard. Ellen and the owner of the lingerie shop were moved in like manner to the floor below us, but the lingerie shop was gone. The family who was forced to take us in consisted of a woman and her two daughters, Lily and Zora; her husband had been arrested and taken away. The woman, Mrs. Cohen, did not look upon Esther and me as two refugees who were forced into her apartment, but rather tried to make us feel at ease, sharing her meals and making a bed for us in the corner of the room.

Lily became good friends with Esther, as they were both eighteen years old. I became fascinated with Lily's near helplessness. Raised to be a lady, to marry young and hire servants to help her do everything, she had never worked at a job outside her home. She asked endless questions about our work when Esther and I returned at the end of the day.

"Where did you go today?" she would ask me, peering out through the very thick glasses she groped for the first thing in the morning, as a crippled girl reaches for her cane.

"I went to a suburb outside Budapest. I'm making a suit for a businesswoman, Mrs. Schwartz."

"You went all that way? By yourself?"

"Why should anyone go with me? I sew the suit by myself. Should I take someone along just to hold my hand on the way there?"

She blushed and lowered her eyes, her long brown hair falling about her face. She was as pretty and delicate as Louise had been as a young girl.

"I'm teasing you," I laughed. "What did you do today?"

"Oh . . ." She looked around the room as if the answer to my question were lying on the table or on a chair or perhaps on the worn burgundy rug. "I don't know . . . embroidered, I guess. Would you like to see what I'm working on?"

"I would love to see it," I said.

She ran to get the hoops with a piece of linen stretched between them, and held up the filled-in picture: a young girl wearing a long, pink dress reclined in the middle of a garden of red roses, white doves flying to her hand and a silver stream trickling at her feet.

"It's lovely," I said.

"I'm glad you like it. I'll give it to you when it's finished," she said.

"No, you save it for your hope chest. Your fiancé, David, will want to see it hanging in your house someday."

She blushed again. "Yes, he might." She pulled out her needle and began to fill in a dove.

ONE EVENING AS I WAS COMING UP THE STAIRS TO our room, I saw Zipporah on the landing above me. It was the first time I had seen her in months.

"Seren!" she called. "Wait there."

She came down the stairs slowly, cautiously, not at all in the manner she usually descended—in little leaps taking in three or four steps at a time.

"I need your help," she said as soon as she was three steps above me. She looked down at me steadily, directly into my eyes. "I know you don't approve of me, but you must help me. You must!"

"What is it?" I asked. "Are the police after you? Do you want me to find a place to hide?"

"No, no, nothing like that. It's . . ." She looked down and began to stroke her skirt, her hands curving up around her hips and down across her stomach. Finally she looked at me again. "Can you guess?"

"No! Zipporah, don't go on like this. What is it?"

"I'm pregnant."

"Oh, Zipporah! Oh, my God, Zipporah . . ."

"I didn't mean to. Aaron and I were so in love. We couldn't wait. We just couldn't. Now he's in the labor force. I don't even know when I'll see him again."

Her face slowly became mottled, dark red blotches appearing on both cheeks. A tear slid down one side of her face, fell on the collar of her jacket. She continued to look at me.

"Zipporah," I said, "what do you expect me to do?"

"I've thought about it all day. I want you to help me find one of those doctors."

"Me? You got yourself into this! You wouldn't listen to me when I told you to leave Aaron alone! Now all of a sudden you want me to become involved."

"Please help me, Seren. You're my sister! I have no one else."

I wanted to run back down the stairs and out into the street. Zipporah had betrayed everything our mother and father had taught us; no respectable Jewish girl even thought of such intimacy with a man until she was his wife. I looked up at her again. She was circling her stomach with her hands as before, tears gathering at the corners of her eyelids.

"How far along are you?" I asked.

"I'm not sure . . . three months, I think. When Aaron knew he had to leave, we . . ."

"Do you really want to do this?" I asked impatiently.

"I don't know what else to do. Do you?"

I thought for a few long minutes. No, there was no other solution.

"Will you help me?" she asked again.

"Tomorrow I'll ask one of my clients to suggest a doctor," I answered.

She looked at me again, wiped the tears away with the back of her hand, and went past me down the stairs. "I'll be back tomorrow night," she called up.

I turned to look after her.

"Don't tell any of this to Esther," I said in a loud whisper.

"No, I won't," she answered.

She went out the door and was gone.

Fourteen

ON A COLD, GRAY MONDAY MORNING ONE WEEK LATER,
Zipporah and I sat on the streetcar heading toward the address Mrs. Kolman
had given me. Zipporah had said nothing all morning, not even greeting me
when we met, and still sat silent, her eyes fastened on a spot she had fixed on
in the lower part of the window. Only her hands moved, trembling, the left
hand lying loosely in her lap, the right holding a cloth bag.

"Are you all right?" I asked.

Her eyes slowly left the window, traveling across the front of the streetcar, coming to rest on mine.

"Are you all right?" I asked again.

"I'm scared," she said. "It will hurt, won't it? I know it will hurt." She
shifted in the seat, turning her back to me, and fixed her eyes again on the
same spot. We rode the rest of the way in silence.

The trip took over an hour as we traveled to the edge of Buda, changing streetcars twice. Finally we arrived at the intersection closest to the address I had been given, got off the streetcar, and began walking down the

wide street past old mansions set back from the sidewalk and almost hidden by towering trees. Lawns of lush green grass rolled beyond wrought iron gates, and beds of yellow chrysanthemums blossomed along the bottom of high fences.

"Where are we?" Zipporah asked. "I didn't know such places existed in Budapest."

"This is a very wealthy area. Only Gentiles live here."

"How do you know where to go? What if we get lost?"

"Don't worry. I know where we are. A client of mine lives on the next street."

"You have Gentile clients?" she asked.

"I don't tell them that I'm Jewish."

"Oh . . ." She looked at me quickly.

"Are you ever asked for your identification?" she asked.

"Never. No one has ever asked to see it."

"I'm always asked. Why do I have to look Jewish when you don't?"

"But Zipporah! I have admired your dark eyes and hair since we were children."

"You have?" She stopped walking, turning to look at me again.

"Come on," I said. "We better hurry. I don't want anyone to see us here."

Beginning to walk faster, we covered the next few blocks quickly and were within half a block of the address when a car coming up the street from behind us began to slow, following us as we walked.

"Keep walking!" I said. "We're almost there."

"Who is it? What do they want?"

"I don't know. Try to ignore them."

With a sudden slam, a man in the uniform of the Hungarian National Guard bolted from the car and ran up to us, drawing his rifle as he ran.

"Halt!" he shouted.

I grabbed Zipporah, who was bracing herself to run, her arms drawn tightly against her side, head lowered. "No!" I whispered.

The soldier ran directly in front of us, blocking our path, while another man came from the back of the car to stand behind us, rifle pointed at our heads.

"Jews are not allowed in this part of the city!" the soldier in front of us shouted. "Get in the car!"

"Oh, please, let us go," Zipporah said. "We'll go back to where we came from. Please . . ."

"Get in the car!" he shouted again, moving a step closer.

The thought of being taken to prison again was like a fire burning in my breast. There was a possibility that my earlier arrest and imprisonment had been recorded and that I would be treated even more harshly because of it. Would I be sent away like Emma?

After a few minutes it became apparent that we were not being taken back into the city; the car was speeding past fields of wheat and peasant huts. Finally we turned onto another road, bumping along for half a mile or so, and came to a bridge that had been destroyed. Several women were walking toward it carrying long planks while other women stirred what looked like cement in big tubs, soldiers standing beside them with drawn bayonets. The car came to a stop and the men jumped out quickly and flung open both back doors.

"Out!" they commanded in unison.

We were herded to a tent a few meters from the bridge. There, we were each handed a shovel and told to start digging holes for pilings on both banks of the river. We were in a work camp, I realized, and I was somewhat relieved that we were not taken to a prison; we would probably be treated decently as long as we did the assigned work. Then I remembered: Esther! She would be frightened when I didn't come back at night. *She will think that I am dead,* I realized.

THAT NIGHT WE SLEPT ON THE BARE GROUND UNDER the trees, huddled beneath a thin, worn blanket thrown to us by a guard. Zipporah had fallen asleep as soon as she stretched out between me and another woman, but I lay there listening to the leaves, to the stream trickling below, for hour after hour. Aspen trees rustled with each sweep of the night wind. The sound was familiar; the wind in the trees in Fulehaza had made the same sound the night my father prepared the boiling water to use against the students coming to burn down our house, and the other small children and I had been hidden in the garden. Again I was beside Zipporah, now exhausted with her pregnancy, breathing deep, even breaths in the cool October air. *How can she sleep and I lie awake?* I wondered. *If it weren't for her neither of us would be here.* At last I must have drifted into sleep, for the high, shrill cry of a young rooster crowing from a distance startled me awake.

The days merged together: we carried boards, poured cement, lifted rocks, dug holes, cleared roads, ate, slept, moved to a new location, began again. Our group consisted of other Jewish women from Hungary who, like us, had been seen in the wrong place at the wrong time. The heavy work kept us from becoming acquainted, the rifles trained at our backs discouraging any conversation. Each of us was alone.

By the end of November snow fell daily from the gray sky that hung above us like a heavy, dark cloak. Every evening we cleared the drifts from a space on the ground and threw a tarpaulin cover over the frozen earth, but we might as well have slept on the snow. The chill penetrated our cover, our clothes, our flesh, until it seemed as if a quilt of ice enveloped us from all sides, from above and below.

One night Zipporah stopped shivering, settled into a spot near my left shoulder, and was almost asleep when she gasped, "Oh!"

"What is it?" I asked. "What's wrong?"

"I felt something. I don't know what it was."

"Where did you feel it?"

"In my stomach, I think . . . There! I felt it again. Yes, it's in my stomach."

"Does it hurt?"

"No, it's a strange feeling—like my stomach is moving."

"Oh, Zipporah, it's the baby."

"What?"

"The baby. It's quickening."

"What are you talking about?"

"Rose told me about it when she was expecting Elena. It means the baby is big enough to move around."

"Oh, Seren, what am I going to do?"

She began to cry, heaving against my shoulder with sobs that grew in intensity until I was afraid she would grow sick from crying. I thought of reaching over, stroking her hair, telling her that everything would be all right, but I could not promise her that when anything might happen. We were alone, almost frozen, dead to our family. I lay there, silent. Finally she stopped sobbing and fell asleep. I drew the blanket up around her shoulders, turned over, and settled for the night.

TWO MORE MONTHS PASSED. HANUKKAH CAME, although I did not know the exact date as we could not distinguish one day from the next. I thought of our mother and hoped she was still safe. Surely Herman or Rose had taken her in when she didn't receive any rent money from me these last three months. Was Esther all right? Lily's mother was probably looking after her. And what would happen to us? How could Zipporah give birth to a baby by the side of the road like a farm animal? She was growing bigger; a small mound rose beneath her coat and she left several of the buttons undone.

One day she and I sat on a rock eating supper in the dim light of late January. I was looking at her, wondering how a healthy baby could grow inside her here in the snowy fields with barely enough for her to eat, no vitamins, no milk. She did not seem to notice my stare and sat kicking some loose stones.

"Do you remember when we used to fight those peasant boys on the way home from school, the ones who called us 'dirty Jews'?"

"Yes," I answered. "I hated them."

"Weren't they terrible? Remember the time two of them had you pinned against the bridge and were threatening to throw you in the river? Then I came up from behind and hit one over the head with a rock and kicked the other in the seat."

"No, I don't remember."

"Well, I do! They ran all the way across the bridge and didn't look back once. One took your hat, though."

"Oh, I do remember now," I said. "I had forgotten. They took the brown hat Mama knitted for me . . . You were a feisty little girl, weren't you?" I asked, laughing.

"So were you! Remember the time you burned my hair? We were playing under the kitchen cot and you lit a candle."

"Yes!" I laughed. "Mama yelled, 'What's scorching?' It was your hair!"

Zipporah smiled. "I wasn't always bad."

"Oh, Zipporah, I know . . ."

She looked away into the darkening sky and said no more.

The next evening we lined up for supper as usual before walking past the food tent. Snow was falling in hard, tiny bits that stung my face as I trudged forward slowly, Zipporah in front of me, the wind slipping into the space between us and blowing her long scarf across my face. As I was leaning forward to tell her to wind the scarf around her neck so it would not hit me, a guard shouted, "You! Halt!" He was pointing to Zipporah.

She jerked around to look at me, her eyes asking, *What is it? Why is he singling me out?*

"Step forward ten paces!" the same guard shouted.

Zipporah began to walk away from me. I knew instantly that this was wrong, that I should grab her, stop her, stop her. I could not move.

She took the ten required paces. The guard strutted to a place a few feet from her side, raised his rifle, and in one quick, terrible instant, in one movement that almost stopped my heart, he fired. Zipporah fell to the ground.

"No! No!" I screamed, and ran to her, lifting her from the ground. A trickle of blood ran down one side of her face from a deep hole in her temple, ran past the black mass of hair around her neck, dribbled into the snow in a thin, red line. She slumped against my shoulder, dead.

"What is the slut to you?" the guard demanded.

I looked him straight in the eye. "She is my sister."

"She shouldn't have gotten herself pregnant, the whore!" he sneered, and walked away.

I cradled Zipporah's head in my arms and rocked slowly back and forth, back and forth. She was so still. She who had whirled about on the dance floor joyously, in complete abandon, now lay quiet, arrested. The pale winter light fell across her high cheekbones in slanting rays, lingering on her slightly open full lips, rested on the hair falling about her face and over my arm in a rich, black cascade.

How can this have happened? I asked myself over and over. *How can I have allowed this to happen?* The guard was coming back with a cart. Slowly I lowered her head to the ground and covered her face with the long red scarf. She had loved red. "It is like fire!" she said once. "It suits me."

Finally, I backed away and looked at her lying there in the snow, her hands covering the small mound. Shuddering, so cold that I felt naked in the dying light, I walked away behind the other women to the far end of the field.

All night I cried, trying to think of how it could have been prevented. If I had been kinder to Zipporah, if I had not forced her to move out of Aunt Terry's house, she might not have become pregnant; I could have looked after her more and none of this would have happened. No, I decided, she would not have listened to me. Then I should have grabbed her today when I knew that something was going to happen, thrown myself in front of her. I had stood there, not moving at all, until she was shot and it was too late. It was all too late. Over and over the same thoughts surged through my mind relentlessly, until I must have lapsed into a half-sleep toward morning.

As I lay there a loud voice suddenly called out to me in the darkness: "Seren!"

"Who is it?" I answered, bolting up from under the blanket.

No one was there.

Fifteen

ONE MORNING AT THE END OF FEBRUARY WE WERE told our special detail had completed its work and we were free. Immediately I began walking back into the city, reaching the edge of Buda late one afternoon. Wide expanses of land, empty except for solitary, blackened chimneys, stretched before me where once had stood rows of apartment buildings and businesses. Jumbled piles of broken bricks were scattered amid the pitted dirt. Sometimes a single building was left standing, nothing left of the windows except holes through which pigeons flew in and out.

After crossing the Danube I began to run, stopping to catch my breath every few blocks. I was encouraged by all the buildings still standing and thought, *Esther and the others are safe. I know it! They're safe!* When I came to 7 Sziget-utca at last, it looked almost the same as when I had left it early that morning to meet Zipporah. Three or four windows were broken and stuffed with cloth and a hole was gouged out in the front, but the building stood.

Ringing for the elevator three times with no response, I realized that it must not be working and began to climb the stairs to Mrs. Cohen's apartment on the fifth floor. I hurried up the first two flights, paused on the landing for a minute, and was beginning to ascend the third when I heard someone slowly coming down the stairs above me. The steps got closer and a girl rounded the landing, her head bent downward, one hand listlessly sliding along the banister. It was Esther. Oh, it was Esther!

"This is a fine welcome," I called out. "You don't even say hello!"

Her head jerked up so quickly that it snapped, and her eyes grew wide. "Seren?" she asked quietly.

"Who else?" I answered.

Flying down the remaining steps almost as if she had wings, she reached me in an instant. She hugged me again and again, kissing my cheeks and hair, finally sinking against me and sobbing.

"Come, Esther," I said, holding her close. "It's all right. I'm back."

I TOLD ESTHER EVERYTHING—EXCEPT ABOUT ZIPPO-rah's pregnancy. And for the next few days I enjoyed the luxuries of sleeping between clean sheets and warm comforters, bathing as often as I liked with soapy, steaming water, eating hot meals at a table. Mrs. Cohen greatly enjoyed cooking for me. She was one of those rare people who can prepare a nourishing, appetizing meal out of nothing more than rice, a few vegetables, and a sprinkle of seasonings. I ate, rested, scrubbed off months of grime and perspiration, and looked forward to acquiring new customers and working again. Within a week I found several women in the outlying reaches of Buda who needed a dressmaker. Once again I was in business.

The first few days of March 1944 came clear and cold. There was a tension in the air, however. I had sensed it as soon as I returned to Budapest. Germany was losing the war, her troops retreating from the advancing Russian army across the snow and ice fields of Russia to the Hungarian border. By the middle of the month swarms of German soldiers were converging on the city. I could not go through the streets without seeing mile-long streams of motorized divisions moving like slow, brown armadillos.

Each day we felt less free than the day before. There was no escape: to the east was Romania, from which we had been deported; to the west, Austria; to the north, Slovakia and Poland; to the south, Yugoslavia—all controlled by the Third Reich. Even if we could have escaped through these countries and the rest of Nazi-dominated Europe, who would have welcomed us? Where could we have gone? A few Gentiles took in small numbers of Jews and hid them. Sweden produced small miracles in saving us. The Norwegian Resistance fought long and hard. However, for the most part, we felt abandoned.

On the twenty-ninth of March, I came home to find Esther, Lily, Zora, and Mrs. Cohen all making Stars of David out of yellow cloth. "Has it come to this?" I asked.

"Yes," Mrs. Cohen answered. "A notice was tacked on the door to the building this morning. All Jewish people have to start wearing the star by tomorrow."

"What if we don't wear it, Mother?" Zora asked. "I don't want to."

"Oh, you must!" Mrs. Cohen answered. "You'll be arrested if you're caught without the star." She looked at me then. "Seren, I guess you'll have to give up your clients. That's too bad."

"Why?" I asked. "We need the money."

"Your clients are Gentiles. When they see you coming up the sidewalks of their fine homes with the Star of David pinned to your coat, they'll turn you away."

"I won't wear it then."

"You have to!" Esther exclaimed.

"You don't look a bit Jewish, do you?" Mrs. Cohen said to me. "You could easily pass for a Gentile, even now."

"I have before. I can again. It's all right, Esther," I said, turning to her. "I'll be very careful."

"You're so brave," said Lily.

"No," I answered. "I'm practical. I don't want to give up my customers!" Laughing, we sat down together to supper.

More restrictions were imposed: the few remaining Jewish stores were painted with large signs saying, "Shopping forbidden here." Jews could walk only at the curbs of the streets. All butter, eggs, and rice were forbidden to us. Sugar, fat, milk, and meat were rationed. Telephones, cars, radios, and books were taken away.

A few weeks later a Jewish mother and her four young daughters were moved in with Esther and me, while another family joined Lily, her mother, and Zora. Ellen and her former employer were forced to take in two families. Our building had become a ghetto filled almost entirely with women whose fathers, husbands, and brothers had been arrested and taken from them. All over Budapest that day and the next, thousands of Jewish women and children were evacuated from their apartments and forced to leave behind all of their furniture and most of their clothing. As I walked through the city I saw them herded along the streets by the Hungarian National Guard, mothers holding the hands of children, babies wrapped in blankets and nestled against their breasts. One or two children sometimes trailed behind, stumbling sleepily in the cold morning air and crying, rubbing their faces with both fists. When one lagged too far behind, a soldier prodded the child with the butt of his rifle, causing the small boy or girl to run blindly, screaming. The mother would look around in terror, hearing her child's cry, and then grab the child to her desperately.

Late one morning toward the end of April, I was shopping for some vegetables in the small grocery store near our building when I overheard two Jewish women talking.

"A ghetto has been made for all the Jews in my village," one was saying. "The SS roped off an area on the outskirts of the town and forced the Jews into it. Then they put guards all around it. No one can come in or go out. My mother still lives there. I am so worried about her!"

The other woman looked out from under a white wool scarf tied under her chin and pulled out over her forehead. "What's the name of your village?" she asked.

"Reghinal-Sasesc," the first woman answered. "I left it many years ago. If only I had taken my mother with me!"

I ran up to the first woman and touched her on the arm. "Are you sure that this has happened in Reghinal-Sasesc? Maybe you have the villages confused. My mother lives there and my brother and sister. They haven't written anything about a ghetto."

"Yes, I'm sure," she answered. "My nephew escaped from there only last week. He stopped to visit me on his way to Sweden."

I hurried back to our room, completely forgetting to buy the vegetables. When I arrived I went to Esther, who was talking to several of the other girls in our room.

"Esther," I said as soon as she and I had withdrawn to one side. "The SS has made a ghetto in Reghinal-Sasesc. We must try to get Mama out and bring her here! Do you have any money hidden away?"

"No," she answered. "I had a little but I was forced to spend it when you were gone."

"It's all right. We'll have to think of something."

By the end of the week I finished a dress I was making for a client and received payment. On Sunday I wrote a letter to Mama enclosing the money for the train ticket, but on Monday another notice was posted on our door, stating that travel was forbidden to all Jews in Hungary. *Oh, Mama,* I thought. *When will I ever see you again?*

ONE EVENING ESTHER RAN UP TO ME AS I WAS COMing in the door to our room. "Do you know what?" she asked. "A soldier from the National Guard was here today and said that our mail is being held at the Jewish Federation. Every day they receive cards from the villages. Before the people are moved they let them write to their relatives. Maybe Mama has written or Rose. Can we go tomorrow and see?"

"Of course we'll go," I answered. "If this is true, Mama will have written. Maybe a postcard is waiting for us!"

Early the next morning Esther and I went to the office of the Jewish Federation and found many other people on the sidewalk in front of the building, all waiting for the office to open. Finally an older man in a black flannel suit, a large Star of David pinned to the upper right pocket, limped to the door with the help of a wooden cane and unlocked it. Slowly, in a dignified manner, he removed his gray homburg and motioned for us to come in. As many people as possible crowded inside the office, the rest pressing against the doorframe. Esther and I found an opening beside his small desk.

"Have you all come seeking mail?" he asked in a quiet voice.

"Yes," a young woman near him answered. "That's why I'm here."

"Yes! Yes!" others around her answered, bobbing their heads up and down, their eyes serious, wide.

"I'm sorry to say that I have only a few postcards," he said. He picked up a small pile of mail. "Is Anne Tenenbaum here?" he asked. "Anne Tenenbaum?" Our eyes darted to one another's faces. No, she was not among us. *Hurry!* I thought. *Go on to the next one!*

He picked up another card. "Herman Kuhn?" he asked. "Is Herman Kuhn here?" An old man with a short white beard shuffled forward and grasped the postcard in his hands. "My daughter . . ." he said, the card trembling in his frail hands.

Another name was called out. "Miriam Zhitamir . . . Miriam Zhitamir . . ."

A dark woman whom I had noticed because of the red plaid shawl she had lavishly draped around her shoulders shouted, "That's me! I'm Miriam Zhitamir!" She made her way to where Esther and I were standing, grabbed the card and pressed it to her chest with both hands, rocking back and forth for a few long moments. "It's from my mother," she finally said. "Do you want to see? Oh, I'm so happy!"

I took the card from her. "Dear Miriam, my love," it read. "I am still well. Mama." I wondered where her mother had been when she wrote the card, where she was being taken, why she had not written more. The handwriting was hurried, uneven, as if she had written it while riding on a train.

No more names were called out. We were told that perhaps a few more postcards would be dropped off in the afternoon. For the remainder of that day, for many days afterward, Esther and I stood in front of the office and waited.

No postcard ever came.

THEN ONE MORNING I CAME DOWN THE STAIRS AND found a chain and padlock on the gate going across the building's courtyard. Two guards were posted on the other side. For one hour, between ten and eleven o'clock in the morning, the gate was unlocked and we were able to go out of the courtyard to the markets. Fortunately our building had by now become a smoothly running entity in itself. When the ghetto was made, each apartment building had selected a committee to oversee daily operations. In our building the committee was composed of a few elderly Jewish men who had not been taken into the labor force because of their age. They were intelligent, reasonable men, former doctors, professors, and heads of businesses, who tried to make life as pleasant as possible for us. Several men kept the shelters cleared of debris and ready for us. Other men constantly repaired the pipes so that we were never without running water. If a problem arose, such as whose responsibility it was to keep the hallways clean, a meeting was held in the courtyard and any conflicts were resolved.

Our life was bearable. No one contracted a disease because of unsanitary conditions; the building was always kept clean and orderly. No one went hungry; if one roomful of people did not have enough to eat, we shared. We were Jewish women who had been taught from childhood to respect the judgment of men without stopping to either analyze or criticize their pronouncements.

In the afternoons the priests came. First we would hear the ringing of a bell, jingling in the warm air of late May. Then snatches of sermons would come drifting up to us from the courtyard, where many of the women had gathered to hear these missionaries. The Catholic Church had not believed any of the decrees defining a Jew as one who had Jewish ancestors. It still regarded "the Jewish question" as a religious one while the Nazis saw it as one of contaminated blood. Not realizing the real significance of this view of us as "spoilers of the race," as none of us did, the Catholic Church continued to try and convert as many of the Jews as possible.

Several of the young girls who lived with us went to a meeting in the courtyard one afternoon and came back to our room with flushed cheeks, gold crosses dangling from their necks on metal chains. I could not help smiling at seeing the cross hanging inches away from the yellow Star of David pinned to their chests.

"I see that you've converted," Mrs. Cohen said to them.

"Yes!" answered Mira, a young girl of sixteen. "The priest promised that we won't be deported to another country now that we're Christians. We can stay here in Budapest. The Church will save us!"

A few days later, at the end of June, there was a knock on our door in the morning.

"I'll get it," Mrs. Cohen called. She stood by the door for a few minutes, her voice rising and falling excitedly. "No!" she said once, and then I heard the low murmur of a man's voice again. Finally she closed the door, went to a chair and sank down into it, her face ashen.

"What's wrong, Mother?" Lily asked. "Who was that?"

Mrs. Cohen looked up at Lily, her eyes ringed with deep lines. "That was a man from the building committee with a new order from the National Guard. It's happened," she almost whispered. "They're coming to take us away. The committee must have everyone ready."

"Who, Mother? Who's coming?"

"The National Guard. In three days all the women between the ages of fifteen and forty will be taken into a labor force . . . Oh, Lily . . ." she said louder. "That includes you!"

Lily began to weep loudly against her mother's shoulder.

"What will happen to the children?" I asked. "Surely they won't be left alone?"

"No, no . . ." Mrs. Cohen replied. "The women who have small children won't be taken. They don't want to be bothered with old people or children. Zora and I will be left here alone."

Mrs. Cohen buried her face in Lily's hair. Each of us sat separate, looking into ourselves to see how we would summon up the courage to face the very thing we had dreaded for so long.

As we sat silently, Mira suddenly shouted, "Wait a minute! I won't have to go! I've converted. The priests will come and rescue me and the other Christians. You must have forgotten to tell us that. I'm so glad I remembered!"

Mrs. Cohen looked up. "No, nothing was said about Christians being excluded."

Her eyes reddened and tears burst from them. "It isn't fair!" Mira shouted.

Lily's mother stroked her hair for a few silent minutes. Then, turning to me, she said, "Lily's a very delicate child. She's so young . . . All she's ever done is attend school. How will she be able to endure a labor camp? Why couldn't she stay here with Zora and me? Couldn't she? She doesn't look old. We could say that she's younger."

"No, she would be arrested and taken to prison," I said. "I'm sure they know exactly how many of us must report to them for the labor force. The police have each of us on file—our names, ages, addresses. Let her go with us. Esther and our friend Ellen are very young too. We'll take care of her."

"There's nothing else we can do?" Mrs. Cohen asked.

"Nothing. I've been in a labor camp before. I know what to expect, what to take along. She'll be fine with us. In fact, I have something that will be perfect!"

I took from the closet the box of clothing that Samuel had left, and found four pairs of trousers. "Girls," I said, "we're in luck. These will keep our legs from freezing."

"But they're men's pants!" Esther said. "I've never worn pants in my life!"

"Is this a fashion show we're going to be in? No. We'll be outside in all kinds of weather. The trousers will keep us nice and warm!"

Esther and I tried on a pair. Hers almost fit. Mine hung like a sack and dragged on the floor behind me.

"Wouldn't Samuel laugh to see me now," I said, "wearing his clothes!"

I paraded back and forth in front of the girls, stumbling along, almost falling once, until Esther and Ellen were doubled up in laughter.

"How can you act like this when in three days we'll be taken away?" Lily asked, beginning to cry again.

"Lily, Lily," I said. "We'll be back as soon as the war's over. They're inducting women now because all the men are already in the labor force. They need us for the war. We'll have to work hard, but working is better than being in prison, isn't it?"

"I don't know. I've never been in prison. But I've never worked outside like a man before either."

"Working is better than prison, believe me! Now come here. I'll get you all fixed up."

Later in the day we were told to bring along a knapsack, warm clothing, cooking utensils, and blankets. Remembering how cold the ground had been during those long months sleeping outside while I was in the special detail, I decided to bring more than blankets. Taking two down comforters that Mrs. Cohen let us use and some waterproof material I had saved, I covered the comforters with the waterproofing. When I finished we had a portable bed large enough for the four of us. Let it rain and freeze! We would remain warm and dry.

AT SEVEN O'CLOCK ON A JULY MORNING, ESTHER, Ellen, Lily, and I reported to the Hungarian National Guard in our courtyard. After a few minutes one of the soldiers ordered us to line up, and then a reading of our names was begun. There were hundreds of us. The soldiers yelled out a name, a woman answered, and she was ordered to step forward. I was surprised to see how young they were; no woman was older than twenty-seven or twenty-eight and most of them were young girls of fifteen and sixteen.

We were marched out of the city. Rain began to fall in a steady, cold downpour, running over the faces of the women who had forgotten to wear hats or scarves. A young girl in front of me, her hair plastered to her head in long, dripping strings, began to cry. "I'm so tired . . . I'm so tired . . ." she said over and over. "We'll never stop walking! I'm so tired . . ."

Finally the girl next to her said, "We should be stopping soon. It's growing dark."

"But I'm tired now!" the first girl replied. "I'm not used to walking. Why couldn't they let us ride the streetcar? I can't keep up. I can't! This pack is too heavy."

In another minute she slid the knapsack from her back and let it fall to the ground. I had to step over it quickly to keep from stumbling.

Esther, who was walking on one side of me, said, "I think I'll throw away my knapsack too. It's just too heavy."

"No you won't!" I said. "You have one of the comforters. What will we sleep on? They won't give us beds! No, we don't throw away anything."

Finally at dusk as the rain was beginning to slow, we came to Kishpest on the outskirts of Budapest. Here we entered a soccer field, walking out onto the rain-drenched grass, and stopped. I looked around, in all directions seeing women gathered in little groups of four or five or standing alone, lost in the sea of women. The soldiers of the National Guard who had marched beside us, among us, in front of us, and behind us with raised bayonets now moved back and forth shouting, "We'll sleep here. Lie down! Lie down!"

We unrolled our comforters and spread one on the ground. Then we stretched out on it, the four of us fitting snugly, and pulled the other one over us. I gazed up at the stars beginning to appear in the sky and shining down upon us, on the women around us curled up on the soggy ground with nothing between them and the dampness, on the women beyond them crying into their coat sleeves, on all the thousands of women sprawled there as the night began to fall.

Sixteen

THE NEXT DAY WE MARCHED OUT OF BUDAPEST. IN the middle of the afternoon we came to a wide, green, rolling field where cows would normally graze, but I saw none, only broken fences and wood stakes sticking out of the ground at short intervals. We stopped and then, even before we had a chance to sit down, each of us was handed a shovel and told to go to the far end of the field to dig a pit for our toilet.

In about an hour we had the toilet dug, but before we had a chance to relieve ourselves the soldiers ordered us back to the middle of the field and lined us up again. One of the soldiers began to shout, "You will dig trenches to trap enemy tanks. They must be three meters wide and three meters deep. You must complete one hundred trenches by nightfall. Failure to complete one hundred trenches will result in punishment. The sites are marked with poles. Begin!"

Esther, Lily, Ellen, and I ran to one of the marked sites and began to dig. The digging was easy at first, like working in our garden at home, but then we came to hard, compacted dirt and our shovels hit against it with a clang, barely scraping away an inch or two at a time. The soldiers, who were standing over us with their rifles aimed at our backs, began to shout, "Faster, you bitches! Work, you lazy Jew whores!"

I was working beside Lily and she cringed, covering her ears with her hands.

"I can't stand it," she gasped. "I have never been called such names." Tears ran down her face and fell onto her hands, already blistered and raw.

"Keep working," I said. "Please, Lily. Dig!"

She bent over her shovel again and resumed digging. "I am not a whore!" she said, the tears still falling.

"Of course you're not!" I said. "Just keep digging."

An hour passed, two. The blisters in the crease of my right hand between my thumb and first two fingers puffed up until they broke, the raw skin burning each time I pushed against the shovel, and still we dug. There were about twenty of us working on this trench and we had by now removed two meters of soil and thrown it up above our heads. We were digging ourselves into a black hole as we went deeper and deeper into the earth.

We still had not been given the chance of going to the toilet. Finally I could stand it no longer. "Do you want to ask if we can go to the pit?" I said to Ellen.

"You ask first," she answered.

I yelled up to a soldier, "I have to use the toilet."

He nodded his thick, round head and beckoned at me to come up, keeping his bayonet pointed at my chest. I climbed out of the trench and walked ahead of the soldier, who followed me all the way to the toilet pit. There I saw pairs of people all along the edge of the pit: a woman squatting over the edge, her coat drawn up around her waist, eyes squeezed tightly together, and a heavy, thick-middled soldier in a dark green uniform standing directly above her, his legs far apart, bayonet pointed, eyes staring at the white flesh suspended over the cold, damp hole. In the small camp I had been in before, we were granted privacy. *I won't be able to do anything,* I thought to myself. *How can I with those old, fat men watching me?* The need was great, however; I walked to the edge of the pit, lowered myself slowly, raised my coat as little as possible, and tried to let go the pressure that had been building up inside me since the day before. I could not. I could not relax the muscles with the soldiers staring. Straightening up again, I began walking back to the trench.

We worked while the afternoon faded away, worked into the early evening, worked until it was so dark down in the pit that we could barely see. Sometimes, just as we were lulled into the weary mindlessness of shovel, lift, throw, shovel, lift, throw, a series of explosions sounded directly above our heads. I looked up to see a soldier shooting his gun over the pit.

"Faster, you lazy bitches!" he yelled. "Next time I'll shoot you. It's not deep enough. Faster!"

We willed our arms to continue moving up and down, trying to ignore the aches of our shoulders and backs. It made no difference. Finally we were marched back to the area where we had left our knapsacks, trembling, realizing for the first time that we were alone in the middle of a barren field, surrounded by soldiers who wished us all dead.

Later that evening we were taken to the end of the field where a kitchen had been set up, and given a cup of vegetable soup and a piece of bread. As our group was near the beginning of the line, we were served. Those at the end reached the serving area to discover that the food was all gone.

When I awoke in the morning the pressure inside my bowels was so great that I could think of nothing else. I decided to try again to see if I could relieve myself. The procedure was the same; a guard marched behind me and then stood near, his bayonet drawn. Again I squatted at the edge of the pit. I could not relax. I gave up trying and rejoined the others.

"I'm very constipated," I whispered to Ellen. "I think I'll explode."

"You have to go," she answered. "You'll get sick!"

"I can't. I just can't."

"Why does a soldier have to go with us?" she asked.

"I don't know. We're homeless. We have no identification. Who would take us if we did try to run away? Where would we go?"

That day passed the same as the one before. We worked all day in the trenches as the soldiers shouted, "Faster! Faster! Faster!" firing their guns repeatedly over our heads. In the middle of the afternoon a girl who was digging on the other side of our group next to Esther suddenly pitched forward in the dirt, falling down on her face, arms raised above her. Long, dark hair fanned out around her head, around the shoulders of the brown coat, trailed through the fresh, loosened dirt.

"Damn you, son of a bitch!" a soldier shouted down. "Get up!"

She continued to lie there, soundlessly.

He yelled again, his gun pointed directly at her back. "Get up, bitch! Now!"

The little finger on her left hand moved once very slightly. The gun fired—one! two! three! four!—opening holes in the back of her coat. The girl lay perfectly still.

"Pick her up!" the same soldier yelled.

Several women on the other side of her gently lifted her body, and as they did, her head rolled back. Lily gasped, grabbing my hand. The dead girl was the same one who, walking beside us with dress shoes and no hat, threw her knapsack away when it became too heavy as we left Budapest. She had lasted for two days.

"Work!" a soldier yelled. "Faster!"

The dead girl was passed from hand to hand above our heads until she was lifted out of the trench. We jammed our shovels into the hard earth. That evening, when we climbed out, she was almost buried under our pile of dirt; we would not have known she was there except that one of her hands reached out from under the mound of dirt, palm up, the fingers spread wide.

The next morning I was in such pain that I could barely walk. Summoning a soldier, I went again to the toilet pit. I sat there in the pale, cold light, a woman straining on each side of me, and tried to let go, tried again and again, until tears were squeezed from my eyes from the effort, but I could not. *I will die if I don't,* I thought.

After another day of digging trenches evening came. I decided that I had to let go. That night I strained against the blocking stone until I was soaked with sweat and dizzy with exhaustion. It came out. The body can become accustomed to almost anything.

———

THROUGHOUT THAT MONTH OF JULY 1944 WE MOVED back and forth across the plains of Hungary, digging ever more trenches for the tanks of the enemy. The weather grew hot, but at night the heat lessened and we found comfort in the cool darkness of sleep. In the mornings we would shake the collected moisture from our hair, like horses in a dewy pasture. Often, there were twenty or thirty who did not rise, remaining curled up on the ground, dead. They would be left as they were, their bodies no more than small mounds on the grassy field, as we moved on to a new field.

We, who numbered about ten thousand women at the beginning of July, were down to nine thousand by the end. Over and over we were counted, once every morning, once every night. Sometimes the counting was interrupted by the roar of planes overhead and we were ordered to lie down. As we got closer to Budapest the bombing was more intense. At night we looked out from our comforters into a sky blazing with explosions of light as "Stalin candles" were dropped over the city. A few minutes later the bombs detonated and the earth exploded all around us; the ground shook, the smell of burning drifted over us, and the entire sky was on fire.

By now my emotions were numb. I should have been curious—no, eager to see Budapest. But I felt nothing as we walked through my beautiful city, across blocks of crumbling bricks.

We cleaned the streets of debris. Sometimes a solitary building was left standing while all around it only scarred earth remained. One day we came upon an entire stretch of nothing but the exposed shells of buildings, walls sloping down at angles from the open rafters to the base, standing like ruins in an ancient city. Two or three times we came upon water gushing from a broken pipe and hurriedly splashed our grimy faces and arms. Once I even found a sliver of soap amid the rubble and knew again the pleasure of having clean hands. At night we were brought to a field outside the city and here we ate supper and slept. When the streets were clear we moved into the countryside again.

Often as we worked in the fields, we heard the low whistle of a train from far away and then the steady chugging of the engine, the clacking of the wheels against the rails. Stealing glances whenever I could, I watched these long, long trains running day and night. Sometimes they were made up entirely of freight cars, sealed and bolted. At other times passenger car after passenger car rolled by, the faces of mothers and their children pressed tightly against the glass, looking out at us.

"Where do you think all those trains are going?" Esther asked me one night as we lay on our comforter beside Ellen and Lily.

"I don't know," I answered.

"The people on them are Jewish, aren't they?"

"Yes."

"You don't think that Mama is on one of those trains, do you? It would be so terrible for her if she was going right by us and we didn't know."

"It would be just as bad for us . . . to have her so near and not know," I said, hearing the rumbling of an approaching train.

"Let's not even imagine it," she said, turning over to go to sleep. "Mama is safe. She's fine."

A FEW NIGHTS LATER AS I WAS BEGINNING TO DRIFT into sleep, I heard a man's voice calling. I lay there, startled. Who would be out there on the other side of the field? Then I heard it again, louder, stronger. "Deborah Eliad . . . Deborah Eliad . . . Deborah Eliad," it called.

Another voice from the same, distant place began to call, "Eloise Eskin . . . Eloise Eskin . . . Eloise Eskin . . ."

By now many of the other women were sitting up on their blankets and looking around, frightened. Had the ghosts come to call on us lying there all alone under the cold stars? Then a woman from somewhere behind us called out, "I'm Eloise Eskin . . . I'm Eloise . . . Who's calling me?"

"Norman Eskin," the voice called back. "Norman Eskin . . ."

"Father!" the woman yelled. "I am Eloise."

My eyes filled with tears. My father would never call me again.

"Who are those men out there?" Esther asked.

"Could it be the men's labor force?" Ellen answered.

"It could be!" Esther said. "They must be camped on the other side of the clearing."

I thought of all those I knew who might be in the group: Samuel, my brothers Eliezer and Shlomo, the men who had worked near Valea Uzului several years ago. Perhaps someone would call me. Perhaps someone would remember me!

Soon a jumble of voices filled the air. Names of women drifted over the field in low voices reaching out into the night; flying back in high arcs lilting across the low shrubs, the grassy hillocks, were the names of men. "Adam Davidow . . . Adam Davidow . . . Adam Davidow . . ." a woman next to me kept calling. I lay there hour after hour, hearing names all night long, but not my name. No one called me.

The following evening it was the same. Voices reached out through the dead night until they found someone—touched them. A woman who had felt so alone that she sometimes thought of falling down and letting herself be shot now heard the voice of a loved man calling to her out of the blackness and was alone no longer. Again I listened for my name. I did not hear it.

ONE EVENING WE WERE CAMPED OUTSIDE BUDAPEST near Cvespol, where an airplane factory was located and the bombing was particularly heavy, the explosions so near that fragments of metal came hurtling through our camp. I looked for something to cover my head with but could find nothing other than the knapsack, which was soft and would not have given me much protection. Then I remembered the cooking pots. We had been carrying them all over Hungary and had not used them once. Quickly I took a black kettle with a long handle from my knapsack and put it over my head. It fit perfectly. When Ellen saw me she burst out laughing.

"Have you gone crazy?" she asked. "Or is this the latest fashion for labor camps?"

"You can laugh all you want," I said, "but my head will not be knocked off by a bomb."

Esther looked at me, her mouth open. "But what if a bomb falls on your foot?" she asked. "Maybe you should wear the pot on your foot."

"I can live without a foot," I said. "I can't live without a head." I curled up to go to sleep, still wearing the pot. In the morning when I awoke I saw Ellen, Lily, and Esther all wearing pots on their heads, the handles sticking out behind them.

AS SUMMER WANED, OUR WORK DID NOT SEEM QUITE as hard as before. Our hands had developed thick, hard calluses and the muscles in our backs and arms ceased to ache throughout the nights. On our long treks we began to find small gifts of food left for us along the wayside by the Hungarian people: a loaf of bread, some boiled eggs, a few cooked potatoes. When one of our group was able to pick up one of these gifts she shared it with the rest of us. We walked along together, nibbling at our prize, and felt a little less lonely, knowing that someone cared about us.

The calling back and forth between the men's camp and ours resumed when we were camped next to each other outside Budapest. Again many of the women heard their names and felt comforted by the voices of loved ones separated from them. Every night for a week I listened for my name, lying there in the dark for hours hearing names: fathers calling for their daughters, husbands for their wives, brothers for their sisters, young men for their sweethearts. Each night I thought, *No one calls for me. Not a single person. Doesn't anyone remember me? Not one?* I fell asleep listening to the names drifting above me. When I awoke in the morning I thought, *Maybe tonight someone will call my name,* and went to work, hopeful.

One night as I was lying there listening, almost despairing of ever hearing my name, I heard "Seren Tuvel" come across through the tumble of voices. *No,* I thought. *It was another name that sounds like mine.* Then I heard it again: "Seren Tuvel . . . Seren Tuvel . . ." It was my name! I wanted to jump up and run to the men's camp to find out who was calling me.

"I am here . . . Seren Tuvel . . . Seren Tuvel . . ." I called back.

There was no answer.

I called again, louder. "This is Seren! Seren Tuvel!"

A deep voice shouted back, "Seren."

It was Joseph, Herman and Tamara's youngest son! He was one of the last people I expected to hear. *Why does he call me?* I wondered. *He is much younger than me. Esther is more his age.*

"Joseph Tuvel," I yelled back. "Joseph Tuvel . . ."

Again and again I called out his name, and while he may have answered, I could not tell. All around me women were shouting; names were jumbled, scattered, lost amid the strained cacophony of voices. After half an hour I quit calling his name and lay down to sleep. To think that Joseph had called me! I had always assumed that he never felt any affection for me; I was nothing more to him than an older aunt he had to tolerate. But he called me! I was not forgotten. Oh, I was not forgotten!

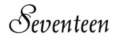

Seventeen

*L*ATE ONE NIGHT WE MARCHED AGAIN INTO THE
blackness of Budapest, walking through the silent streets until we found
ourselves climbing an incline. Like animals being herded up a chute, we
were shoved against each other in the pitch-dark, stumbling over women
who had fallen and had no chance to rise again. The four of us, Esther, Ellen,
Lily, and I, clasped hands—so tightly that our fingers seemed welded together. How could I have survived these weeks without them? They were
each like a part of me; as much a part of me as my leg, or my skin. Together
the four of us had a strength that the other women lacked.

"Where are we going? What's happening?" Esther cried.

"I think we must be going up into a building," I told her. "Hang on!
Don't let go of my hand whatever you do!"

In a few minutes we were crammed onto a narrow ledge inside the
building, a railing on one side of us and a wall on the other. We could see
nothing, determining our surroundings entirely by touch. Still clasping

hands, Esther, Ellen, Lily, and I struggled to find a place where we would not be shoved from all sides. Putting my free hand in front of me, I felt the air and inched slowly forward. My hand bumped against a cold, rounded structure and then another like it. *Pipes,* I thought. *They must run along the side of the building. Maybe we can squeeze into the space next to them.* Pulling the other three along behind me, I eased between two pipes. There was not enough room to sit comfortably, but we nestled amid the cold columns, out of the way of the screaming women who continued to fall over each other. As soon as we were settled, I took off my shoes and tried to place them beside my feet. Before I realized it the left shoe was gone. I felt a hole beside the pipe where it should have been.

"Be careful!" I cried out. "This place is full of holes. My shoe just went down one."

"What will you do now?" Ellen asked. "You have only one shoe."

"Who says I have only one?" I asked. "Why do you think I carry around this knapsack?"

In the morning we were marched out of the building, which we saw in the dim light was a brick factory, I wearing a hiking boot on my right foot, an oxford on my left. Every day after that we walked. We did not dig any more trenches but marched to the east past rolling fields of wheat ripening in the yellow sun, past corn stretching in rows like waves on an emerald sea, marching in the sun, in the moonlight, in the cool, cricket-singing air, marching ever away from Budapest. One day we were told we were going to a factory on the border between Hungary and Germany, the next day we were told that we were being relocated, the third day it was the factory again.

In the late afternoon of a day three weeks after we began marching away from Budapest, we reached the border patrolled by soldiers of the German National Guard, all wearing swastikas on their sleeves. We crossed the border and marched a few more kilometers to the depot of a small town in Austria. A long, dark passenger train was steaming on the tracks.

"Get on the train! Hurry!" the soldiers yelled suddenly.

The masses of women became a mob surging toward the cars. Anxious to be out of the wind and the rain, to sit down, they pressed against us from all sides. I grabbed Esther by one hand and Lily by the other. "Get Ellen!" I yelled to Esther.

"I have her!" she yelled back. "She's here!"

The four of us, Ellen first, then Esther, then I, and Lily last, clung to each other's hands so tightly that the bones of our fingers seemed to be breaking. From behind us, from every side of us, women were falling against our backs, against our hands, pushing us forward. Ellen reached the steps leading up to a platform on the train and pulled Esther behind her as she stumbled up the stairs, looking back to make sure that we were all still together. I shoved forward, squeezing Lily's hand even tighter. "Oh, you're hurting me!" she cried. In another instant we were up the steps and being pulled into the interior of the train.

Two rows ahead of us I saw a long empty bench on the left. "Ellen!" I shouted. "There—to the left!"

She veered toward the empty bench, throwing the weight of her body out from the onrushing flow of women. The four of us heaved into the waiting space, collapsing with a heavy thud on the hard wood.

"My hand!" Lily gasped. "The fingers are so twisted I can hardly bend them."

I looked down at my own hand to see why it was still hurting. The ring Samuel had given to me was pressed hard into the flesh, the joint red and swollen.

The women were still streaming past us, their faces anxious, eyes darting over the filled benches as each woman looked for a place where she would fit in, belong.

"Look!" Esther shouted. "Isn't that Mira from our apartment? It is! Mira! Over here!"

Mira turned from the flow and eased to the side, pulling another girl with her. Moving closer together, we made room for the two of them at the end of our seat. We were now sitting so constricted that I could not move an arm without bumping into Esther on one side or Lily on the other.

"This is crazy!" Mira exclaimed.

"Have you been with us all this time?" I asked. "I haven't seen you since we left our room in the apartment building."

"Yes," she answered. "Delia and I have been together. Do you remember her? She lived in the room next to us."

"I recognize your face," I said to Delia.

"Where do you suppose they're taking us now?" Mira asked. "I think it's to a factory," she continued without waiting for an answer. "I don't believe any of those stories about resettling us all somewhere in Germany. Why would the Germans take care of us when they could still get more work out of us?"

While she was speaking more and more women had been streaming by us, but now the surging stopped abruptly.

"The other door is locked!" a woman in the aisle next to our seat was shouting. "Turn around! The door is locked!"

Slowly the mass of women shifted so that they were facing the other way, the direction from which they had come. As they began to edge toward the door, the harsh, metallic clanking of a bolt being shoved into place was heard at both ends of the car. We were locked inside. The women still standing in the aisle looked bewildered. The seats were filled, the exits bolted. As the train suddenly moved forward with a jerk the women began to scream, clinging to each other's backs and shoulders to keep from being trampled. Then as the train began to pull out of the station, one by one the women worked their way in between the rows of seats and eased themselves into the spaces on the floor. A tall woman wearing a thick black coat sank in front of me, squashing my left foot.

"Excuse me," I said to her. "You're sitting on my foot."

She half turned to look at me, her eyes dull, eyelids lowered, and then turned back again without moving.

I suppose she imagines that I am comfortable sitting up here, I thought, *even though I can barely move.* I wiggled my foot loose until it was wedged between her and the woman sitting at Esther's feet. The train jolted again and slowly rolled out of the station.

Night came, darkness total inside the locked cars as the train moved on, our bodies swaying back and forth against each other. Unable to sleep, I looked out past the window into the blackness, waiting for the towns and villages to pass by the glass. First I would see a flicker of light on a hillside, another, then a sprinkling of lights as the train neared a stop. Finally we pulled into a city. The stations would be stirring with activity even in the middle of the night; German soldiers from other trains ran back and forth to the faucets always left running so they could quickly fill their canteens and board the trains again. When we began moving once more, I dozed off, only to wake with a start when the train began to slow for the next station.

In the morning the locked door at one end of the car opened and two guards entered and began to pass out chunks of dry, dark bread and small slabs of brown cheese.

As the day wore on I began to crave a drink of water. Normally I went for days without one, sometimes not even drinking liquids with my meals. While we were in the fields the other women became so thirsty from working in the hot sun, the dust and dirt flying about their heads, that they could barely speak. At night they could not drink enough water with the evening meal, while I drank a cupful and was satisfied. Now, however, I could not get the thought of quenching my thirst out of my mind.

The air was becoming increasingly rank. When I reached to open a window it would not budge; like the doors, it was locked. *We will all suffocate in here!* I thought. Glancing out the window, I saw that we had pulled into another station. Several guards had jumped from the train platform and hurried to the faucet that was running, running, the stream of fresh, cool water coursing to the ground. *No, I won't look,* I decided, and turned my head away. As the train began to leave the station my eyes stole back to the faucet. It was still splashing, the water from the flowing stream bubbling into the drain.

The next morning and every morning thereafter we were given the same meal of dry bread, cheese, and once in a while, a cup of cold coffee. Seeing the guards each day pushing through over the women sitting in the aisles, I thought, *I won't eat today. It will make me even more thirsty.* When a guard reached me, however, my stomach cried out, rubbing against itself, and I grabbed the bread and cheese before he had passed by. I ate and was even more thirsty.

The women on the floor at our feet began to complain. "How can you be so selfish?" one asked me. "Let me sit on the seat for once!"

"She's right!" the woman beside her said, looking up at Lily with dark, angry eyes. "You're no better than us, are you? Well, are you?"

Lily looked at me, her eyes wide and blinking rapidly behind her thick glasses.

"Do you want to change with them?" I asked her.

She continued to look at me and then nodded her head.

"Come on, girls," I said. "To the floor."

With a great deal of stepping on each other's feet and hands the six of us on the seat managed to trade positions with the women on the floor. Just as we were all settled Lily said, "I have to use the toilet. I've waited for a long time . . ."

"All right," I answered. "We'll go."

As the four of us had made it a practice to never be separated from each other, our clasped hands the links between us, we and Mira and Delia went together to the toilet at the end of the car. A chorus of "Watch out!" followed us all the way there as we climbed over the backs and heads and feet packed solidly together. We arrived only to find that the toilet had become blocked and feces were piled up almost to the rim of the bowl. The stench was overwhelming. When Lily saw it she shuddered, her face blanched, and she held a hand to her mouth.

"I'll go first," Ellen said, and took her turn. Finally, after the rest were through, Lily gingerly lowered herself.

When we returned to our place in the car we found that other women were sitting where we had been, easing themselves into it from the crowded aisle.

"I think I see a place over there," Mira's friend said, pointing to the front of the car.

Threading our way as carefully as possible, we climbed over the women in the aisle again and finally collapsed against the side of the train in the area behind the last row of seats. Slightly more room was available here, as no seat pushed up against us. Ellen began undoing her knapsack and pulled out one of the comforters.

"Why sit on the hard floor?" she asked, and slid the comforter under us.

"What a good idea," I said, smiling. "I'm almost comfortable. Do you have some water for us too?"

"No," she said, smiling back.

We leaned against each other and closed our eyes, the clicking of the rails lulling us into a soft doze. I began to dream. A woman was singing, the notes rising up strong and clear, rising like thrushes, lifting me with them above the cars, above the long body of the train, above the hills turning white with frost, above the pale clouds of snow drifting over the forests.

It's Tamara! I thought in my dream. *I'm at home and she's come to sing for us in the evening beside the fire.*

The voice sang on, now in Hungarian. It was no longer the voice of Tamara but I did not mind. The song was one a lover would sing to her beloved softly, at the closing of the day.

I awoke with a jolt. The train had stopped again.

"Isn't her voice lovely?" Esther was saying.

"Did you hear it too?" I whispered, looking at her quickly.

"Of course. We all did. The woman who is singing is sitting only four rows ahead of us. Mira says that she heard her sing in an opera in Budapest."

"Then it wasn't a dream . . ."

"What wasn't?" Esther asked.

"Nothing . . ." I closed my eyes, hoping to be carried out of the train once more. In a few minutes I heard the voice again. I knew that I was awake this time, and strained to see who was singing.

"I remember so well the time I saw her," Mira was saying. "My father took me to *The Magic Flute* on my fourteenth birthday. This woman had the leading role. Her dress was pink—yards and yards of pink satin. I decided to become an opera star just like her. Now look at me! My hair is so dirty and matted I can't even run my fingers through it."

The song began again. It did not matter that we did not even know the singer's name. We stopped talking, the car became perfectly still, and she sang.

I am lonely, I thought. *I am afraid.*

Let me sing for you, the opera singer seemed to answer. *Perhaps it will ease your sorrow.*

For two weeks I counted the dreary nights, the days; fourteen days without water. After that I lost track of the time. The train continued to stop and start, stop and start, sometimes remaining at one location for days, sometimes just long enough for the soldiers to jump off and fill their canteens at the ever gushing faucets. The doors and windows remained locked. No woman was allowed off the train unless she was dead. A few did succumb to the thirst, the stifling, the wretched smells. The rest of us became one with the hard, wooden seats or the floor. Every time I awoke after a few hours of fitful sleep I could not move without a great amount of pain permeating my sore legs and back, stiff shoulders and neck.

"I ache. Oh, I ache," Esther moaned over and over. We were going into the third week on the train and sitting again on a bench, I squeezed next to the window. We seemed to be traveling east as far as I could tell from the direction of the sun. The signs at the stations were all in German. Every depot had the faucet open wide, the water pouring out.

One day late in the afternoon as the sun beat in through the windowpane, my head began to grow heavy, thick, my tongue to feel like it was tasting sand. The inside of my throat began to close and I became terrified that I would not be able to swallow. Water suddenly began to pour into my mouth. I held it open as wide as I could, stretched, taut, the liquid pouring, pouring, ever flowing into my mouth. The cool, silvery wetness ran over my chapped lips, over the blistered lining of my throat, and slid down the red, dusty valley of my gullet to my stomach. It cooled, cooled, cleansed, satisfied as nothing had ever done before. Still I drank, mouth open, never choking, on and on, the water having no end.

A screeching of the wheels jarred me back into consciousness. I was thrown back against the edge of the seat, my mouth open, my tongue sticking to the bottom lip, my throat raw and burning.

"Seren! Seren! Are you all right?" Esther was asking, touching my shoulder.

I could not talk. I nodded my head.

"You were delirious," she said. "I couldn't wake you."

I turned from her, remembering the sensation of the delicious, sweet water gurgling down my throat. A drop of moisture fell onto my lips. It tasted of salt.

Outside the window a child, a small girl of four or five dressed in a red coat and hat and black boots, skipped along on the platform beside her mother. Seeing a vendor at the other end of the station, the little girl pulled her mother to him and danced around the vendor while he prepared a cup of juice for her. Handing it to her with a smile, he tipped his hat; she laughed and then went with her mother, holding the cup carefully in one hand. *Thank God I don't have a child,* I thought. *I'm so glad that I never married and had children. How unbearable it would be to be locked on this train with a child crying for a drink of water.*

Then one day when we were traveling through a forest, pine trees stretching away from the window for as far as I could see, the train slowed and came to a standstill.

"Where are we?" Ellen asked. "There is no station."

"I can't tell," Mira answered. "It looks like nothing but a forest. I don't see any buildings."

A great sense of hopelessness overcame me. *Everything is ending,* I thought. *We are in the middle of nothingness. They have brought us all the way here to the middle of a deep forest to shoot us. Who will stop them? Who can save us now?*

"Everyone out!" the German soldiers began to yell.

We started to rise, barely able to move our legs; they had turned into boards while we were not looking.

"Hurry! Hurry!" the guards shouted.

A line of women began to move toward an exit, carrying their blankets and knapsacks in their arms.

"No!" the soldiers shouted. "Leave everything! Out!"

We put our knapsacks back down on the seats. My suspicions were confirmed; the soldiers were going to shoot us. Dead women did not need blankets, extra clothing, and their mothers' rings. I said nothing. There was no need for the others to also feel the fear tearing at my own heart.

As soon as we struggled down the steps, breathing fresh air for the first time since we boarded the train, we were ordered to line up, five to a row, and to begin marching. The four of us, hands clasped, formed a line beside a young girl. At first many women stumbled, clutching each other's arms so they would not fall. The ground was rough, sticks poking up at our feet. After the hot staleness of our compartment, the air outside was biting and cold. Half an hour of marching passed; they did not order us to halt as I expected. *Maybe they want to take us far from the railroad tracks so no one will find our bodies,* I thought. We marched for several hours more until darkness was beginning to creep through the bottom of the trees, the pale light rapidly receding from the trees' crowns. The cold grew more intense and I began to shiver inside my coat. *We will never stop marching,* I thought. *Through all eternity we will be marching.*

Then I saw it—a bit of red and yellow between the trees. What was it? We marched closer. We were approaching a huge gate with a sign suspended over the top. As we drew nearer I could read the words printed in huge letters on the sign: *Das ist dein Tot* (This is your death). Below the words was an enormous insect painted in garish red and bright yellow. A long, flat body with a small pointed head and six legs, each with a hook on the end, crawled across the sign.

"What is it?" I whispered.

"A louse," Ellen answered.

We halted before the gate briefly and then marched on, coming after a few minutes to another gate and another huge sign. This one read: *Arbeit macht das Leben süss* (Work makes life sweet). Stretching out from the gate on both sides were high walls with barbed wire above them, extending so far in both directions that I could see no end to them. Again we were ordered to halt briefly and then marched on beneath the gate, beneath the sign promising us a pleasant life. We passed through, the guards hurrying us inside with their raised rifles, and the gate clanked shut behind us.

We were lined up alongside a road coming from the other end of the camp. The light had faded to a dull gray but I could still make out the forms of women slowly dragging by on the road. Some of them were carrying buckets, some hoes. As I stared at them in the dim light, the women's pace seemed to slacken even more, their feet barely leaving the surface of the road. One foot moved forward, then the other, slowly, slowly, heads dropped, arms hung loosely at their sides. When one group of women had passed, another began, row after row coming by, ever coming by—women with green, red, or purple markings on their coat sleeves, women barely more than children, old women.

This can't be true! I thought. *I'm having another nightmare. When I wake up this will be gone and I'll be back on the train.*

Then as the last group of women passed us, the sounds of their shuffling feet fading into the night, a guard ordered us to enter a low, gray building across the road. I followed the row of women ahead of me into the building.

Eighteen

"*NACH RECHTS! . . . NACH LINKS! . . . NACH rechts! . . . Nach links! . . .*" a woman guard was ordering as we approached the building; alternate lines of women were being sent to the right and to the left. Our line went to the right, the four of us and twenty-five or thirty other women entering a large, open room with low wooden benches all along one wall. The air was chilly, the floor damp, shallow puddles here and there darkening the cement. While we were nearly beyond thirst after weeks of being deprived of almost all water, for an instant I visualized sprawling on the floor, lapping up the few drops of water with my tongue.

"*Achtung! Achtung!*" a voice began shouting. I turned to look in the direction which the voice was coming from. A person wearing blue-gray pants and a jacket with a green triangle and bar sewn on the sleeve was speaking. The soldiers of the German National Guard who had accompanied us on the train and during the march into the camp had evidently turned us over to these camp guards.

"*Achtung!*" the voice commanded again. While the voice was deep and harsh, the face was soft, intriguing; I could not tell whether a man or a woman was speaking. We were ordered to form lines and to undress completely for a bath.

"A bath!" Ellen whispered to me. "I can't believe it."

Neither could I. The accumulated grime and dust had by now so mingled with the secretions of our bodies that the creases in our necks, wrists, and ankles held solid lines of dirt embedded into the skin.

What was the most disheartening, however, was my hair. Since I was seven or eight I had washed it often, immensely enjoying combing out the wet strands and letting them dry on my back into a flowing mass of waves. Now my hair protruded from my head in thick, twisted coils, matted and oily. When I tried to comb it with my fingers I was stopped by tangled snarls. *Maybe they will even give us combs,* I thought, picturing my hair soft and sweet-smelling once more.

The women began to undress, glancing quickly at the guards as they unbuttoned their blouses and slipped off one sleeve. We were ordered to fold our coats, pants, blouses, sweaters, skirts, socks, and underwear and place them in piles at our feet. Our shoes were to be set to one side. When I had finished undressing I was so cold that I could not stop shivering. The windows were broken and the wind was blowing in on us in strong gusts. Glancing around the room covertly, I saw one girl with trembling arms crossed over her breasts while another was bent over, arms folded tightly together. Several women still held on to the last piece of clothing they had taken off—an undershirt, a white pair of underpants—and draped it over the lower part of their bodies. The two guards stood together in the front, arms around each other's waists.

"Beeilen Sie sich!" shouted one of the guards. As I understood German, I realized that she was telling us to hurry. Most of the women, however, spoke only Hungarian and could only guess what they were being ordered to do. One by one the women still holding on to a piece of clothing met the narrowed eyes of a guard staring at them and let the garment fall.

Two more guards wearing the same uniform entered the room, one carrying scissors, the other a bowl of water and a razor. Walking up to the first row of women, the guard with the scissors grabbed the hair of the woman first in line with her left hand; with the right she made one quick cut at the base of the neck. A mass of black hair fell away. The guard walked to the front of the room, threw the shorn-off hair on a bench, and went back to the same woman. Her scissors moved quickly; here, there, and there a chop was made. Disparate tufts stuck out in one place while in another the hair was cut so close that the whiteness of the scalp was visible.

The guard moved on down the line of women in front of me, making separate piles in front of the room: one for blond hair, one for brown, one for chestnut, one for black.

When the guard reached our row she quickly slashed off Ellen's hair, Esther's, and Lily's; I was next. She grabbed me with a hard yank that hurt deeply, as if she were pulling my hair out by the roots, and then paused for a minute.

"Just look at this!" she yelled.

Who is she talking to? I wondered. The women in front of me turned around to look.

The guard with the razor walked over to us from the opposite end of the room. Her hands were covered with curly hair. "Hah!" she laughed. "Isn't she a fine one!"

The first guard took her scissors and made several quick, sawing movements. My hair fell into her hand. Four more rapid snips were made around my head and finally the guard walked to the blond pile and threw my hair on it with a careless toss. It began to slide from the top of the pile, slowly at first, and then, picking up speed, tumbled to the floor, landing in front of the bench. The guard, going by with a length of black hair, gave it a kick with her boot.

A hot burning stung my eyelids. Tears gathering behind them pushed out in clusters, collected in the lower portions of my eyes. I could not pull my gaze away from my hair. Finally I forced myself to look at the other women huddled into themselves, shivering, diminished, like sheep after a shearing. One woman had no hair at all except for a tuft sticking straight up from the top of her head. Another had a short stubble over one ear, a longer layer above the other. I could only guess at my own appearance but I imagined jagged lines, ragged edges.

As I stood there, drawn deep inside myself, the other guard approached and ordered me to spread my legs apart. My body obeyed, my mind remained dark, numbed. I felt a sharp pull on my pubic hairs followed by a biting pain as the razor made two, three swipes across. The guard moved on, swishing her razor in a bowl of water black with hair, traces of red floating on the dirty scum. I looked at my legs. A trickle of blood was easing down the inside of one calf. *I would almost rather die than suffer this,* I thought, and crept back into the softness inside my head.

The piles of clothes at our feet were picked up and put into large bins at one end of the room. A few minutes later wooden crates were brought into the room and a guard began to move down the rows. Each woman was handed an undershirt, regardless of its size. I was given a gray, soiled piece of thin cotton that hung to my feet. Next the guards came down the rows with crates of dresses; again we were given whichever piece of clothing was closest to the guard's reach. A dark green jersey dress, the kind of garment an older woman might have worn to an afternoon tea in Budapest, was thrust at me. Across the front and the back were large stripes made of a dark cloth and sewn on so that a large X was made across both my chest and back. All of the other dresses bore the same markings. It slid over my head and fell about my ankles, the waist coming almost to my knees, slippery and cool on my body. I began to shake, trembling violently, moving my hands up and down my arms, trying to warm them. Lily, who was standing immediately to my right, must have touched Esther beside her and pointed to me; Esther and I never lined up directly next to each other for fear that we would be recognized as sisters and separated.

"Are you all right?" Esther whispered across to me.

I nodded my head, glancing at her. I was relieved to see that she had been given a woolen dress. The right sleeve was torn, the midriff was soiled, and there were several holes in the skirt, but it would be warm.

The guards came through again, handing out coats. I could not understand at first why they took away all of our clothes only to give us in return garments that must have been worn by other women entering the camp. But as I looked around at the women beside me withdrawn into their meager, worn rags, I saw that we were no longer the strong women who had been able to endure hard labor, wartime conditions, and separation from our families and friends. The shearing of our heads and vulvas, the stealing of our clothes and everything we had owned, took from us the last traces of who we had been. My knapsack on the train, my mother's chains and rings, would never be given back. I felt their loss almost as much as the loss of my hair. All I had left was Samuel's ring.

When the guard reached me she held out a long gray coat. Without thinking I took it from her with my right hand. Immediately the guard circled the ring with her fingers and thumb, giving it a hard yank. My finger felt as if it were being pulled from me. The ring would not come off. Her grip tightened; the flesh around the ring was squeezed tightly. I cried out in pain.

"Quiet!" she hissed.

Again she pulled, spitting on the ring twice while she wiggled it back and forth. Finally, in one smooth movement, she scraped it over the ridge of my knuckle and slipped it off the end of my finger and into her pocket. Quickly she glanced around. Satisfied that no one had seen her, she shoved her crate of coats forward and moved on.

One more time a guard passed through our lines. Each of us was given two red cloth triangles with numbers at the top, two yellow cloth triangles, two strips of yellow cloth, and a needle and thread. We were instructed to sew one red triangle on the sleeve of our coat, the other on the sleeve of our dress, and then to sew the yellow triangles crossing them, forming Stars of David. The yellow bars were to go beneath the stars. When we were finished sewing, the guards walked up and down our lines to make sure that we had all followed orders correctly. Finally we were ordered to pass our needles and thread to the end of the row. *I'm going to keep mine,* I decided; I was never without a needle and thread. Slowly I slid my right hand inside my left coat sleeve as if I were trying to warm my fingers, and stuck the needle into the lining of the sleeve.

The guard collecting the needles took them from the last person in each row and began to count them silently. Finished, she looked up and yelled, "There's one missing!"

My heart began to race, but then I thought, *What more can they do to us?*

The guard began to walk up our aisle, stopping before every woman, shouting, "Did you steal a needle?" Each woman shook her lowered head, eyes fastened on the floor. How like cattle we had become. Then I spotted a needle lying on the floor in front of me, left there by the last group of women. When the guard approached me I pointed to the needle and she pounced on it. Satisfied, she went on to the next row.

The two guards who had marched us into the room and remained standing at the front, now moved apart. One began to speak to us in German.

"You are in Ravensbrück, an all-women camp. There are no men here except for a few doctors in the hospital. You are our first Jewish prisoners. We have honored you by giving you the Star of David." The speaker glanced quickly at the other guard, barking a short laugh.

"Every woman is in here for a reason," she continued. "The color of the triangle on the sleeve will tell you what it is: criminals have green triangles; prostitutes, purple; those arrested for political or religious reasons, red; and Jew bitches like you, yellow. In case you're wondering why I'm here, you can see by my triangle that I'm a criminal. Does anyone want to know what I did?"

No one made a sound. The realization that she was a woman and a criminal as well was more than we could absorb at one time.

"Well, I'll tell you anyway," she went on. "I killed someone . . . stabbed her with a knife! Anything else you want to know?"

Again there was silence.

"From now on," she continued, "each of you will be known by your number. Each of you will be accounted for twice a day. We know exactly how many of you there are by the numbers."

I looked down at my sleeve and again read the number: 85803.

"From here you will be taken to barracks twenty-one and given supper. Tomorrow morning you will begin work. Now, put your shoes back on. Quickly!"

She and the other guard began to move among us with long, slender poles, hitting the women who were bent over tying their shoelaces. The shoes were damp from the long walk through the forest and would not slide onto our bare feet. We were not going to get stockings, I realized, or underpants. We were not going to get a bath or even so much as a drop of water to drink. I tied my shoes in loose knots and stood up again before a guard reached me.

A few minutes later we were driven out of the building by the guards, who stood to one side, striking out randomly at the passing women with their poles. We came into a yard lit in areas by floodlights beaming down from the high walls and were marched between more long, gray buildings stretching out on both sides of us for as far as I could see—rows and rows of unpainted wood shacks with empty, black windows.

We stopped before the building marked "21" and were made to form a line outside. After a long wait in the wind each of us was ordered to remove her shoes and then allowed to enter a room immediately to the right of the large entrance hall. Here flush toilets were laid out in rows. All but one, however, were roped off. The line moved forward very slowly as each woman took her turn and then joined another line moving through the entrance room. As Esther, Lily, Ellen, and I passed through the toilet line and joined the second line, the comforting smell of hot soup and the warmth and light of the spacious room gradually eased through me. At last we were out of the cold. Surely now we would be given something to drink.

As we passed by a table, each of us was handed a metal cup and spoon. Ahead of us I could see a large pot of soup and a metal plate piled with bread. To be given something to drink at last, even if it was not cold water, was almost enough to take my mind off the despair that had been growing in me since we entered the camp. Finally I reached the soup and held out my cup. A woman prisoner, also with a green triangle on the sleeve of her uniform, dipped a ladle into the pot and held it above my bowl. Beside her stood another prisoner with a long fork, holding a plate with small pieces of meat. When a piece of meat was about to fall into my cup the prisoner with the fork picked it out of the ladle and put it on the plate of meat. My cup was filled with a few bits of turnip and clear broth.

Next another guard picked up a slice of dry, stale bread, splashed it with a spoon of pink liquid slightly resembling jam, and handed it to me. I followed the line, looking back to make sure that Lily, Esther, and Ellen were still behind me. Passing out of the entrance area, we continued down the large hallway which ran the length of the building and came to two doors, one on the right and one on the left. Another guard was standing near the doors and hitting the women as they passed by, yelling *"Achtung! Achtung!"*

The soup in the cups of the struck women splashed out and spilled onto the floor. This caused the guard to hit them again. Ducking away from her flailing pole, I squeezed against the far side of the door on the right and hurried through it. *If only the others follow me,* I thought. I looked back to see Ellen entering the room in the same way I had done, Lily and Esther following close behind her. There was no guard in sight here. The four of us moved together and looked around the room.

"This must be where we sleep," Ellen said.

"In those?" Lily asked.

We were in a cavernous room, dim and bitterly cold. A row of rickety wooden bunk beds three tiers high reached up above us. Every five tiers were nailed together so that a unit of fifteen beds was made. A narrow aisle ran between the units stretching as far as I could see in the pale light coming in from the hall. Other women had already crawled onto the row of bunks nearest us. A guard at the far end of the room began to shout, "Four to a bed! Four to a bed!"

"We better hurry," I said, "if we want to sleep together."

"Let's look on the far side of the room," Ellen said, beginning to run to the area next to the windows. We followed her and came upon a unit still completely empty. Lily sank into one of the beds on the bottom bunk.

"No, no," I said. "We're going up."

"I don't want to," Lily answered. "How can we even get up there? I don't see any ladders."

"Look!" I said, grabbing one side of the beds. As I pushed against it very slightly, the whole set of fifteen beds rocked back and forth. Bits of straw from the second and third tiers rained down on the bottom tier. An icy wind, blowing in through the broken windows, picked up the falling straw and whipped it into our faces.

"But it will be too hard to climb up there," Lily said.

"Just put your foot on the bottom bed and pull yourself up to the next bed. In a minute you'll be on the top."

"But I'll spill my soup."

"Then drink it first. Up! Up!"

Esther went first, Lily second, Ellen third, and I last, the beds creaking and leaning precariously as we climbed. After a few minutes of turning, placing a foot so it did not stick into someone's side, or removing an arm from between two legs, the four of us were lying on the bed, two on each side, propped up on elbows and eating our bread. We had gulped down the cup of soup before we climbed up, yearning for ten, twenty more cups. The bread tasted like sawdust. A few minutes after we had finished a guard came through and told us to save the bread for the morning; it was our breakfast.

"Where are we?" Esther asked when the guard had passed by.

"I think we're in Germany—near Berlin maybe. We traveled very far north," I answered.

"Yes, but what is this place? What's happened to us?" she asked again.

"We're in a prison," I told her, "much worse than the one I was in before."

"The guards scare me," Lily said. "I've never seen women act like they do. I saw two of them kissing each other!"

"One of the German guards even killed someone!" Ellen said.

"Yes!" Lily answered. "I am so frightened . . ."

Tears began to roll down her face, falling on the soiled blue coat she had been given. "Why did they have to cut off all our hair . . . even the hair . . ." She began to cry louder, hiding her face in her hand.

We looked at each other in the half-light—at the naked heads, the bare necks, the big, terrified eyes. Each of us saw herself in the others and was ashamed. One by one we eased down onto the straw, the narrow, hard slats sticking out at both ends, and tried to lose ourselves in sleep. The cold found us lying exposed in the night with no blankets to cover us, no mattress under us—creeping up a leg, inside a coat sleeve, around a neck. We pressed to each other's backs and shoulders, trying not to think of the warm, soft comforters left on the train, of the beds we had once slept in beneath fresh sheets and thick blankets.

Within half an hour the slow, regular breathing of Lily told me that she was asleep; Esther and Ellen were still. A piece of straw had worked its way inside my coat and was chafing against the back of my neck. I tried to reach up with my right hand to pull it out, but Lily was lying so tightly against me that I could not move my arm. Wiggling my shoulders inside the heavy coat, I moved the straw further down my neck where it did not irritate.

Lying still once more, I thought, *I should try to sleep like the others. Who knows what tomorrow will bring?* I closed my eyes. Immediately I saw my hair falling to the floor, the boot kicking it up onto the pile. My eyes popped open; the image disappeared. I focused on the dim shapes of the sleeping women in the bed next to us and in all the beds beyond them. Distant cries echoed in the huge room: one woman called out, "No! No!"; one sobbed in deep anguish; one moaned in a soft, mournful lowing like a cow bereft of her calf. I thought to cover my ears so I would not hear them until I remembered that I could not move my hands. Again my eyes closed; again the vision of my hair falling flashed into my head. It was this that Samuel had fallen in love with, my long, long hair that glistened in the sunlight like ripples in a field of ripening wheat. Who was I without my hair?

I remembered the time I had gone to the school contest in the fourth grade with my teacher; his wife had combed and brushed my hair endlessly, setting me on her lap as we rode along through the hills of Transylvania. "If your mind is as sharp as your hair is beautiful," she told me then, "you'll be sure to win the contest."

"It is!" I had answered, causing my teacher to burst out laughing.

Suddenly I felt a sharp stinging on my legs. I was being bitten. There it was again! Whatever it was must have also been attacking Lily, for she flung her arm across me and then drew it back to scratch at her leg. The painting of the louse at the entrance to the camp flashed into my mind. Shuddering with revulsion, I worked my arm loose and tore at the itching with my fingernails until my legs bled. Finally I sank back down on the straw.

So this is how it all ends, I thought. *My struggle to leave home, to become independent, to make as much as possible of my life. It ends in my lying here amid an entire barracks of women—homeless, having nothing, not even my hair, freezing, filthy, attacked by lice. It would be better to be dead.*

SHARP CRIES AWOKE ME. "DON'T HIT ME! OH please," a woman in the next aisle was screaming.

"Get up, you Jew bitches!" a guard shouted in Polish. "Get up, pigs!" With each command her heavy, long stick came down on a bed of women with a whack. While I was still trying to struggle up from sleep, the guard was below us and striking at the women on the lower bunk. I shook Lily and then the other two. Quickly we slipped our tied-together shoes around our necks, grabbed our cups and spoons, and began to climb down the three tiers. The other women who were being herded toward the door pressed against us as soon as we reached the floor. I grabbed Lily's and Ellen's hands, Ellen grabbed Esther's, and the four of us joined the women rapidly surging out of the door, through the hallway past the entrance room, and outside into the ice-cold air. The sky was dark, the faintest traces of light only beginning to appear on the horizon.

"*Zielappel! Zielappel! Schnell! Zielappel!*" a guard began to shout. The first of hundreds of hours spent in counting us had begun. We were grouped into lines five across while the four guards who were in charge of our barracks counted. I stood in the dark, wondering how they could see to count, an arm's length from Lily on my left and Ellen on my right, Esther next to her. The air was clear, the stars above us sparkling dots of light in the blackness. A numbness began to creep through my fingers and I flexed and unflexed my hands inside the deep coat pockets. My feet suffered more; we were forbidden to move and could do no more than wiggle our toes back and forth inside our damp shoes. How I longed for my warm, woolen stockings and Samuel's slacks.

An hour must have passed as we stood there, silent, rigid, freezing cell by cell. One of the two German guards continued to count us. The other had already moved up and down our rows twice but had evidently come up with a different number each time. The counting continued through an-

other hour, the sky turned a pale gray, then white, the cold entrenched itself firmly into our bodies, and still they were not finished with us.

Across from us was the barracks where we had slept. As I was wondering how many hours more we would have to endure this, wondering how
long we would be able to go on without slipping off to death like so many
women before us, two guards came out of the door carrying something. I
could not tell at first what it was, as their backs were turned to us. Then an
arm fell, swayed back and forth as they walked. The body of a woman was
thrown against the side of the barracks, hitting the rotting boards with a
dull thud.

The guards returned with another body, throwing it down beside the
first, and then another. As I watched, body after body was carried out, flung
down, stacked into a pile in a pattern of horizontal lines repeated sixteen
bodies high, five bodies long. I became almost hypnotized by the stacking
of body upon body, the absence of any curves or angles, the endless piling
up of long, faceless lines with only a slight resemblance to anything alive,
anything human. Then, with a sudden shock, I thought, *They're women! Last
night they went to sleep in the same building as I. This morning they're dead.*

The image of that pile of bodies frozen in the cold, gray light never left
me. I would not be in that pile, I decided then. I would not die. Somehow,
in whatever way I could, I would remain alive; Esther, Ellen, and Lily, as
well. As long as I had strength we would live. I would see to it.

Part Four

Seren and Meyer in front of the community hall for displaced persons. She is in the last row, farthest to the left, in a striped sweater. Meyer is directly next to her, slightly in front. Her hair is still quite short, after her head being shaved during their internment. All those in uniforms are United States Army personnel.

Nineteen

How do I begin to tell how it was that Esther, Ellen, Lily, and I survived Ravensbrück concentration camp while all around us death prowled like a pack of starving dogs, devouring nineteen out of every twenty women? Some of them were too young, some too old; some were frail, some ill; some were simply without hope. Ellen and Lily were also quite young—Ellen sixteen and Lily nineteen. Esther was not much older; she would turn twenty in December. I was twenty-six.

Esther gladly relinquished all organizational matters to me, but this aspect of her personality predates the war. From as far back as I could remember, she was a classic worrier, always. Responsibility for important decisions caused her tremendous anxiety and concern. Even while we were living a peaceful life at home, Esther could get herself worked up well in advance of any impending event or trip. Often, she would anticipate scenarios and consequences in every imaginable permutation. Yet there was a certain naïveté in her, a wish to see the best in everyone's character; there was always a childlike sweetness to Esther, quick to forgive and ready to smile. Esther was a gentle, sweet, and good girl, eager to do the right thing and to conduct herself in a moral way, yet seeming to need looking after.

I felt completely responsible for these three young girls; to me we were all sisters. I had to do everything in my power to enable us to remain alive. Survival became a matter of establishing rules and adhering to them religiously. I was the oldest; I made the rules. We were of the old European school of thought: you listened to the oldest even if she was a fool.

The first rule was: do not drink the water. That the water was contaminated became apparent the first day we were in the camp. After the guards were finally through counting us that morning, four hours after we had begun standing outside in the cold, we were lined up for our work assignments without being given anything to eat or drink. The four of us and many other women from our barracks were put in the work detail that unloaded ships at a harbor located about three miles from the camp. Once crates of vegetables were carried off the ship, we unpacked and sorted them in a large storage cellar, the *Kartoffelkeller*. There were bins for each type of vegetable: turnip, radish, carrot, cabbage, and potato.

Ravensbrück was a large camp, imprisoning eighty-five thousand women, the majority of them Gentiles who had been arrested for political reasons. There were many nuns, prostitutes, Gypsies, and women who may have harbored Jewish people or been associated with a group regarded as detrimental to the Nazi cause. We only heard about these other women, however, as we Jews were kept separate from the other prisoners. We went out in the morning to the harbor and returned again at night without seeing anyone except our guards. The other prisoners remained within the walls of the camp, working in factories.

That first morning as our work detail walked the three miles on numb feet, guards on both sides of us holding the leashes of German shepherds straining to be free, the four of us joined hands as before, fingers interlaced tightly, soup cups swinging from strings in our buttonholes. On reaching the ship we climbed a ramp leading up to the deck and immediately were ordered to carry the crates of vegetables back down the ramp and up a small hill to the *Kartoffelkeller*. Finally at noon a pot of soup was brought to the door of the cellar. We lined up, held out our metal cups to receive the thin broth, and went inside the cellar to sit down and eat. At the end of the meal we were, of course, still thirsty as well as hungry. Several of the women noticed a faucet near the door on the outside of the cellar and drank from it. During the afternoon many other women also drank from the faucet, snatching a few gulps of water whenever they could.

Late in the day, as Lily and I were standing above the bins, she said, "I'm going to get a drink outside. I'll be right back."

"No you're not!" I ordered. "I don't want any of us to drink the water."

"But I'm so thirsty," she said, looking at me through her thick glasses, eyebrows drawn together. "Why can't I have water?"

"I don't trust it. Remember that time in the labor camp when the water was bad one day? A lot of the women got diarrhea after drinking it."

"How do you know that this water is bad? Maybe it isn't."

"But maybe it is. We'll wait and see. If no one comes down with diarrhea after a few days, we'll drink it. I'm going over to tell Esther and Ellen the same thing. Do me a favor: stay right here."

She sighed. "All right."

We worked in pairs, each woman holding a handle at either end of a wooden crate as we walked down the ramp and up the hill. Lily and I often composed one pair while Ellen and Esther made up the other. Every day, seven days of the week, we unloaded and sorted until late in the afternoon and were then marched back to the camp, marched through a back gate, marched past the long rows of barracks, finally coming to a halt in the counting area directly across from our building. There we stood in lines to be counted again for several hours while the sky grew dark, the wind even harsher. We were forbidden to leave our lines for any reason. As we waited a guard moved back and forth, counting us one by one with an outstretched finger.

There were four SS guards who were responsible for our barracks: the two German guards who had supervised the cutting of our hair and distribution of our clothes and two Polish women, political prisoners who wore red triangles on their sleeves. Each woman spoke to us in her native tongue. If you understood neither German nor Polish your life was filled with terror as you tried to guess what you were being ordered to do before a club came down on your head for not obeying fast enough. Esther and I understood German, having learned it in school as children, and Ellen understood Polish. Most of the other women, including Lily, were from Budapest and spoke only Hungarian.

On that first night in line to be counted, several women in front of me began to shift slightly, bending over at the waist, standing first on one foot and then the other. One moved over a pace, provoking a guard to shout, *"Achtung!"* The woman stood briefly but then doubled over as if in great pain. *"Achtung! Achtung!"* the guard shouted again, and in an instant was at the woman's side, beating her on the back with a heavy stick. After a series of hard, heavy blows the guard strutted back to the front of the group, glared at us, and stamped to the front row to begin counting all over again.

A minute later I heard the sound of someone defecating, smelled the sickly sweet odor. Then the woman in front of me who had been struck by the guard removed something from under her coat and set it beside her on the ground. It was her soup cup overflowing with watery feces. Within the next hour many of the other women did the same, all victims of the bad water.

When we were dismissed from counting we formed a long toilet line outside the barracks door and stood several more hours while the line moved slowly forward into the building. When I reached the door I saw a set of guards waiting. As I entered the hall one yelled for me to raise my arms high into the air, the other rapidly moving her hands down the sides of my coat, checking the pockets carefully, finally turning them inside out. *"Beeilen Sie sich!"* she ordered, and I moved forward, wondering why I had been searched.

Esther, Ellen, and Lily were behind me and I tried to see if they too were stopped. The procedure was the same: each was ordered to halt and raise her arms. They all passed the inspection. I was breathing a sigh of relief and turning again to face the front of the toilet line when I heard someone behind me yell, *"Diebe! Diebe!"* (Thief!). Quickly I turned again to look. One of the guards at the door was holding a radish. The prisoner beside her stood with eyes squeezed shut, all color drained from her face. The second guard began to hit the accused woman on the head with a piece of metal. When the woman tried to cover her head with her arms, the guard yanked the arms away and hit her again, over and over, until blood was pouring from the woman's forehead and down into her eyes. Abruptly the guard put down her metal pole and shoved the woman forward with her foot.

By now I realized that the other toilets had also been installed for our use. The guards had simply closed them to us so that each of them could have an individual toilet roped off in a separate area. As I waited in line, a guard walked to her area, slipped under the rope, urinated, made use of one of the many rolls of toilet paper stacked beside her toilet, and went across the hall to a room containing sinks and showers also roped off into separate areas. There were no doors to either of these rooms; everything was visible. Thus, the five hundred women in our barracks had only one toilet, no toilet paper, and no way to wash our hands and bathe our bodies.

As the line approached the toilet I saw the woman who had stood in front of me during the counting reach the stool and pour into it the contents of her cup. A few minutes later she would hold out the same cup, having no way to rinse it before it was filled with soup. Beginning in the pit of my stomach and rapidly streaking up through my chest and throat, a wave of nausea swept over me. Quelling the revulsion quickly, I was left with simply pity. I knew the backgrounds of these women in line with me; they were predominantly from refined homes in Budapest, from intellectual homes where one discussed current politics while dining from delicate china by candlelight.

I made the second rule: Each of us must use the toilets either at the *Kartoffelkeller* or at the ship late in the afternoon every day. This practice would save us the misery of having to wait an additional two hours outside to use the barracks toilet after already standing in the counting line for two or three hours. We would then be able to obtain our supper and go to bed that much earlier.

THAT FIRST EVENING WE WENT BACK TO THE SAME unit of beds that we had slept in the night before. "Up we go!" I said.

Again Lily asked, "Can't we sleep on the bottom bunk? I'm so tired I can barely move."

Ellen looked at her, mouth open, jaw dropped. "Didn't you see all those poor dead women this morning?" she asked. "They had all slept on the bottom level next to the open windows. They froze to death. Seren is right! We're going up!"

I smiled to myself; they were learning.

When we were settled on our bed I took off my coat and began to tear a foot-wide section away from the bottom. The coat was old and fairly worn and tore easily.

"What are you doing?" Esther asked.

"What does it look like?" I answered.

"You're destroying your coat! It's the only one you have."

"I'm just shortening it," I said. "All day long I tramped around on the hem. With the material I tear off I'm going to make myself a hat!"

As I pulled off the strip, part of the hem came undone and a pile of Hungarian paper money fell into my lap. "Look!" I said. "We're rich!"

Unraveling the entire hem, I found almost a hundred bills; the woman who had the coat before me must have hidden her money there while en route to Ravensbrück.

"What will you do with it?" Ellen asked. "If the guards see the money they'll take it away."

"You could take us all out to a nice restaurant," Lily said.

"That's a wonderful idea!" Ellen exclaimed.

"I've thought of the perfect way to use this money," I said.

"What is it?" they all asked.

"Toilet paper!"

"Are you serious?" Ellen asked.

"Why not? There isn't the slightest chance that we'll get to spend the money. And wouldn't you like to have something to use when you go to the toilet?"

"I would!" Lily said. "I've hated having nothing all this time."

"Here's one for you, one for you, one for you, and one for me," I said, giving each of us a bill. "I'll hide the rest of the money under the straw. It should last us for a while."

That night, after I had sewn up the new hem of my coat and made myself a snug, warm hat, I lay down beside Lily, who was seemingly asleep. After a few minutes, however, she began to giggle.

"What's so funny?" I asked.

"Mother always said that she would like money to burn. I was just wondering what she would think about having money to wipe yourself with."

"Lily, Lily," I said, patting her head as if she were a small child. "Go to sleep."

She turned over, fell fast asleep. A voice began to sing very softly. I recognized it immediately as the voice of the singer from the Budapest opera who had been on the train with us. Now she sang a Hungarian song, a slow, peaceful lullaby that eased out over the bunk beds, the rows and rows, tiers upon tiers, of women huddled in the darkness. We were all children again being lulled to sleep by a calm voice singing of a pale moon, of stars up in the sky, of a good, sweet night.

THE MONEY LASTED FOR THREE WEEKS. BY THEN IT was the end of October and the cold had come to rival starvation as our most deadly enemy. In the mornings when we rose I glanced at the bottom bunks as we hurried out to be counted. They were filled with women lying rigid, a layer of snow drifting over their coats, over their bare heads, over their eyes open and still. Several times I warned those on the bottom bunks not to sleep there, not to expose themselves to the open windows, but the women always answered, "Where will we go? All the beds are full." And they were. As soon as a woman died, her empty bed was filled with another Jewish woman transferred to Ravensbrück from a different camp. I came to know the other sixteen women in the four top bunks beside ours; we occupied the first bed in the row and they had to crawl over it to get to theirs. The rest of the women, however, remained strangers. If I had also made friends with them I would have been taking the risk of coming to care for them, of missing them when they were taken away, of grieving for them when they died.

Even the women who crawled over our bed I knew by their faces only. They handed their shoes up to us first and we carefully took them. When we held out a hand to pull them up several of the women broke into a smile and murmured, "Thank you." Sometimes one added, "My name is Helena," or, "I'm Ruth."

The one woman I became friends with was the one who slept in the bed next to ours. She was slightly older than most of us, in her early thirties. She had been a surgeon in a prestigious hospital in Budapest.

She told me these things one evening as we sat on our beds talking for a few minutes before lying down to sleep.

"It's such a waste!" I said to her. "Your life is being completely wasted working in a potato cellar when you could be saving lives."

"Yes," she answered, "that grates on me almost more than anything. But aren't all of us being wasted? Aren't we all of value? I am just grateful that they did not put me to work in the hospital here."

"Why?" I asked.

"Have you ever seen any woman come back? I have yet to see a woman who has reported sick and been sent to the hospital be returned to the barracks. Everyone disappears."

"What do you think happens to them?" I asked.

"They very likely become subjects for experimentation," she answered.

"Do you think so?"

"I am almost positive. The Nazis have become interested in doing research on the effects of different substances on the human body. I wouldn't go near that hospital!"

About a week after this conversation another woman from our group of twenty on the top layer of beds motioned me to her side as we worked in the food cellar.

"Tonight I'm reporting sick," she whispered to me. "I'm going into the hospital. I wanted you to know."

"No, you can't do that!" I told her. "No one in her right mind reports sick."

"But my feet are becoming so swollen with frostbite that I can barely walk. My sister, Alda, also has frozen feet, but she is afraid of the hospital."

"She's right. You must not do this!"

"I can't stand it any longer. I have to!"

That night she entered the hospital. She never came back. One day her sister was gone as well.

It thus became increasingly apparent that there was no middle ground in Ravensbrück. You were given two choices: life or death. If you did not get out of bed at four o'clock in the morning when a guard came through yelling, "Get up, lazy Jew pigs!" flailing as she shouted, if you lingered in a half-conscious state because throughout the night your body had been ravaged by hordes of lice, if your whole system was so exhausted from bouts of diarrhea or vomiting that you could not will yourself to rise up and join the lines for counting, you had chosen death whether you realized it or not.

While the rest of us stood in the counting lines from four o'clock until seven or eight, endlessly being counted, those women who had consciously or not chosen death were carried out and stacked beside the barracks door in the same manner as the first day—like piles of firewood. The Gentile barracks also had dead women beside their doors in the morning, but they lost only the very old or the very sick, not more than four or five each morning on one pile. At our barracks the number of women grew almost daily, reaching up higher and higher, ten, eleven, twelve feet into the ashen sky.

On a number of mornings we were still in line when a large, open truck came to take the piles of bodies to the crematorium burning somewhere in the camp. As the SS guards picked up the bodies and threw them into the truck one by one, a woman being carried would sometimes cry out, or the hand of a woman in the pile would rise, her fingers feeling the air, and then fall back. Some were still alive! The SS, however, did not recognize illness. If you got up and went to work, you were alive. If you did not get up, you were dead.

When I came in from working each day, sometimes in freezing rain or thick snow, so hungry that I had thought of nothing all afternoon but the cup of broth and crust of bread I would be given for supper, I wanted to scream when a guard carefully picked out the pieces of meat from my soup.

She would dine on nothing but meat while I had to be satisfied with a thin broth and a dribble of half-cooked turnips.

To the rules concerning water, toilets, and beds I added one more. The meals we were given each day never varied: that cup of broth twice a day with the addition of a potato or turnip at noon, if we were lucky, and a piece of hard, tasteless bread with watery jam on top at night to be saved for the morning. One night I was not as hungry as usual, having helped myself to carrots and radishes all afternoon while working in the *Kartoffelkeller*. We all did this; the guards could not watch us every minute and it was necessary to eat whenever we could if we were to survive. I decided that night to save my piece of bread for the morning, hiding it between my shoes, which I used for a pillow. The next morning while my eyes were still closed I thought of the bread, glad that for once I would not have to go to work without anything to eat. Sliding my fingers into the space between the shoes, I found nothing. Someone had stolen my bread.

I knew that Lily, Esther, or Ellen would never take anything from me, as we always shared everything. The thief had to be someone from the next bed, someone I had held shoes for while she crawled over our bed, or whispered to in the still hours of the night. I realized that when people are desperately hungry they will do things they would never do otherwise, that they will steal even though their hearts are burning with shame. But that was the last time anyone stole anything from us. The fourth rule was established: never save food. The corollary to it was: never pass up the chance to obtain food—as much as possible.

To this end we always tried to work in the detail that unloaded the ships and sorted the vegetables. There were other work details that did such things as shovel sand all day and were nowhere near food. During the first few days of camp one of the German SS supervisors learned that I understood German. One day she asked for an interpreter and I volunteered. Normally I volunteered for nothing unless it involved food, as our best chance for survival was to stay as inconspicuous as possible; anyone gaining the attention of a guard was usually singled out for punishment. However, I could not bear the beating of the Hungarian girls simply because they could not understand the orders. I especially worried about Lily, as she was timid behind her glasses and would not ask for anything. I translated for her and the other Hungarians.

This supervisor was not much taller than I, quick, with glinting dark brown eyes, and often walked by me as we marched back and forth to work. She seemed to enjoy having someone to converse with in German as well as translate for her. We had polite conversations about the weather—the amount of rain that had fallen the day before, the thickness of the snowfall, the direction of the wind. I did not mind these conversations, for if a Polish guard ordered our line to come with her that day to carry sand, this German guard barked, "No, this line is in my detail!" As a whole line of five women was never broken up, Esther, Ellen, Lily, and whoever else was in our line went off with me to the *Kartoffelkeller*. Once there we popped a radish or a carrot into our mouths at every opportunity.

One day I thought, *Why should we only be able to eat while at work? Why not bring some vegetables back to the barracks? Maybe we can even trade them for bread.* I had come to realize within a few weeks after our arrival at Ravensbrück that we Jews were given food different from that of the other prisoners. In the mornings the guards had occasionally begun to offer us what they called coffee but was actually a lukewarm, gray liquid with a rancid taste. The four of us used it to wash our faces. Whenever a guard asked for a volunteer to obtain the coffee at the kitchen building that served the whole camp I volunteered, always on the lookout for food. Often I was chosen to go.

The first time I came into the kitchen and saw the huge, boiling pots filled with pounds and pounds of thick meat and whole potatoes, I knew that it was only us who were being starved. The kitchen was filled with food, the aroma of real, freshly baked bread so strong that I nearly grew faint. I wanted a slice of that bread so badly; the piece of stale, caked bread that we received each night was nothing more than flour mixed with sawdust and drugs to keep us from menstruating. If somehow I managed to sneak radishes or carrots back into our barracks, perhaps I could trade them with someone who received real bread.

One day as we worked I broke several radishes in two and hid them in the shoulder pads of my coat, one on each side. Next I slid two carrots into the hem of my coat, also one on each side for balance. For each vegetable I hid, I ate two. I did all this without attracting the attention of a guard. Esther, however, saw me hide the carrots in the hem.

"What are you doing?" she whispered, her eyes wide. "You'll be caught. Don't do it. Please!"

"I won't be caught," I whispered back. "Don't talk to me about it! Just pretend you don't know anything."

That night after we were released from the counting lines and were entering the barracks one by one to be searched, I sent Esther in first and then Ellen and Lily. As my turn came my heartbeat quickened, but I knew that the guards were mainly interested in the pockets. I was stopped and the guard hurriedly passed her hands down my sides and emptied out my coat pockets. Then she paused. I could already feel the metal pole coming down on my head, remembering suddenly the beatings in the prison with my father. Then, without a word, the guard ordered me to move on.

Later in our bed I brought out the vegetables. Once we were all in bed the guards did not leave their heated, lit dining room for our cold, dark cave.

"Look what I have for us," I said, fishing a radish out of the padding.

"Did you hide it there?" Lily asked.

"It didn't grow there," I laughed.

"I know that," she said, hurt. "I just didn't think you would dare to steal it."

"It wasn't that hard. I'm hoping to trade it for bread. I'm fairly sure that the Gentile women from Poland two barracks over from us get good bread. Oh, I would love to have some!"

"I'll go over there," Ellen said. "I speak Polish."

"You aren't afraid?" I asked.

"Yes, but I'll go anyway. You stole the vegetables. I'll trade them."

She took the vegetables, hid them in her coat, climbed down to the floor, and jumped out of a broken window. Minute after minute crept by and she did not return. After at least half an hour had passed and she was not back, I thought, *I should never have let her go. She's still a child. I should have gone instead.*

Then I heard her climbing in the window. In another minute she was back up in our bed. "I got some bread!" she whispered. "The Polish women were glad to trade it for some fresh vegetables."

"Ellen!" I said. "I can't believe it. Real bread. Just smell it!"

We handed the large chunk of dark bread from one to the other, inhaling the intermingling odors of yeast, oil, and flour, stroking the thick, moist texture with the tips of our fingers. Finally it came back to Ellen. She broke it into four pieces, dividing it as evenly as possible, and we slowly ate, savoring each bite. When we were finished we lay down to sleep, almost content. I closed my eyes, planning how many radishes and carrots I would steal tomorrow.

Twenty

Y DECEMBER WE NUMBERED LESS THAN A THOU-
sand out of the ten thousand who had walked out of Budapest. At night we
did not dream, ever. If we had held our mothers' arms, our fathers' hands,
even in our dreams, we would not have been able to let go of them in the
morning. It was better to fall into a deep, exhausted sleep, a dreamless sleep,
where one was not tempted to slip off to memories and never return.

When the weather turned cold our feet became frostbitten and swelled
inside the tight shoes, making it almost impossible to walk. Shoes began to
disappear during the night as each woman tried to find a pair that would allow her to walk without pain. The four of us slept on ours to prevent them
from being stolen. Those women who woke up without shoes went to work
barefoot until a guard decided to give them another pair from the camp
storehouse.

By mid-December my feet were so swollen that every morning at the
counting I clenched my fists until my feet froze to keep from crying out in
pain. Once they were frozen they lost all sensation; I walked around all day

on two blocks of wood. In the evening the whole process began again. When my toes turned dark I knew that I had to get different shoes, but they were given out only if you had none and then if and when a guard chose to give you a pair.

Then sleep was taken from us. In the middle of the night the guards came into our barracks shouting, "Get up, pigs! Up, you lazy, filthy swine!" They whacked us into consciousness, hurried us out into the sleet, into the piercing cold, into the snow, to unload trains that came to Ravensbrück day and night carrying car after car of plunder. Forced to unload these trains while the Gentile prisoners slept undisturbed, we walked by their barracks, glancing through unbroken windows at the softly lit rooms, at the layers of blankets on each bed, ever on the outside looking in.

Once we arrived at the trains we climbed up into the cars and began to unload them, making piles for each kind of goods. Paintings went in one pile; white down comforters covered with satin, embroidered in silk, went in another; linens in a third. Women's lingerie in pale yellow, light blues, was heaped beside the delicate dresses of little girls, pink and green ribbons twined into the bodices. Doll carriages trimmed with shiny chrome made up still another pile and to the side of them, dolls tossed every which way, soft faces thrown against the ground, legs sticking out in all directions. The trains came endlessly. Night after night we unloaded boxes and boxes, cars and more cars, coming from all parts of Europe, especially from the Scandinavian countries. Sometimes I found a name and address sewn inside the lining of a coat and wondered about the man or woman who had owned the coat, about the Jewish home and family that had been destroyed. After a minute, however, I threw the coat down into the proper pile and went on with the unloading, hoping that if we worked fast enough we would be able to return to our barracks before morning.

One night while I was unloading a train I came across a pair of wooden clogs like the ones worn by the Gentile prisoners. Immediately I took off my old, shriveled shoes, threw them into the pile of shoes on the ground, and put on the clogs. They were not very warm as the top was made of canvas, but they fit my feet comfortably; I could wiggle my toes for the first time in months.

The next morning when we lined up for counting, two hours after we had returned to the barracks, I stood again with clenched fists until my feet froze, anticipating how much easier it would be to walk to the harbor in my new shoes. Then, as one of the German supervisors was counting us, she stopped suddenly and stared at my feet. I panicked. This was the same supervisor who walked beside me back and forth to work, engaging in conversations, but that did not mean she was my friend. First and foremost she was an SS officer; first and foremost I was a Jew bitch.

"Take off those shoes!" she ordered, her brown eyes flashing.

I removed them as quickly as I could.

"Get your own shoes, thief!" she yelled.

The blood pounded in my head. How could I get my shoes? They were at the bottom of a pile by the trains. Then, for no apparent reason, the other German SS supervisor walked over to the first one and said, "Oh, let her have the shoes. She was about due for a new pair anyway."

The first SS woman stared at me for another minute, hands on her hips, mouth drawn into a thin, tight line, and then turned abruptly and strutted to the head of the row. She did not walk beside me that day, either coming or going, but the next day she was back, remarking on the delicate texture of the snow that had fallen during the night.

These two SS supervisors, as well as the Polish SS women, were infinitely interesting to us; our lives sometimes depended on determining exactly what pleased them and precisely what angered them. However, knowing these things helped us only in the slightest, as most of the time the motivation for their actions was incomprehensible. You could expect a beating if you were caught stealing vegetables or if you did not understand an order, but you could also be hit for no reason.

The short, quick-tempered SS supervisor who walked beside me must have heard the woman from the Budapest opera singing to us at night as we drifted off to sleep. One day during lunch in the *Kartoffelkeller* she walked briskly over to the opera singer and commanded, "Sing for me! Here!" and pointed to a box in the middle of the floor. Startled, the woman walked to the center of the room and sat down on the box. Very softly, she began to sing a popular song in German, *"Du, du, du bist mein Herr."*

As she sang the damp, chilly air, the murmur of the rain upon the roof, the hollow faces of the women staring at her with empty eyes, seemed to slip away from her, and she began to sing louder, her voice filling the underground room. The song she sang was in waltz time, the slow, sweet beat moving like a strong tide through us, up . . . down . . . down, up . . . down . . . down, washing each of us upon a calm, sun-dappled shore, back into the flux, up on the shore once more.

The song over, she stopped. We slid into the sea. Deep silence hung in the air for long minutes while tears ran down the face of the SS woman. In another instant, before any of us knew what was happening, the SS woman was beating the singer, hitting her again and again with the ladle she had grabbed from the pot, striking her on the head, on the arms, on the back. Just as abruptly she stopped, put the ladle back, stood up and ordered us to begin working. The singer struggled up from the floor and stumbled to a sorting bin.

Three days later this command performance was repeated, and continued thereafter several times a week. The scenario never varied: we sat down to eat, the woman was ordered to sing, the SS woman's face became bathed with tears, the singer was beaten.

One day sometime in December the SS supervisor inflicted a particularly brutal beating to the singer, striking her repeatedly with the heavy club she was carrying that day. I wanted to rush at her, grab the club, and hit her over the head, but I knew I would only be arrested and thrown into solitary confinement. Finally the beating stopped and the supervisor ordered the singer to get back to work. The singer did not move.

"Get up, I said!" the SS woman commanded. "You godforsaken sow! Get back to work!" She kicked her in the side but still the singer did not move. She was lying on the floor, facedown, arms curled around the patches of hair on her head beginning to grow out again. The supervisor was by now scarlet with rage, clenching the club with both arms, ready to begin the beating once more. But the listlessness of the body on the floor, the way the legs sprawled out far apart from each other, must have aroused her curiosity; she put the club down and stooped beside the singer, turning her over. A line of blood ran from the woman's open mouth, dribbled down her chin onto the floor. Already her eyes were sinking into their sockets.

"Damn bitch!" the SS woman shouted. Rising quickly, she stalked out of the room, not looking back. We filed out into the pouring rain, the water rushing over us from all sides.

That night we sat on our bed talking for a while longer than usual. We were continuing to trade vegetables for bread as often as we could. Sometimes Ellen came back with one or two slices, sometimes with none. I did not allow Esther or Lily to hide the carrots and radishes in their coats and told Ellen, "Don't bother. I'll steal enough for all of us." I do not think that any of the other women in our barracks brought back vegetables. The fear of being caught and punished was overwhelming. On this particular evening we sat very quiet after having shared our extra bread.

"She had such a lovely voice . . ." Lily said finally.

"She did," Ellen replied. "I will miss it so."

"What if the SS supervisor finds someone new to pick on?" Lily asked. "She terrifies me more and more. What if she decides to pick on me?"

"Lily, Lily," I said, reaching out to hold her hand. "She won't hurt you. She picked on the singer because—I don't know why. Because she was beautiful, I guess. She made her cry."

"I know, but I'm so scared!" Lily answered, her fingers tightening around mine.

"Do you know what!" I said. "I've thought of another place to hide carrots!"

"You have? Where?"

"In my shoes! These boats I wear are so big that I could slide a carrot along the side of my foot. That's two more carrots to trade."

"But what will they smell like after they're in your shoes?" Esther asked. "The Polish girls won't eat them."

"They'll eat them! So they'll smell like dirty feet. We eat bread that has lice crawling all over it when the guard takes it out from under the rag cover, don't we? They'll eat smelly carrots."

I was right. The carrots I sneaked into camp in my shoes were also traded for bread, when the Polish women had extra, and gave us the strength to keep getting up in the morning for the counting. Our feet continued to swell and freeze, swell and defrost, but we were dragging along from day to day as well as possible.

Then one afternoon while we were unloading a ship, the SS woman who often walked beside me ordered me to report to the other end of the deck. When I arrived I found a guard stamping furiously back and forth on the planks. She had commanded several of the Hungarian girls to separate three different kinds of crates and put them into piles. As the orders had been given to them in German, they did not know what they were to do. I translated for them and hurried back to Lily, whom I had been forced to leave by herself.

When I returned to the area where she and I had been pushing crates across the deck, I could not find her. "Have you seen Lily?" I asked Esther and Ellen.

"No, we were at the cellar," Esther answered. "We just returned."

"We've got to find her!" I said.

After searching as much as we could while looking like we were still working, I finally spotted her slumped behind a large crate, her face in her hands.

"Lily?" I asked. "Are you all right?"

She looked up at me, cheeks pallid, blue-white patches encircling each eye. A bruise on her temple was turning dark, the center already purple.

"Your glasses are gone! Oh, Lily, did someone hit you?"

She kept looking at me, but no sound came from her. She seemed to be in shock. Then a woman from our top level of bunks came up to us and said, "One of the SS women, the short Polish one, beat her. She gave her an order in Polish and Lily didn't obey it."

"She doesn't know Polish. Come, Lily," I said, putting my arms under hers. Ellen went to her side and the two of us raised her up. She stood quietly, still not speaking.

"I can't see . . ." she said finally in a low whine.

"Do you know who I am, Lily?" I asked.

"You're Seren. I know your voice. But I can't see your face."

"What can you see? Can you see anything?"

"I can make out a few shapes—some colors. That's all. What am I going to do? I've never been without my glasses." She began to weep, hiding her face in her hands again.

"It's all right," I said, pulling down her hands and taking them in mine. "I'll stay with you. I'll see for you."

After that at least one of us was always by her side. When we walked back and forth to work I took one arm, Esther or Ellen took the other, and we half carried Lily along. If the SS woman marched beside me I was terrified that she would notice Lily stumbling along, nearly tripping every few steps. Ellen and I considered trying to hide her somewhere in the barracks during the day, perhaps under a pile of straw in our bed, but we could not count on being taken back to the same barracks again at night. We also thought that the barracks might be inspected during the day and Lily would be discovered and taken to the crematorium, so we decided to keep her with us at all times. If she slipped and fell against me while I was listening to the SS woman talk about the weather, I did not turn toward Lily, continuing to listen attentively.

"Isn't this a fine day?" the SS woman would often ask.

"Yes, indeed!" I always replied, taking no notice of Lily nearly knocking me to the frozen ground.

Once we were at work, it was easier to take care of Lily. If we were unloading a ship, I put her at the back end of a crate and I went in the front as we carried it off the deck, down the ramp, and to the cellar; she simply followed the crate. If we worked in the cellar, one of us stood beside her, putting a crate of vegetables at our feet. The location of each bin she could distinguish by color: a red haze was radishes; orange, carrots; green, cabbage.

Often while we worked together I told stories, partly to keep Lily's mind off her lack of glasses, partly just to hear the sound of my own voice. I have always loved to talk. Since Lily and many of the other women in the camp were children of mixed marriages where Jewish customs had ceased to be observed generations ago, I loved to tell her how it was in my home. I explained how my family observed each holiday, how the cycle of the year, the quickening of spring, the dying of summer, the advent of fall, moved us from season to season, from year to year, like the violets coming up each April on the mountaintops or the leaves of corn whispering in the summer suns.

"TELL ME AGAIN ABOUT THE POLENTA," LILY SAID one day. Like all of us, she could think of nothing but food.

"My father normally never touched anything in the kitchen," I began.

Now he's dead, a recess of my mind reminded me. No, I would not think about that. *Go on with the story!*

"Preparing food was women's work!" I continued. "But for some reason or other he decided that he and only he could cook polenta. In the summer we often had dairy for the evening meal and this is when my father made the polenta. He had a special kettle that could only be used for cooking the corn down into mush. Once it was cooked he took it—oh, it was as smooth as silk—and layered it in a large pan. On the bottom he melted butter and cheese, then he put a layer of polenta, a layer of cheese, more polenta, and so on, making three or four layers. On the top he put a big mound of sour cream and spread it all around. After it baked for about an hour he took it out of the oven. The cheese and butter and polenta had all melted together and smelled so delicious that we could barely wait until my father was through saying the prayers. Finally he cut it into thick slices and we poured cream over it that our mother had skimmed from the milk. It was like tasting a piece of heaven when I took that first bite! With it we had tall glasses of milk cooled in a barrel in the spring and—"

"Stop! Stop!" a woman next to us cried, interrupting me. "I can't bear to hear about all that food!"

We turned to our bins, sorting in silence. After a long while Lily said, "The time goes too slowly when you don't talk, Seren. Tell me about something else. Tell me about Shabbat."

"Shabbat!" I answered. "How I loved Shabbat! On Friday mornings I woke up to the smells of baking rolls and challah. The odors came into my bedroom early in the morning, when I was still asleep beside Esther and Zipporah, and entered my dreams. I used to imagine that I was in a room piled to the ceiling with bread—loaves and loaves of sesame bread, poppy seed bread, braided bread warm from the oven, the butter melting into the crusts."

"You're talking about food again!" the same woman interrupted.

"Oh, I forgot . . . Well, I can tell you about the ceremonies. It was very important that everything and everyone be absolutely clean for Shabbat. All of us—my mother and father, Herman and Tamara, Rose, Berta, Mendel, Meyer, Louise, Shlomo, Eliezer, Zipporah, and I—went to the bathhouse at the mill on Friday afternoons to take a bath in separate rooms, one for the men and one for the women. Esther couldn't go at first because you had to be eight years old. Then before we sat down for the evening meal we had to wash our hands in the kitchen basin with water brought in from the spring, even if we had come directly from the bathhouse. Finally, my mother lit the candles she used only on Shabbat and we all sat down at the table, my father at the head, my mother next to him, Herman and Tamara next, and so on down the line from the oldest to the youngest. Each face turned toward my father was softly lit by the candle's flame, subdued, at peace.

"Then my father blessed the challah, broke off pieces, and gave one to each of us, beginning with the oldest and finally working down to Zipporah, Esther, and me. Sometimes I thought I would never be able to wait until I could bite into the soft bread just waiting for me beneath the crust. Would you believe that on Saturday morning I took the leftover challah and cut off the crust because I thought it was too hard? Oh, I would give anything to have a piece of challah now!"

"You've done it again!" the woman said. "I can't stand it! Can't you talk about anything besides food?"

I quit talking for the day.

ONE EVENING AFTER WE CAME BACK TO CAMP AND stood in the counting lines we were not dismissed for supper. Over and over we had been counted, but the supervisors were never satisfied with the total. Finally one said, "A woman is missing! You will all stay where you are until you tell us where she is!"

I looked quickly down our row past Ellen, Lily, and Esther and then at the row behind me. Many of the older women were also looking, their eyes darting back and forth. Each of us probably had the same thought: How could anyone have escaped? All around us constantly were guards holding the leashes of German shepherds. If a woman fell to the ground during the marches to and from work and did not rise quickly, the dogs were let loose, one flying at her throat, another at her chest, a third at her legs. Around these dogs and guards, around the entire camp, were high concrete walls topped with a solid layer of barbed wire. At regular intervals were towers holding guards with guns, loaded and pointed down at us. If, by some miracle, a woman did succeed in eluding the dogs and guards and escape while at work outside the camp, where would she go? Ravensbrück was located in the heart of the Third Reich. When the Germans heard rumors of the camps, of the smoke smelling like burned flesh and belching from the crematorium stacks, they believed that their Führer would not do these things without good reason. Why even attempt escape?

On that evening we stood in our lines for four hours, for five hours, wondering where this woman could have gone. Snow began to fall, settling on our heads, on our coats, piling up in little hills on our feet. After several hours we were no more than rows of white poles in a drifted field.

Across from us was a barracks full of Gypsy women, additional "spoilers of the race," who had been brought into camp after our arrival. Many of the women had entered the camp with their small children. They were made to stand outside in lines all day, all night, with bare feet, bare legs, babies crying ceaselessly in their arms. They stood so tonight, barely visible in the flurry of flakes piling up around us.

As my feet froze solid, legs and arms becoming completely numb, my mind began to drift with the snow, with the softness. I was six years old again. It was late spring and the Gypsies were returning to Fulehaza. As soon as Berta and Rose heard that their crimson-and-yellow wagons had been spotted jingling toward the village, they began to talk about the fortune-teller. Every year a woman dressed in a long black skirt and white blouse embroidered all along the flowing sleeves with brilliant red roses went from door to door telling fortunes. This year the Gypsy woman finally came to our house late one afternoon when the sun had already begun to slide down behind the tallest trees on the mountaintop. She climbed the steps to the house quickly, the silver bracelets on her wrists jangling, and knocked on the door. I watched from the swing under the tree in the side yard as Rose let out a squeal and said, "Come in! We've been waiting for you."

In a few more minutes I went inside too, sitting on the far end of a bench by the kitchen table. The fortune-teller was seated at the other end of the bench, Rose, Berta, and Tamara all grouped around her. She was holding Rose's hand and gazing at it intently, her long braids swung forward. The coins entwined in her hair glinted in the light from the front window slanting across the table in long, yellow sweeps.

"Ah," she said after a few minutes. "I see a handsome young man in your future. He will fall in love with you as soon as he sees your lovely face."

Rose broke into laughter that bounced in the soft, warm air. "That's wonderful!" she cried. "Will he be rich too?"

"Rich enough," the Gypsy answered, tossing her braids behind her and smiling. "Who is next?"

Tamara had her fortune told and then Berta, who was promised a fine young man and a happy, happy life. Then the Gypsy woman saw me watching her from the end of the table. "You, little one, wouldn't you like to have your fortune told too?" she asked. I had been afraid she would never ask me. I held out my hand and she stared at it for only a minute.

"Oh, you are going to travel over a big body of water," she said. "Someday you will marry a dark young man and have two children."

My mother, who had been watching from a corner of the kitchen, spoke for the first time. "So my little bird will fly away!" she laughed. "I've always known she would someday." She pressed several coins into the Gypsy's hand. The woman rose and left the house.

What a silly fortune! I thought, and ran back outside, swinging up into the highest branches of the tree.

———

"*ACHTUNG!*" AN SS SUPERVISOR WAS SHOUTING. "*Achtung!*" She had come out from the barracks where she had been warm and dry, leaving us with several of the lesser guards. It was at least midnight. "We have found the missing woman," she announced. "One of the guards remembered that a woman died while at work this morning. You are dismissed." We stumbled toward the door, barely having the strength left to shake the snow from our bodies, and fell into bed, starved, frozen to the bone.

In the morning the number of women who did not get up was doubled, the pile of bodies by the barracks door so large that it had to be broken down into two piles. As we waited in line I looked across at the barracks where the Gypsies had still been standing when we went inside at midnight. Not one woman or child was to be seen, only piles of snow heaped into great white mounds.

Twenty-one

BY NIGHTFALL THE END OF THE BIG TOE ON MY right foot had turned completely black. When I showed it to the surgeon in the next bed she said, "Gangrene has set in. Every time your foot freezes the circulation is cut off. Little by little the flesh dies. The black part of your toe will have to come off or the cells will continue to deteriorate. If you like, tomorrow night I can cut off the gangrenous part with my penknife while it's still frozen."

The night passed in fits and starts. My toe throbbed, a sharp, persistent pain shooting out from the foot, traveling up the leg, circling around my back and chest, gyrating into my consciousness in endless, repeating spirals. Once toward morning I fell into a light sleep only to be awakened by a loud boom followed by screams, prolonged moans. One of the top bunks in the row next to us had fallen down on the two bunks below it, crashing on the sleeping women, carrying them all through the darkness to the floor. This happened often; in the mornings the women still lay as they fell, handfuls of straw sifted over the living asleep on the bodies of the dead.

When the guard came through the rows to wake us I climbed out of bed and hurried to the counting lines with the others, anxious for the cold to seep into my toes, freezing out the pain. I wanted to forget about the part of me that would be cut off and thrown away at the end of the day, but my mind worried it, turned it over and over.

It was one of those mornings when the guards decided, "Yes, they can have some coffee. Maybe it will make them move a little faster—the lazy pigs!" When a volunteer was requested, I piped up, "I'll go!" before any other woman had a chance to say anything. *Perhaps it will take my mind off my toe and I might even see some extra food,* I thought.

I entered the kitchen and began walking toward the large, black iron stove where the pots of bitter coffee were left. As I passed an enormous wooden table where women from the Gentile barracks were often cutting up vegetables, I saw a large iron kettle three feet across and three feet deep filled to overflowing with cooked potatoes steaming in their jackets. They were solid, mealy and white inside, the kind of potatoes my mother had grown in her garden, looking nothing at all like the half-rotted gray lumps that we were occasionally given at lunch. Glancing at the women prisoners stirring pots a few feet away, their backs to me, I grabbed four of the hot potatoes, opened my coat, and slid them down the front of my dress. They tumbled to my chest, bouncing against my breasts, and came to rest at the string tied around my waist. I jiggled up and down, tossing them from one spot to another as the burning skins pressed against my flesh.

From the other end of the kitchen a guard from another barracks started toward me. *Has she seen me?* I wondered, my heart thumping against a potato. I walked quickly to the stove and picked up a pot of coffee, summoning up all my strength to lift it with one hand while holding the other across my waist to keep the potatoes from slipping out and falling to the floor. Shuffling along as fast as I could, I carried the coffee back to our barracks and set it before a guard.

"You took long enough!" she said.

I said nothing, crossing my arms, cradling the outline of a potato in each hand. She heaved the pot of coffee up on a table and I padded over to where Esther, Ellen, and Lily were standing. When the coffee was poured we took our cups and edged away from the guards to a corner of the front hall where we were served all our meals. The three of them began to splash the liquid on their faces. I turned my back to the room, slipped a hand inside my dress, pulled out a potato, slid it up my sleeve, took Esther's hand, and dropped it into her palm. Her eyes grew so large that I had to frown at her, telling her with my expression, *Don't react!* She received the message, lowered her eyes to the floor, and inched the potato up under her coat sleeve. I followed the same procedure with Ellen and Lily. Throughout the morning each of us raised a hand to the mouth as if to cover a yawn, grabbed a bite of potato, chewed it slowly, teeth coming together only once in half a minute. It was almost dusk when I realized that I had not thought about my toe since morning.

That evening, as soon as we were all on our beds, the surgeon took out her penknife and asked, "Are you ready?"

"Yes," I answered.

"Good."

She sat directly across from me, the three other women from her bed behind her, watching. Ellen was on one side of me, Esther on the other.

"Put your foot here, in my lap," she said. "I'll cut as fast as I can."

"Yes, hurry," I answered. "I never liked that toe anyway."

"Always the fool," she laughed. "You play the role well."

"Don't be so sure that it's a role!" I answered.

She bent over my toe, head lowered, one hand cradling my foot, the other clasping the knife. She was completely absorbed in her work; I could see how well she must have performed in the hospital in Budapest. I took Esther's and Ellen's hands in mine and closed my eyes.

My little Gypsy friend, Smarvana, and I are trying to cut the huge log in two with a rusty saw. The saw slips, rips a jagged line in my foot. Oh, how it swells! Mama carries me to the mill doctor early in the morning fog. I ride around all day on the tall shoulders of Gunther like a white heron on long, long legs, dipping and gliding, dipping and gliding as he lopes through the rolling fields of Transylvania. How grand it is to be tall like my father. . . .

"Finished!" the surgeon said.

I opened my eyes. I had not felt anything.

"I grabbed some pieces of packing paper from the ship today," she was saying. "I'll wrap your toe in them. The bleeding should stop in a few minutes."

Blood was gushing from my toe, running steadily onto the straw, spreading in a pool around my foot. I wondered briefly where the dead piece had been placed and then saw some paper wadded into a ball, red-soaked, tossed to one side. *What's done is done,* I thought, and pressed my hands tight against the flow.

"Thank you, my lady doctor," I said.

"You are welcome. I will expect an office call again tomorrow night to see how you are progressing."

"Certainly."

The next morning my toe burned with pain as if the knife were cutting, cutting, ever cutting. Halfway through the counting, however, the foot was frozen again and lost all feeling. Over the next few days the same process occurred. The open wound drained when the toe had defrosted and hurt with a dull pain that never went away, never lessened.

ONE MORNING WE WERE TAKEN OUT TO BE COUNTED as usual at four in the morning but when the counting was over, the dead taken away, we were brought back inside the barracks for coffee. Then the guard said, "We won't work today. It's Christmas."

Christmas! The word was repeated, each woman forming the word over and over, the sibilants singing in the air. We were Jews and this was a Gentile holiday, but for the first time since we arrived we would not have to trudge over the frozen dirt, trudge up and down the steep ramps, hills, and steps, trudge back again at night. En masse we came back to our beds and lay down, grateful for the opportunity to gain some extra sleep, as we were still unloading train cars during half the night. After a few hours, we woke up one by one, stretched, smiled at each other, and began to chat as if we were at home on a holiday, whiling away the quiet afternoon.

Again Lily asked me about the polenta; again I told her in detail. Then the surgeon wanted to know if I knew how to make chicken soup with kreplach and I said, "Of course I know how," and told her exactly how much chicken to use, how much broth, how you added a pinch of this seasoning, a pinch of that, how you formed the dumplings, how you let the broth bubble until the dumplings were tender, perfect.

Once I started talking about preparing food, there was no stopping me. I gave the recipes for gefilte fish, for stuffed cabbage, for baked sweet potatoes laced with honey and sprinkled with nutmeg, for rich, moist honey cake dripping with honey-orange sauce, for roast chicken, for goose, for lamb. Finally, when I paused for breath, a woman from the next bed asked, "Did you do most of the cooking when you were still at home? I'm sure you were a great help to your mother."

"Well . . ." I said, suddenly remembering how my mother had constantly chased me out of the kitchen with her stirring spoon because I would not stop sticking my finger into all the bowls for a taste. "I helped some."

"Were those her recipes?" the same woman asked.

"Oh . . . some were hers. Some mine," I answered her, hoping that she never found out that I could not boil an egg without either burning my fingers or cracking the shell. My mother never let me stay in the kitchen long enough to learn how to cook. I watched, noshing away, until she cried again, "It will pour on your wedding day if you don't stop all that nibbling in my pots!" and whisked me out. I wish I had those recipes I gave out that day; I would love to see what I made up.

THE DAY AFTER CHRISTMAS WHILE WE STOOD IN THE counting lines we saw healthy, well-dressed Gentile prisoners line up outside their barracks and begin marching toward the back gate. The next morning more barracks, all Gentile, were emptied of prisoners, more women walked to the gate. At first we thought that they were being transferred to another camp. That night, however, Ellen came back from trading vegetables for bread and said that the Polish women had told her they were being sent home.

"Do you think they will let us go too?" Lily asked. "Oh, I hope so. I don't know if I can stand this much longer. You don't know how terrible it is not to be able to see. All day I stumble around as if I'm in the middle of a bad dream where everything is blurry and terrifying."

"I know it must be very hard for you, Lily," Esther said. "It's hard for me and I can see. I can't even remember the last time I was happy . . ." She buried her face in the sleeve of her coat and began to cry.

"Come, girls," I said. "The war will end sometime. I want more than anything to see how it all ends. I want to see it to the finish! We've made it this far. We can make it a little further, can't we?"

"I can," Ellen said. "Anyway, I can as long as nobody shoots me."

"Good girl!" I said, smiling at her trusting face, so full of courage for one so young.

"Esther, you can't give up," I said. "You're my sister and I won't let you! And Lily, you can't give up either. We'll carry you if nothing else."

She put her hand on my shoulder. "Could we go to sleep now?" she asked. "I'm so tired I can barely keep my eyes open."

The four of us lay down—settling into our positions easily, knowing by now every board on the bed, the slot for each arm and leg among all the other arms and legs—and fell asleep, Lily's hand resting on my shoulder.

The next day while we worked the air became almost balmy. The sun came out once more after it seemed as if it had been lost forever behind the layer of clouds arching over, thick and gray. Melting began and while we had to walk through mud and slush, it was better than trying to hobble on the clogs; the packed snow stuck to the bottom of our shoes and we walked on a wedge of snow all day long. However, the snow and freezing wind were replaced by the increased infestation of lice; they thrived in the warm weather. During our noon break the four of us went to a corner of the *Kartoffelkeller*, removed our coats, and picked off the lice one by one. Once we had our coats deloused we started on our arms and legs, plucking at the flat, hoary parasites stuck fast by their claws and sucking mouths. When Esther, Ellen, and I were finished one of us deloused Lily.

One day when it was my turn and I was picking them off her neck—

one! two! three!—and throwing them to the ground, Ellen teased, "For someone who didn't know what a louse was when we walked through the gate, you sure are doing a good job!"

"But I learned, didn't I?" I laughed, and with the heel of my shoe, ground to a pulp all the lice crawling at my feet.

THEN ONE NIGHT WHEN WE CAME BACK FROM WORK, the SS guards did not take us back to our barracks. We were marched instead to an enormous canvas tent pitched near two tall, brick smokestacks. The first thing I noticed was the stench of burning flesh swelling through the entire tent, pressing against our nostrils, assaulting our mouths and throats. On days when the wind was blowing toward us from the crematorium we went to sleep pinching our noses closed.

There were no bunk beds in the tent, only an inadequate number of cots with boards for mattresses. If a group of women came in late from work and the beds were full, they had to sleep on the ground. We longed for that which only a few days earlier had seemed unbearable—our crowded barracks beds and a single toilet. We wondered: Is Germany losing the war after all? The camp seemed to be in the process of disintegration. The small amount of food that we had been given became even less: some days we got soup; some days we did not.

Another night when we returned to camp, filing into the tent one by one or two by two, shoulders slumped, heads sunk against our chests, we sensed that something was different and raised our heads. With great curiosity a number of Jewish women were staring at us from the cots. They were dressed in striped pants and striped jackets, their faces full, bodies rounded. As we passed by them, trying to find a place on the ground to lie down, they yelled at us in Yiddish, a language most of our group could not understand. When no one responded to their yells they began to kick at some of the women, screaming even louder than before.

As quickly as we could, Ellen, Esther, and I pulled Lily to a corner and sank against the wall. "Who are they? What are they shouting?" asked Lily.

"I don't know who they are," I answered. "They keep saying, 'What kind of Jews are you that you don't speak Yiddish?'"

"What do they mean by that?" Esther asked.

"I recognize the dialect," Ellen said. "These women are from Poland. They think all Jewish people speak Yiddish, I guess."

"They must have been sent here from another camp," I said. "From the looks of them it was a better one than this one."

"Those warm pants!" Esther said. "I wish we had some like that."

"I don't like it," I said. "These women won't do us any good. I'm sure of it."

In the morning the new prisoners pushed their way in front of us as we went outside to be counted, pushed to the front of the line for coffee, pushed their way into the line for the *Kartoffelkeller*. They did not know where they were being taken; we wanted to be in that line, so they shoved us out as a matter of course. Our days of nibbling on turnips and carrots at work, of hiding radishes in my coat, were over. We spent the long days shoveling sand into a cart, hauling it to a pile across a field, dumping it, and trudging back for more. This work was especially hard on Lily, who tripped often while walking across the plain of dim shapes and dull colors mottled by the dust.

"Have you talked to anyone? Have you found where these new prisoners are from?" I asked Ellen one night.

"They have been in a camp in Poland for three and a half years," she answered, "in a special labor detail."

"What was the name of the camp?"

"Auschwitz."

"I never heard of it."

"No, neither have I."

ONE MORNING AFTER THE SS HAD BROUGHT IN THE prisoners from Auschwitz, we were ordered to line up for counting as usual. The weather had turned cold again and I was waiting for my foot to freeze, head down, hands clenched inside the pockets of my coat. Then a color in front of me flicked briefly in the corner of my eye and I looked up, brown and beige squares weaving in and out in front of me. So astounded that I could not put into thoughts what was startling me, I kept staring at the colors, at the plaid. Then, with a jolt, I realized what I was staring at—the jacket I had made for Tamara. The woman in front of me was wearing the jacket I had sewn for Tamara! She had been wearing it the last time I saw her in Reghinal-Sasesc. I would have known the cut, the fabric, the hand-stitching anywhere. *It can't be! It can't be Tamara!* I thought. *She's shorter than this woman.* Only one thing could have happened: Tamara had been deported to Auschwitz, her clothes taken from her and handed out to other prisoners. The woman in front of me from Auschwitz had been given the jacket I made for Tamara almost eight years ago.

All this time I had continued to imagine Tamara and Herman, my mother, all the others, as I had left them in Reghinal-Sasesc—alive, as well as possible, still living in those rooms. *Have all of them been taken to Auschwitz?* I wondered. *Have they been put in work details like us? Even my mother?* It was not until years later that I came to know the full implications of being taken to Auschwitz if you were not a young, healthy woman with no small children.

Sick at heart, I shoveled sand all during that day, and the rest of the days we were in Ravensbrück, thinking of Tamara. I considered speaking to one of the women from Auschwitz about her, but I knew they would never be able to tell me anything. None of us had names, only numbers. Some of the girls from our group knew my name; after I was asked to translate for them a number of times they asked me who I was, and I told them. But I did not think anyone would know Tamara's name, and how could I describe her? She was short, but so were many other women. She had a voice so beautiful that I used to pretend I was in a great theater when she sang to us in the kitchen after supper, but she would not sing in a camp. Then I remembered the opera singer. Oh, if only Tamara did not sing! Let her not have sung. But can a bird not sing? Even in prison it swells into song.

———

AROUND THE MIDDLE OF JANUARY 1945 WE WERE all marched to the front of a building I had not seen before and told that we were going to be taken to a different camp. "Remove all of your clothes!" an SS guard ordered. "Inside this building you will take a bath." We undressed in the middle of the street that ran through the camp. Those of us from Budapest were by now no more than little twigs shivering in the cold. This time we threw off our clothes quickly, all embarrassment gone in the face of the promise of a bath. Our clothes were crawling with lice, inside and out, our hair nested with lice, more lice creeping over our skin.

We entered the building, lined up in rows, suffered the cutting of all the hair on our bodies once more, were handed ragged summer dresses marked with large crisscrosses like before, and thin raincoats—all covered with lice. We had given up our old, familiar lice only to be given new ones. We came out again into the cold, a drop of water never touching our bodies. Half of us were put in the room on the left, the other half on the right.

That night an SS supervisor came to us and announced, "In the morning there will be a transport to a new camp. Not all of you will be going. I'll read off the numbers of those who will leave."

She started to read the numbers and after a long while read 85803, my number. A few minutes later she read Lily's. She finished, having read neither Ellen's nor Esther's numbers, and strode quickly out of the room. A great cry went out, a moan that welled up from the bottom of despair. Each pair would be cut in two, leaving every woman far less than half of what she had been in a pair. Having a sister, a cousin, or a friend in the camp with you was sometimes the only thing that gave you the courage to go on; each lived solely for the other.

Esther and Ellen sobbed hysterically, clinging first to Lily and then to me, while on the bed beside us two young girls had their arms around each other, crying into each other's shoulders. Finally, one broke away. Sensing me looking at her, she turned and said, "My sister and I have never been apart. I would do anything to stay with her. She's all I have left."

"You know what?" I said to her, wondering why I had not thought of the idea sooner. "Nobody knows your name and nobody knows my name.

All anybody knows is the number of our coats. Our new dresses don't even have a number. I'll just change coats with you. Then I can stay here with my sister and you can go with yours. Or we can do the opposite, whichever you like."

She grabbed me, hugging me fiercely. "I'll stay!" she said after she let go, tears running from the corners of her eyes. "You go."

"Fine! I would love to get out of here!"

Ellen was able to make the same kind of trade and the four of us lay down to sleep.

Early the next morning when the four of us and the other women whose numbers had been called were sitting on the floor of a large, flat wagon, I saw the same girl with whom I had traded coats come out of the barracks, hand in hand with her sister. We were *all* being taken to a new camp; the counting off of numbers, the separating, was simply an exercise. I imagine a bored SS supervisor said, "Let's tell half of those Jews that they're going away and the other half that they're not. Their reaction should be amusing, to say the least." We did not know it at the time, but the Russian army was rapidly advancing toward Germany. The eastern camps were being closed and the Jewish prisoners taken to camps further west and south. As the wagon rolled out of camp I asked a guard for the date, wanting to know exactly when we were able to leave Ravensbrück at last, even if for another camp.

"It's January nineteenth," she answered, "as if that means anything to you."

We had been in Ravensbrück for four months by calendar time. There are other kinds of time, however; immeasurable time, when the days and nights fall into a vast, black wasteland as deep and wide as the immensities of space. Such was the nature of time in Ravensbrück.

WHEN WE ARRIVED AT THE RAILROAD TRACKS WE were ordered to line up beside a long train sitting on a side rail. The four of us clasped each other's palms so tightly that the SS would have had to chop off our hands to get us apart. We followed the line of women up high, metal steps into a cattle car, an enormous wood box whose plank sides reached up high around us. A small amount of straw was scattered on the floor. Toilet buckets stood by the door. Otherwise there was nothing but the cold. As we filed into the car an SS guard counted us one by one. The four of us sat down near the door.

"That's a hundred!" a guard yelled shortly after we entered the car.

"Good!" the SS supervisor standing by the next car replied. "Don't put in any more. A hundred to a car should do it."

"How many cars do we have?"

"Five. There are about five hundred of them, so it should work out perfect."

"Good planning!"

"Yes!"

"Where are we shipping them?"

"To Dachau."

Half an hour later, a guard came through the cars and gave each of us a small chunk of cheese and a slice of bread. It was our ration for the next three days. Then the steps were taken away and the heavy metal door was pulled shut, the loud clang reverberating in the frigid air like the crack of a glacier crashing into the ocean. A pale shaft of blue-white light filtered down on us from a small opening in the ceiling of the car, fell on the four of us huddled together near the center. We formed a square, Esther and Ellen on one side, Lily and I on the other, face to face, leg touching leg, a small island in the sea of women.

When the shaft of light had faded to a dim gray, finally disappearing altogether, it left nothing but the icy blackness clutching at our arms, hands, legs, chest, and feet, at our very insides. Those who had been crying the night before at the separations, those who had sisters or cousins in the camp, must have been separated after all when we were packed inside the cars; in our car were women, many of them the prisoners from Auschwitz, who were all strangers to each other. Yet as the cold became even more bitter, the darkness complete, individual women began to move toward each other, seeking the warmth of another body.

The four of us moved even closer together. "I can't stand this much longer," Lily whispered to me. "It's so dark. It's so terribly dark! And I'm cold! I'm cold! Oh, I'm so cold!" She was shivering violently, her whole body convulsing.

"I'll try and warm you a little," I said, putting my arms around her. Esther and Ellen leaned against our legs, their feet curled under them. If we could have crawled inside each other's bodies we would have done so. In the morning all of the hundred women had crept so close together that half the car was empty.

For six days and six nights we counted the coming and going of the light in the roof opening. The door was never opened. At the beginning of the seventh day a guard knocked on the side of the car. *"Ist der Tote?"* (Are there any dead?) she asked. We looked around. Here a woman sat with head fallen to one side, mouth hanging open; there a woman lay pressed against the side of the car, legs bent backward. *"Der sind Tote,"* I called back. The door was unbolted, opened, the dead shoved out into a cart sitting beside the tracks. The fresh air blew in, pouring over us like a cool draft of water. As we traveled into a warmer climate the air inside our sealed cars had become thick and rancid. The SS guard returned with a box of dry bread and handed each of us a piece—our first food in six days. Then she picked up our toilet pails, which had barely anything in them; if you are not fed you do not need to eliminate.

"Who wants to get some water in these pails?" she asked.

I volunteered, wanting desperately to get out of the car for a while.

"No, no, don't leave me . . ." Lily cried, her eyes welling with tears.

"I'll come right back," I said. "I promise."

Another woman and I stumbled down the steps to a faucet in the station. We filled the bucket only half full, knowing we could not carry more, and dragged it back to the train. However, we could not lift it up into the car. As I was struggling with it, I spotted three frozen potatoes lying under the train, set the bucket down, grabbed the potatoes, and called to Esther, "Take these, quickly!" Finally, with the help of three other women, I lifted the bucket into the car. "Well, where are the potatoes?" I asked Esther as soon as I was sitting again.

Someone else had grabbed them. The door was closed, bolted. The next morning we began to move again for the first time after sitting for three days on a side rail.

As the heat, the stale air, pressed in upon us over the following eight days, the women fought for the absence of bodily contact as fervently as they had once sought it. We took off our raincoats and our dresses and sat in our thin undershirts, almost naked, but nothing helped. In the daytime the light coming from the skylight made possible a distancing and we carefully avoided touching each other. The presence of light served as well to chase away the demons that came to torment us in the cars where we remained day after day after day. The nights, however, became infinitely long nightmares.

"Ahhhhiieeeeee . . ." a woman would scream as the skylight grew black. Another would take up the wild cry and then another, the screams bouncing back and forth on the walls of the car as we moved through the dark countryside or stood on a lonely platform. When the screeching began to die, the sobbing to become less hysterical, a sharp whack sounded as a woman struck out at the unknown arm or leg that dared to touch hers.

"Oh! Oh! No! Oh! Noooooooo . . ." a voice would howl. The crying would resume again, beginning in loud, forlorn sobs and gradually lessening to a prolonged weeping like that of a child taken from her mother. Often one of the women from Auschwitz attacked a Hungarian girl, pounding at her with her fists. These women had come into our camp well fed and still had strength. When one Hungarian girl was attacked in this way she often cried out, "Seren! Seren! Help me! Seren . . ." I had translated for her in the camp, saving her from a beating, and she thought I could save her again, but I was so weak myself that I could not help her.

On the tenth night as we were sitting back to back, Lily by my side and a Hungarian girl leaning on my back, I began to hurt from the pressure of her against me. She weighed very little, each of us by now so thin that almost all the flesh was wasted away. We often sat with our hands under our buttocks to ease the pressure on the upper thigh bones protruding from our skin. I knew that this Hungarian girl leaned her back against mine because she was too weak to sit up in any other way, but I could not bear even her slight weight upon me. Finally I said, "Please don't lean against me."

She did not move; she could not. After a little while I asked again, "Could you not lean against me? It hurts me so." Still she did not move. Finally I decided, *I'll have to give her a little shove.* I raised my arm. It fell to the floor like a lead weight before I could touch her.

Thus I could not help the Hungarian girls who were abused mercilessly by the Polish women, hardened and bitter after having been in Auschwitz for so long. They asked repeatedly, "When were you taken to Ravensbrück?"

"In the fall of 1944," I answered.

"That is nothing! We have been in Auschwitz since 1940." Then they struck out at the Hungarian girls, who did not understand Yiddish. Perhaps because I understood the language they did not harm me. However, they taunted me unceasingly. Finally one day when one of them said for the hundredth time, "Your time in Ravensbrück was nothing compared to mine in Auschwitz!" I answered, "Was it my fault that you were in a camp for so long?" After that they left me alone, and Esther, Ellen, and Lily as well.

By the eleventh night the number of women in our car was less than half the original hundred. A guard had knocked on our door several more times, asking only after the dead. The toilet buckets were removed as well. The last bits of straw had been eaten several days ago. On this night the SS women did not come near the car. We were parked on a side rail as we had been for the past three days, never moving, and the women's screams seemed to have reached an even greater intensity. The hunger gnawing at our flesh was eating at our sanity as well. Suddenly the door was unlocked and thrown open. Two men wearing the Wehrmacht uniform stood at the door, staring.

"Jesus Christ!" one of them said.

The other said nothing, turning abruptly and walking away. In a few minutes he was back with an armful of turnips. He flung them into the car and closed the door again. Quickly I reached out and grabbed a large one that had landed near my feet. It seemed to weigh far more than a turnip normally did, until I remembered that I was weak. Esther took hold of one end and I the other and we broke it in two and then in four pieces. I put Lily's portion in her hand and began to chew on mine. She ignored it, continuing to lean against my shoulders, her eyes closed.

"Eat, Lily," I said. "Someone will take your piece away from you if you don't."

Still she sat, not moving, saying nothing. I shook her. "Lily! Wake up! I have a piece of turnip for you."

At last she sat up slowly and opened her eyes. "You can have it," she said.

"No, Lily! It's for you. Now eat it!"

"I don't want it . . . I am so tired . . . I don't know . . ."

"What, Lily? What don't you know?"

"I don't know if I can go on any longer. The screams . . . and I am so terribly tired. I can't see anything . . . I don't think I can make it."

"Lily, Lily . . . You can make it! You have to! You have to make up your mind that you will make it."

"I don't know if I can anymore . . ."

"You can't if you don't eat. Now eat this piece of turnip. I promised your mother I would look after you. Eat it for me. Please, Lily."

She took the turnip and held it to her mouth, nibbling on it slightly. When she fell asleep, her head in my lap, it was still in her hand. I took it from her and hid it in my pocket to give back to her later.

The next morning, the twelfth day, she looked so pale and lifeless that I picked up her frail, sleeping body and cradled her in my lap. Her skin was translucent in the soft light coming from the opening in the roof, the deep shadows under her cheekbones almost invisible, eyelashes spreading across her face in delicate fans. She woke up, blinking once or twice, and looked at me for a long time, her large, dark eyes filling with tears. Finally she said, "I'm not going to live anymore, Seren." Before I could answer she put her head on my breast and died.

Two hours later the Red Cross opened up the cars and gave us soup.

On the fourteenth day, two days after Lily died, the train reached Turkheim. The locked cars were opened and we climbed down from them at last. Those who had died during the past few days were still in the car, heaped in a corner. I had by now cried all I could for Lily, the tears washing down my face and soaking my dress until I was exhausted. Lily's death was equally painful for Esther and Ellen. The four of us together had seemed indestructible.

With quick glances we looked one last time at the bodies in the corner, their faces to the end wall as if the rows of backs, of shorn heads, would give them anonymity. It was futile. I knew exactly where Lily lay—on the bottom, next to the right wall, one foot curved slightly outward. "Lily! Lily! . . ." I cried one last time, only my heart speaking, and hurried down the steps, grasping Ellen's and Esther's hands.

Twenty-two

ON THE PLATFORM BESIDE THE TRAIN WE LINED UP again for counting, numbering less than two hundred; for over three hundred women the thin fiber of hope, frayed thread by thread during the long months in Ravensbrück, became even more tattered in the locked cars, until the last shabby strand snapped, and they died. The Red Cross had fed us, but they were not our rescuers. They'd given us hope, but it was a false hope. We had been brought to a camp called Turkheim, a small section of the larger camp, Dachau. As we stumbled from the train platform, we passed through a gate and a long corridor lined on both side by high fences edged with barbed wire. Several men were on the other side of the fence, the first we had seen since leaving Budapest. They looked healthy and were dressed in work pants and jackets. I wondered if they were German civilians come to stare at us. However, on second glance I knew them to be Jewish men.

Then I noticed a peculiar thing. The women walking ahead of me kept stopping and half turning back, raising an outstretched arm in my direction. As I drew near to where a man was standing on the other side of the fence, I heard one ask, "Do you know Seren Tuvel? Is she with you? . . . Seren Tuvel—is she here?"

"Yes," the woman a few yards ahead of me answered. "She's right behind me."

When I reached the man who was asking for me, I knew immediately who it was. "Joseph!" I said, stopping opposite him.

"Seren?" he asked. "Are you Seren Tuvel?"

"Yes! Don't you recognize me?"

His eyes looked blank. In an instant I was outside my body, looking at myself as he must have seen me: a skeleton with a few patches of hair on her skull, clothed in scraps of rags, bits of skin still clinging to the frame. When we removed our coats and dresses in the sweltering cars, we had nothing between us and the sides and floor but a thin undershirt. As day after day passed and we were not fed, our bodies began to devour themselves, the flesh to disappear, the skin to chafe between the pressures of the bones on the inside and the hard surfaces on the outside. The knuckles on my hands were rubbed raw, dirty skin curling around the ridges, my ankles also raw. The white of bone showed on my lower legs. My buttocks were nothing but bones protruding through the skin. Where the skin was not gone, it separated from the bone, puffing up in bubbles.

I spoke to him again. "You're Joseph, Herman and Tamara's son. You called out to me one night near Budapest. I am Seren! And this is Esther beside me."

"Yes, I see . . ." he answered slowly, as if he were speaking in a dream. Then he pushed a chunk of bread through the holes in the fence. "Here, I brought this for you."

"Ah, Joseph, you never forget me. How did you know I was coming?"

"We heard that a group of Hungarian women was being brought into the camp today. I knew you left Budapest with some women last August. I also knew you would still be alive."

The guards were ordering us to move forward.

"I'll come back later!" he called as we moved away.

We passed through the corridor and came into a huge yard. I saw no barracks, only low flat roofs almost level with the ground. We were taken to one of these cellarlike buildings, descending the steps to an underground bunker. "Over there!" an SS guard, a man, commanded; the SS women guards had left us once our train arrived at the camp. The guard was pointing to a far corner of the room, where two rows of wood planks stretched out on the dirt floor. On the other side of the room a group of Jewish women were edging into the opposite corner. As we began moving toward the planks several of them cried, "My God! Who are they?"

We were given some blankets and then the SS guards left. I stretched out between Esther and Ellen, glancing at these women on the other side of the room. Like Joseph, they were dressed in warm, clean jackets and trousers, with no holes or rips in them. They looked so healthy! Some of the women had rolled up the sleeves of their jackets, exposing thick arms, firm muscles. Their faces were full, without deep hollows, without the cheekbones almost cutting through the skin. As they continued to stare at us, shuddering, crowding further into their corner, a woman with a red kerchief tied around her hair finally called out to us, "Where are you from?"

"Ravensbrück," one of our group answered in a listless voice.

"Have you heard of it?" the same woman asked another in her group.

"No. Wherever it is, they must not have fed them," the second woman answered.

"Do you go out to work here?" a woman from our side asked.

"Yes," the woman with the red kerchief answered. "We go out each morning to the farms around here and work in the fields."

"Are you fed there?"

"Oh, yes. The farm wives feed us well. We have bread and meat and potatoes every noon and all the milk we want. At night we have another meal."

A low moan began on our side of the room, swelled, rose up with one voice as we pictured the hot food, the heaping bowls of potatoes, the plates of meat still simmering in their juices, the pitcher of milk, tall and cool, drops of moisture collecting on the sides.

Suddenly the planks beneath us began to tremble. In another instant the entire room, the very ground, was shaking, deep, low explosions thundering all around us. *This is why we're in bunkers,* I realized. I grabbed Esther's hand before she began to scream. She burrowed into one side of me, Ellen crawled close on the other, and we lay facedown, waiting out the bombing. As we lay still I kept thinking, *If only we can work at the farms! If only we can work at the farms!* I barely heard the roaring as I imagined eating and eating until I could eat no more. After about an hour had passed the bombing stopped. Several of the women from our group left the bunker to wander outside in the early-evening light in search of something to eat—straw, grass, a bit of rotten potato. As I still had the chunk of bread from Joseph, the three of us stayed inside, divided the bread and chewed it slowly, savoring our first food in days. Then one of the women came down the steps and called, "Seren. A man is asking for you by the fence."

"It's my nephew Joseph. I'll be right there," I answered. I began to put on my shoes but Esther and Ellen grabbed hold of me, Esther clinging to the hem of my dress and Ellen to a foot. "It's all right," I said. "I'll be back in a few minutes. I promise. Maybe he'll even have more food for us." They let go and I dragged myself up the steps and to the fence.

"I brought some more bread," he said when I arrived. "Is there anything else you need, anything I can get for you?"

"My toe drains all the time. Part of it had to be cut off. I can barely stand to wear my shoes. Could you get some bandages?"

"There are some in my barracks. Will you wait here while I go and get them?" he asked.

"Where would I go?" I laughed. He looked at the ground, his hands sliding into his pockets. Then he turned, taking off at a run, vigorous like his mother, Tamara.

Joseph was back in several minutes with a handful of bandages which he gave me. "I can't stay long," he said. "A guard might see us and keep me from coming back."

"Do you work on the farms too, Joseph?" I asked. "You look so good!"

"Yes, we eat only breakfast here. We're given dinner and supper on the farm."

"Do you think we'll work there too?"

"I don't know." He let his eyes rest briefly on the raw knuckles of the hand holding the bandages. "I hope so . . . I have to go now. I'll be back whenever I can."

The next morning thin broth and dry crusts of bread were brought to us in our bunker. No one beat us awake, no one ordered us to line up for counting, no one formed a work detail and marched us to the farms. The women on the other side of the bunker ate their meal hurriedly, as if they could not endure being near our filth and lice for a minute longer than necessary, and hurried up the stairs to the outside. Several women from our group also climbed the stairs. As soon as they opened the door we heard a man shout, "Go back! Go back!"

"But we want to work on the farms . . ." a woman answered.

"Go back!"

The women descended the stairs, fell to the floor, buried their heads in their arms, and wept.

I DO NOT KNOW EXACTLY HOW THE NEXT FIVE OR SIX weeks passed. As we realized that we were to be kept in a hole in the earth, kept from any opportunities of obtaining extra food, kept hidden away like half-crazed creatures while the bombs fell and fell, the days and nights began to spill over into each other, blend, come and go haphazardly. Sometimes I was positive that it was morning, that I had slept through the night despite the bombs exploding above us. When I looked up, however, the women who went out to work were still sleeping. Either I had slept through a night and the entire next day or I had been asleep for only a few hours; I could never be sure which it was. Sometimes I went to sleep with the question: Why do they keep us here when we could still work? Seemingly days later the answer would almost come. Then I would lapse into a half-sleep and a few hours later ask the same question, as if I had thought of it anew.

If the bombing ceased temporarily we could go outside and walk around in the yard of the camp. Once in a while Esther, Ellen, and I did this, searching for a sliver of carrot or a potato peel buried in the dirt. Several times Joseph came to the fence in the evening and asked for me. He always came bearing food, whatever he had been able to hide in his clothes. But many times his group worked until late in the night and he could not come at all.

Then one night he came to say good-bye. Perhaps it was the middle of March by this time. The weather was turning warmer. "I'm not coming back tomorrow," he said that night.

"Are you being let go?" I asked quickly.

"No, but the war will end very soon. I'm sure of it. The farmer I work for has agreed to hide me in a shed until it does. It's only a matter of days, weeks, until it's over."

"Why will he hide you?"

"The Germans know that they're losing. When the war's over they will be punished for their crimes against us. He's hiding me to make himself look as if he sympathizes with us. He's been better than some, though. I should let him hide me, don't you think?"

"Of course! Joseph, do you know why we aren't taken out to work too?"

He looked quickly away. Slowly he brought his eyes back to mine. "You would come in contact with the German citizens if you worked on the farms. They believe that throughout the war all Jews have been given what I am given now—good clothes, good food, a clean bed. If the SS allowed them to see you and the other women, then the civilians would know the truth. Bones don't stick out of people who are given enough to eat."

"So we are kept hidden away, like in Ravensbrück. We saw no one from the outside there. Here we see no one either. It's this isolation that's killing us."

"Yes . . . but it will be all over soon. You must believe that, Seren! I'm pretty sure that this camp will be evacuated in a few more days. You must not give up hope!"

"Don't worry! I'm going to live! If I make it on nothing but sheer willpower alone, I will live. I have to see how it all ends. I'll be here on the day when it's finally over. Maybe not the day after—but on that day I'll be alive."

He handed me some more bandages and a penknife. "Whatever happens, take these and use them. I think you'll need them. Wherever they take you, it will be by foot. I'll come and find you when it's over," he said again as he began to walk away. "I promise."

EARLY ONE MORNING SEVERAL DAYS LATER AN SS guard tramped down the stairs and announced, "This camp is being evacuated. You are being transferred to another camp. Be ready to begin walking in half an hour."

As we began to heave ourselves up from the floor, to put on our shoes, wondering where we would summon up the strength to walk for days as we had during labor camp when we were strong and healthy, one of the women from our group came in from the outside. She hurried down the steps, walked over to another woman standing close to me, and whispered something in her ear. The two of them immediately hobbled up the steps as fast as they could. Although I had not heard all they had whispered, I had heard the one word that sent me up the stairs right after them—"potato." I followed the two women outside, hearing Esther and Ellen calling up from the basement, "Seren! Come back! Seren . . ." but continuing after the women anyway. I fast-shuffled across the yard to a food cellar which someone had discovered was full of potatoes. It had very small windows, not over a foot wide.

One of the women began to smash in a window with her foot and in another instant I was also kicking, using the bottom of my wooden clogs. As soon as the glass was broken out, I dived through it, determined to be the first one in the cellar, and scrambled onto a whole pile of potatoes. The other women—there were by now twenty or thirty who had heard of the discovery—fell in after me. Like lunatics we began stuffing potatoes up our sleeves, in our coat pockets, down the fronts of our dresses. When the bosom of my dress was so full of potatoes that I looked as if I had sprouted enormous bulges, I climbed out of the window again, wiggling through sideways. My feet had become so skinny that a shoe fell off as I crawled out and it landed inside the cellar. As a guard was running toward the cellar, I stood up, heaved up my bosom with both arms, and hurried back to the bunker, bobbing up and down with one shoe on, one shoe off.

When I reached the bunker the three of us divided the potatoes, distributing them equally among our bosoms. After we were outside, forming lines to leave the camp, I whispered to Esther and Ellen, "Don't worry! Don't say anything! I'm going back to the bunker to see if I can find another shoe."

"No, don't go!" Esther said, grabbing my arm. "You're always running off. Please stay with me!"

"I can't walk with only one shoe! I'll be right back."

Breaking loose from her grasp, I ducked down the stairs when no one was looking and scanned the floor quickly. There in the corner of the bunker was a leather, laced shoe. I limped over and picked it up. It was for my right foot, the foot that already had a shoe. I slipped it on my left foot nonetheless and clambered back up the stairs, rejoining Esther and Ellen. Locking hands, we slowly began shuffling out through the gates of Turkheim and into chaos.

Thousands of Germans were fleeing, running away from a country that was disintegrating around them. We saw soldiers who had lost their guns headed toward Switzerland, saw wounded soldiers making their way as slowly as we, crutches sometimes falling from beneath their arms as they stumbled on the loose rocks; saw fathers pushing small red carts heaped up with pillows and comforters, a rocking chair tied on one end, as mother and small children followed closely behind. As the Allied armies advanced, civilians were leaving their homes, beds unmade, dirty dishes piled in the sink, the front door open, and were taking to the roads leading out of Germany, fearing for their lives.

Although we did not understand it at the time, the SS was even more anxious to outdistance the advancing armies than were the ordinary Germans. They were still trying to eliminate those of us, only a hundred or so women out of the original ten thousand, who had refused to die. By this time we were too weak and too ill to want to be let go; there was no place to go. We needed food. We needed care. Who would give these to us? We wanted only one thing: the end of the war. We lived for that day—nothing more.

Sometime near the middle of April we reached Burgau, another small camp located in the middle of grassy fields, crops of grain planted all around. The perimeters of the camp were marked by tall electric fences, at each corner a cubicle and a guard, his rifle aimed down into the enclosed area. Inside this fenced-in yard were freshly painted gray buildings with windows clean and sparkling and rows of bunk beds, their images shimmering on the shiny floors. The odor of soap and hot, sudsy water emanated from the doorsills and windowsills, from the bedsteads, from the walls. Again I realized how the concentration camps could vary immensely. If the camp was hidden away in a dark forest, like Ravensbrück, it was no more than a filthy, cold cave, while those camps out in the open, like Burgau, shone full of light, as immaculate as the kitchens of the hausfraus.

The camp was deserted. We filed into the empty rooms quietly and sank down on the hard beds. Those of us who had survived the walk, less than eighty women, were exhausted from the effort of dragging our ragged selves along with nothing to sustain us. It had been weeks since we were given any food, the one meal a day gradually diminishing to nothing at all. Esther, Ellen, and I tried to ration the potatoes I had grabbed, allowing ourselves one every day. When they were gone, two days after we arrived at Burgau, we went out into the yard to look for scraps.

When we came outside, the area around the building seemed different—rougher than I had remembered from the day we'd arrived. "Something's changed," I said. "I can't tell what it is."

"The grass is gone!" Ellen answered. "I'm sure there was grass all around here. Now the ground is all chopped up."

As we rounded a corner of the building we came upon a woman crawling over the dirt on her hands and knees, head down, spoon clutched in one hand. She came to a large board, and after a few, futile attempts, managed to move it, exposing some yellowed grass. With a grunt she began digging at the ground with her spoon, tearing at the roots, cutting them out of the soil. As soon as she had a clump loose, she shook it briefly to let the dirt fall and then shoved the grass into her mouth, roots and all, chewing contentedly.

For a minute we stared at her. In another minute we were also on our hands and knees, looking for hidden grass. Do you know how delicious even the simplest meal tastes when you are genuinely hungry? That's how the grass tasted that day. Several days later anything that resembled grass was

gone—the pale white shoots coming up under rocks, the soft roots of this-
tles, the tender interior of young trees.

Esther was growing weaker, the bones below her waist no more than
thin white lines poking out from her protruding hipbones. She spent most
of the time lying on the bed. If I decided to go outside she immediately noticed that I was putting on my shoes. "Don't go," she begged. "Your toe will
just hurt more if you put your shoes on. Stay here with me . . ."

"Ellen will stay with you, won't you, Ellen?" I would answer, continuing to put on my shoes.

Ellen did not want me to leave either, but she usually answered, "I'll
stay—if you come right back."

"Why are you always afraid I'll leave you? I would leave my sister and
my best, true friend? Is that what you think?"

"No, no," Ellen answered. "I don't think that . . . It's just . . ."

Neither of them had recovered from Lily's death, nor had I. I knew this
was at the base of their fears. Reassuring them one more time, I went outside, spoon in hand.

As I was on my way to a far corner of the yard one day, ready to dig up
worms if I found no new shoots, I passed a window in one of the barracks.
Suddenly I jumped back, terrified, the blood pounding so hard in my light
head that I thought I would faint. An old, wrinkled crone was peering at
me out of eyes sunk deep into the sockets—a bony ghost come to call.
Quickly I looked behind me to see who she was, this head on a stick, frightening me more than anything I had ever seen. No one was there. I looked
back at the window. *It's me,* I realized. *The ghost is me. I've become an old woman
. . .* The last time I had looked into a mirror was the morning I left Budapest as a young woman; now an eighty-year-old looked back at me. *Forget what you saw!* I told myself, and walked on. Thereafter each time I passed
a window I looked the other way.

One warm spring day the three of us were outside, sitting on a step in
front of the barracks, trying not to talk about food but unable to stop ourselves. "Do you remember when we dug out the raisins from Mama's rolls
and hid them under our plates?" I was asking Esther. "How could we have
done such a thing?"

"That was long ago . . ." she answered. Before she could continue, a series of thuds sounded nearby. Something was being thrown over the back fence and landing in the yard.

"Potatoes!" someone began to scream. "It's raining potatoes!"

I hobbled to the fence. On the other side were farmers, baskets at their feet, throwing potato after potato. As soon as one hit the ground three or four women dived for it. If one managed to grab it, another snatched it away and still a third clawed it away from her. I wanted no part of it. It seemed strange that these farmers had come to help us at last. One of them must have caught a glimpse of our skeletal bodies and realized that what he thought were only rumors spread by the enemy were true after all. Then an SS supervisor ran to the tower near us and yelled, "Shoot them! Shoot them!" The guards in the tower opened fire on the farmers, who ran through the fields, leaving the baskets sitting in the dirt.

When all was quiet again, another supervisor walked up to the one who had ordered the shooting. "Why did those stupid farmers do a thing like that?" he asked.

"It's Easter," the first man replied.

THE WARM APRIL LAGGED. WE SAT IN THE SUN, HANDS beneath our buttocks, coats off, our legs stretched out before us like two slivers of bleached wood. Once in a while we were given a dry crust of bread, once a half-cooked potato. Or we lay on our beds resting, almost too weak to move. I passed the time observing the other women, picturing each one as she would look with flesh on her bones, a head of hair, a lovely dress.

One morning a guard came to the barracks and told us that we were evacuating this camp also. As he turned to leave the room another guard came up to him and said, "We have to hurry! Today's the twenty-fifth. They want them by the first of May."

When they left the room Esther turned to me. "It's your birthday!" she said.

"I haven't even thought about it coming," I answered. "There isn't much to celebrate, is there?"

"Well, you are still alive," said Ellen. "That's something."

"Yes, it is," I said.

"Listen!" Esther exclaimed. "Do you hear that? What is it?"

A rat-a-tat-tat was sounding in the far distance. It stopped and then began again.

"Those are machine guns!" I said. "The Allies must be so close that you can hear them!"

"How do you know they are the Allies?" Esther asked. "It might be the Germans."

"The Germans wouldn't shoot machine guns at their own people! No, those are Allied guns. The war will be over any day now. I know it!"

We left Burgau, walking to a station where a long train of cars stretched for half a mile down the tracks. We were ordered to board it. "Oh, God, no!" I cried as the guards pushed us toward it. "Not another train! We are so close to being free!"

The butt of a rifle hit me hard in the back. I climbed up the steps into the open car, pulling Esther and Ellen with me. They packed the eighty of us who were left into one car and locked it. On both sides of us were other cars also filled with prisoners, all men. The doors were bolted, the interlocking of each car completed as the train began to move forward, the motion traveling down its length in a series of clicks and jolts.

It was the worst time of all; it was a time without hope. Each day, each night stretched to the boundaries of finiteness, broke through, eased out into the vast regions of space where time circles in upon itself, cycling around and around. The train went back and forth, back and forth over the same rails. Small English planes flew not far above our open car, their machine guns pocking the earth on both sides of us. American bombers droned high overhead, blackening the sky. We were in the very thick of the war, caught on every side. I did not think we would ever get off that train alive. The cars were opened each night to take out those who had died from despair. By the fourth day there were no more than twenty women still alive.

On the fourth day, April 29, 1945, the train pulled into a little village and stopped. I peered out of a crack in the side of the car and looked up and down the train. Three cars in front of us was the engine, parked near the station of Schwabhausen. Stretching back of our car were seven or eight more cars, some open at the top and some closed. Across from us was a field and beyond that a forest. Then I saw a Red Cross truck pull into the station. In another minute several men from the truck were coming toward us with crates of bread.

"Oh, girls!" I cried. "We're going to get some food!" The three of us were sitting by the door. I had taken off my shoes, as my toe still drained continually, and began to put them on. Whenever I had my shoes on Esther and Ellen grabbed hold of my coat; they knew I planned to go somewhere and they did not want to be left behind. They held on to me now, one on each side. A Red Cross official came up to our car and ordered it to be unlocked. In another minute an SS guard began to slide the door open. Then, when he had pushed it open only eight or nine inches, an air-raid siren in the station began to scream. It rose up high, higher, shrieking in our ears. *Why does there have to be bombing now!* I thought, so exasperated that we were not going to get food that I did not realize how close the bombing was. The SS men and Red Cross officials all ran for cover, leaving us in the locked cars. Esther and Ellen let go of me, covering their ears against the siren's wail.

Then I happened to look at the ground outside our car. There, right below me, was a chunk of bread which the Red Cross attendant must have dropped as he ran. *I'm not going to tell the girls,* I decided as I eased toward the opening, *but I'm going to get that bread!* In another instant I had slid through the opening and was on the ground, reaching for the bread.

A noise suddenly came up from behind me, a monstrous roaring. I glanced quickly over my shoulder. Hundreds of English planes were flying very low, sweeping along the length of the train, their guns firing. I could clearly see the soldiers in the planes take aim at the train with their machine guns and fire at the prisoners in the open cars. Before they could shoot me I rolled beneath the train. *I have come so far!* I thought. *To die like this!*

Miraculously, I survived. The planes flew on. We ran again, to the front of the train. I crawled in to make sure there was no one hiding inside. It was empty except for a blanket, which I instinctively carried outside. I gave it to the girls and then decided to explore inside the remaining cars. Esther begged me not to go, but I had to . . . All I could think of was food. Surely there would be something—a potato, a scrap of bread—that had been left behind. I limped off, closing my ears. Just a few minutes later I heard the planes return. I tried to run, but I wasn't fast enough. I was horrified as I watched the bombs fall. As I saw one of the soldiers aim his rifle at Esther.

God forgive me! I thought. *How could I have left them for a piece of bread?* Esther had been leaning against the side of the car when the bomb hit, and the car had exploded into her back. In every other bombing we had been through I had ordered: "Cover your head. Get low. Lie flat." This time I was not with her, so she had remained upright, her back leaning against the metal. Ellen must have remembered my warnings; she was unharmed.

Ellen brought the blanket and we spread it on the embankment next to the train and moved Esther to it.

"There's a bullet sticking out of her head!" Ellen cried.

"I see it," I answered, spotting a round shaft of metal protruding from the upper left side of her skull.

While Esther was still in shock I plucked the bullet from her head and threw it as far as I could. Next I removed the thick, long splinters of metal from her back with my fingers. Then I took the penknife Joseph had given me and began to cut out the smaller ones. Some of them were very thin but longer than a darning needle, and I had to cut deep. When the blood began to flow even more profusely I tore off pieces of cloth from my shirt and handed them to Ellen. "I'll cut! You wipe!" I instructed. I continued to cut and Ellen to wipe away the blood until I had removed as many splinters as I could see. We took the few shreds of my shirt that were left, wrapped Esther's back, and folded the blanket around her. Rain was beginning to fall.

Twenty-three

SUDDENLY I BECAME AWARE AGAIN OF THE SCREAMS coming from the other cars, from the embankment, from the grassy slopes beside the train. I looked up. Winged skeletons with rounded skulls were drifting across the field through the falling rain, wild cries coming from the open holes of their mouths. The men prisoners who were still alive had draped blankets over their heads and were moving toward the dark forests. For a moment I was swallowed up by the eerie cries, merged with the graying sky, with the water pouring down upon me, with Esther still moaning at my feet, with the dead sprawled inside the locked cars as they fell, one on top of the other. Blood kept running from the cars, trickling over my feet and down the slope, mingling with the rain.

Then the field was empty, the ghosts vanished. I looked around, blinking rapidly as if I had just awakened from a deep sleep. Coming from the station, which had not been damaged, were three or four SS guards, heading toward the train.

"Come!" I said to Esther. "We must get away from the train. We'll help you."

Somehow Ellen and I pulled her up and dragged her down the embankment and across the field to a space under some pines at the edge of the forest. As we were putting her down on a bed of pine needles two of the guards caught up with us, having followed us across the field. One removed his gun from its holster. "Back to the car!" he ordered.

I looked at him, looked back at Esther, at the train still oozing blood, and decided that I had had enough. I was not going to follow one more order. "I am not going anywhere!" I said. "Here is my sister. She is terribly wounded. She cannot go back on that train with all those dead people. And I won't leave her."

"Back on the train!" he repeated, raising his gun to the height of my chest.

"You can shoot me if you want, but I won't go back."

He glared at me, raising the gun even higher, now aimed at my head. I continued to look at him, straight down the barrel. The gun began to waver, veering to the right and then to the left. Finally he lowered it and began to walk away, the second guard close behind him. When they reached the train they climbed in, the engine beginning to tow the cars full of dead into the distant fog.

When this train was gone a second train, parked directly behind ours, was noticed by some of the prisoners hiding in the forest. Several men crept toward it and broke into the cars, discovering that they were full of canned goods. "Food! Food!" they cried. They began throwing cans down to other prisoners standing at the bottom of the embankment. When one can rolled down ten men jumped on it. While they were all fighting over the can, five or six other cans were rolling by their feet.

I stared at the prisoners, at the blankets flopping from their heads as they ran to and fro from one rolling can to another, wondering how I could get some of this food. Deciding to stand where most of the cans rolled down, I edged toward the train, standing there for only a minute. Two cans rolled to my feet. I slipped them inside the front of my dress and hurried back to Ellen and Esther.

"I have two cans!" I cried. "Two whole cans!"

"What's in them?" Ellen cried. "Oh, what do you suppose it is?"

I glanced at the large, heavy cans. The printing on them was in a language I did not know; later I found out it was English. "I don't know," I answered. "I don't even know how to open a sealed can. Oh, who knows what may be inside them!"

I turned one can over and over, around and around. For five or ten minutes I struggled with the cans, trying to pierce them with my knife. All of the prepared food we ate at home and in Budapest had been in jars sealed with a lid. These metal cans were strange, lidless. As I was banging on one of them with a rock, almost smashing it entirely, a prisoner with a blanket over his head came up to me and said, "I see you have two cans."

"Yes," I answered. "But I can't open them."

"I'll tell you what," he said. "If you give me one of those cans I'll show you how to open the other one."

One open can was better than none, I thought. "Show me how to open it," I answered, giving him one can.

He plucked a metal key from the bottom of the can, stuck it on the edge of a strip near the top, and began to wind up the strip. Like magic, the can was opened.

"You're a genius!" I said. "An absolute genius!"

"Thank you," he answered, and drifted off down the slope, his blanket flapping behind him.

"What's in the can?" Ellen demanded. "What's in it?"

"It looks like milk!" I cried.

Slowly I raised the can to my lips and tipped it slightly. Warm, sweet milk flowed into my mouth, eased down my throat. I gulped another mouthful and then handed it to Ellen. She held the can to her mouth, drank long and deep. Then we propped up Esther and dribbled some into her mouth, a little at a time, until she had had her share. Back and forth the can went among the three of us until it was drained. Then I took out the chunk of bread I had grabbed just before the bombing started and broke it into three pieces. It was our first real meal in months. I felt refreshed, renewed. All the thoughts of dying that had raced through my head as I lay beneath the exploding train vanished. I had some milk and bread in me; I wanted to live!

The question now was where to go where patrolling SS guards would not find us. It was beginning to rain harder, the drops falling through the trees above us and splashing on our heads. In the countryside lights were coming on in farmhouses, twinkling in the gathering dusk. Ellen and I sat under the dripping trees, Esther lying between us, and watched the lights flicker there and there and there. When I saw a light come on in a house a few hundred meters away, I decided to go on another foraging expedition; the milk and bread had revived me, reminding me what it was like to eat again, and I wanted more food for us.

I began walking toward the light. As I reached the house a large collie dog ran out of the yard toward me. *What if he bites me?* I thought. Then the dog stopped a few meters away from me, looked up at my hollow face, put his tail between his hind legs and whimpered. Slowly he turned and slunk away, still whining.

I knocked on the door. An old woman opened it. "Could I please have something to eat?" I asked. She stared at me for a minute or two, looking at my face, at the raw patches on my hands, and let her eyes travel down the blistered, loose skin on my legs, the bones now fully exposed on my feet. Her eyes moved back up again in the same slow manner. When they reached my neck she pulled them away before she would have to look into my eyes, turned and walked away, leaving me in the open door. In another minute she returned and handed me a plate full of greasy pork bones. Without a word she turned and closed the door. I hurried back to Esther and Ellen.

"I got some bones," I said, "but they're pork."

"Pork? But how can we eat that? Won't it make us sick?" Esther asked.

"Even pork is better than nothing," I answered her. "I'm not going to worry about getting sick now. I'll worry about that later."

Ellen, seeing me chew on a bone, took one also. As we ate we broke off small slivers of meat and fed them to Esther. I cannot imagine why we did not become violently ill from eating that greasy pork, especially as we had just drunk all that milk, but we did not.

By now the sky was black and I decided that it was safe to move out from under the trees. Earlier I had noticed a building next to the house I visited. In Europe barns frequently are used only to shelter the animals, while hay is kept in a different building so that if the hay catches fire the animals will not be harmed. It was likely that this building stored hay. The time had come. Ellen and I dragged Esther over the wet field to the building. The large front door was padlocked. What would we do now? Then I heard the rustling of hay and soft whispers drifting through the crack in the door. There must be another way in, I decided, and started around the side of the building, feeling my way along the boards with my fingers. I came to an opening where two boards were missing.

"I'll squeeze in first and then take Esther from you," I told Ellen as I started inside. However, someone just inside the door quickly blocked my path. *He's probably frightened. He doesn't know who I am,* I thought, and began to speak to him in Yiddish. "Please let us in," I said.

"I can't," he replied, also in Yiddish. "There's no room."

"You've got to let us in!"

I realized that this is where all the other prisoners, the men, had gone when they disappeared. "You have to let us in," I repeated. "I'm here with my sister. She's been shot. And it's raining. Now let us in!"

"Where would you go if I let you in? I mean it when I say there's no room."

"I'll find somewhere. You don't need to worry about that. Just let us in. I won't go away until you do!"

With a sigh he moved away from the opening. The three of us crawled in. The man had not been lying; everywhere I looked were men stretched out on the floor. At first I could not distinguish them, but gradually my eyes became accustomed to the darkness and I saw the white faces, the bony skulls sticking out from the hay. Carefully we made our way over them to the far end of the barn and found an empty space next to the wall. We eased down, scattered some hay over us, and leaned back against the wall. We had no bed and we were not very warm, but we were out of the train, out of the rain, out of the camps.

Then I heard footsteps on the other side of the wall. A man called to us through a knothole, "Is anyone there?" He spoke in Hungarian and was obviously another prisoner.

"Yes," I answered, also in Hungarian.

"Where did you get in?" he asked.

"We came in through the side but I don't think you can get in too. It's very crowded in here. A man is standing by the opening to keep any more from coming in."

"All right. I'll try to find somewhere else to spend the night."

"Wait!" I called. "Do you have any food?" After so long without food I could not get enough of it.

"No," he answered, "but I do have a bottle of whiskey. I found it in a farmhouse."

"I would love to have some for my sister. She's wounded. If I put my cup next to the knothole, will you fill it?"

"Certainly. Just hold it up."

I did; he filled it and then went on his way. I gave a sip to Esther, drank a little myself, and handed the cup to Ellen.

"I've never had whiskey before," she said. "I don't know if I should try it."

"Try it!" I said. "It will make you feel a little better."

We passed the cup back and forth, back and forth, feeling a warmth ease down our throats, spread through our chests, melt down into our worn, haggard bodies, soothing, soothing. In half an hour we were intoxicated, at peace, sleeping the sleep of the free.

In the morning we awoke as the light was beginning to stream in through the window high above us in a rich, golden flow. It must have been the sound of the lock on the door that woke us. A German farmer pushed the door to the side and then stood perfectly still, his outline silhouetted in the light coming from behind him. He gazed at his building, at the scattered hay, at the thin, nearly bald heads, the enormous eyes staring back at him. Without a word he turned and left, leaving the door open.

The men began to rise, stretch, limp slowly out the door one by one. Freedom was new, strange to us; we did not quite know what to do with it.

The warmth of the liquor and the hay still permeated me and I was not ready to leave. When the last man had gone, closing the door behind him, the three of us still lay as we were, content. I looked out through the knot-hole. Snow was beginning to drift down, blowing across the field on the cold wind. *What will we do now?* I wondered. *Where will we go?*

The door suddenly burst open. A group of Wehrmacht soldiers from the regular German army, not the SS, came in. They had probably come to change into civilian clothes before fleeing the country. When the soldiers saw us they immediately turned to go again. Before they left, however, one man came closer, stretching out his hand to us holding a package of food. I took it from him. Inside were three crackers, one for each of us, a hunk of Cheddar cheese, and a chocolate bar—a feast! We ate and then sat back again, still not sure of where to go.

As I looked out of the peephole again, I saw smoke coming from a single cattle car parked on a track near the station. Some of the men who had been with us were climbing into the car, evidently joining others who had built a fire. "That's where we'll go," I said to the girls. "It will be warmer there."

We pulled Esther along. She was becoming delirious as infection set into the wounds. Soon after we reached this car several of the men remembered that the train parked on the side rail had food. They began to climb on it once more, ransacking the cars. As I also started for this train, still ravenous with hunger, Esther grabbed one arm and Ellen the other.

"Let me go!" I cried. "There's more food in the cars!"

"No! No! No! No!" Esther cried, and held firm with a strength I could not believe she still possessed.

"Ellen, can't you help me?" I asked. "You know I'll be right back."

She shook her head no. As I was still struggling to break free an explosion shattered the quiet morning air, throwing us off our feet. I looked up to see the food train blown into fragments, not a trace left of the men who had been on it. The SS had placed a bomb on the train and it detonated when someone stepped on it.

We climbed into the single cattle car on the other tracks and held out our hands to the small fire burning at one end. I did not want to stay; a bomb might have been planted in this car as well. Esther was moaning, becoming almost unconscious. I desperately wanted someplace where she could lie down. Then one of the men said, "There's a small barracks on the other side of the tracks where railroad workers lived. Why don't you take her there? I think another woman is already in it."

When we opened the door to this barracks a Hungarian girl from our camp, Sonia, greeted us. "Seren! Come in!" she said. "There are beds here and a stove—and even running water. I discovered this place just a few minutes ago."

"But can we stay here?" Ellen asked. "Will they let us?"

"We will commandeer it," I answered. "It's ours."

While Sonia made a wood fire in the potbelly stove, Ellen and I put Esther on one of the hard beds. We unwrapped the strips of cloth from her back, now no more than one massive, swelling wound, pus draining everywhere. The wound around the bullet fragments still in her head was equally inflamed and sore, her forehead hot and sweaty. I took off what was left of her clothes and sponged her back with soap and water, washed the clothes and draped them around the stove to dry. We stayed in the barracks the rest of the day and through the night.

By the next morning Esther was running a high fever. I knew I would not be able to save her. We had no medicine, no way to remove the slivers of metal festering inside her. I could do nothing.

At midmorning, on the first day of May, a white truck drove up to the barracks. Two men in white coats came to the door and knocked. As they did not appear to be Germans, we let them in. They began speaking to us in a language we did not understand, beckoning us to follow them to the truck.

"Absolutely not!" I told them in Yiddish. "We're not leaving here with someone we don't know."

The men left. *I wonder who they were,* I thought as the truck drove away. They came back in only a few minutes accompanied by a third man. This new man came immediately to the door and yelled in Yiddish, "Open up, please. We're American soldiers. We've come to take you to a hospital."

I opened the door. "What took you so long?" I asked.

———

WE RODE FOR ABOUT FIFTY KILOMETERS UNTIL WE came to a convent, Saint Ottilien, which had been converted into a hospital. As soon as the truck stopped in front of a large tent, the back door was opened and nuns in long black gowns and headpieces came rushing toward it. They held out their arms to us as we crawled out of the truck, and led us to the front of the tent. Here a nun undressed us, throwing our rags into a burning pile. When the nun came to Esther and removed her tattered dress she glanced quickly at her back and cried, "Gott in Himmel!" ("God in heaven!")

Immediately she wrapped a sheet around Esther and ordered two men to bring a stretcher. In an instant Esther was being carried away. "Esther!" I cried. I wanted to follow her. But then I thought, *These nuns are very kind. They will be good to her and give her the care she needs.*

Several other nuns took Sonia, Ellen, and me into a tent where there were women from other trains. We were bathed and disinfected, our heads shaved to rid them of lice, and each given a clean pair of men's pajamas and straw slippers. Finally we were put on a scale to be weighed. I weighed forty-four pounds, including pajamas.

"Now, follow me, please," an older nun said, and began walking into the convent.

I was exhausted and sat down on the ground. Was the war over? It seemed to be, but I was not sure. I was too tired to care, more tired than I had ever been in my life. I closed my eyes.

Then I felt myself being lifted up in two arms. I opened my eyes. One of the American soldiers was carrying me. I closed my eyes again. Drops of water began splashing on my cheeks and running down my neck. *Is it raining again?* I thought. *No, we're inside now where it would not rain.* Then I realized that the soldier carrying me was crying, his tears falling on my face.

He carried me into a large assembly hall where rows of beds were lined up. Gently he lowered me onto clean, white sheets smelling of soap and starch, onto a soft, soft mattress, and covered me with a warm blanket. *Oh, my God! I've died and gone to heaven,* I thought. *Why didn't I want to die all this time? It's so wonderful in heaven . . .*

Part Five

*Seren and Meyer in Germany before their son was born. The older
woman next to her is the German lady who taught Seren how
to cook. The younger woman is a childhood friend with
whom she was reunited after the liberation.*

Twenty-four

E HAD BEEN RESCUED, AND I WAS FLOATING ON A
cloud of pain, grief, and relief.

When I awoke it was evening and a nun was leaning over my bed, her
full, round face framed in stiff cotton. She was looking at me through her
oval spectacles and asking, "Can I get you anything? Is there anything you
would like?"

I could not think of anything I wanted other than to be left exactly as
I was, lying among white clouds, drifting. I closed my eyes and the nun
moved away, her black habit swishing through the aisles.

The next time I awoke morning light was streaming in through the
high windows of the convent, filtering through stained glass, falling in deep
shades of indigo and violet on the rows of white beds, on the small hills and
valleys of our bodies. *It is like the chapel in Valea Uzului,* I thought, remembering how the colored light came in through the windows, how the tall
grass whispered in the wind beside the brook. Letting myself sink into the
grass, I listened to the murmur of the water.

"CAN I GET YOU SOMETHING NOW?" A VOICE WAS ASK-ing again from far away. "Couldn't I get you something to eat?"

With a great effort I opened my eyes. The nun was leaning over my bed. "Yes," I whispered. "I would like some creamed wheat."

"You would like a bowl of cereal?"

"Creamed wheat . . ." I repeated.

"Of course," she answered. "I'll bring it to you right away."

After a few minutes she returned, carrying a steaming bowl of the cereal. "Would you like me to feed it to you?" she asked.

I shook my head no; I was too tired to eat.

"I'll set it here on the table beside you. Whenever you want to you can have some." She smiled, pulled the blanket up over my shoulders, and went to the next bed. *Why did I ask for that?* I wondered. *I don't like it at all . . .*

I AM VERY SMALL, FOUR OR FIVE YEARS OLD, AND quite ill with measles. The mill doctor has ordered me to remain in my darkened bedroom for three weeks. My legs are weak, my body like jelly. I hurt so. Mama comes into the dim room with a big bowl of creamed wheat, smiling, sitting down on the bed next to me. She holds a spoonful next to my mouth. When I swallow it she says, "What a good little girl! You will get better in no time if you eat the whole bowlful."

"Why do I have to be sick all the time?" I ask. "This afternoon Rose and Berta are going on a picnic with Herman and Tamara and I have to stay here in this bed."

"Never you mind them," she answers. "I'll stay here with you. Next time I'll even put a sweet surprise in the cereal."

WHERE WAS ELLEN? WHERE WAS SHE? I OPENED MY eyes, looking quickly over to the bed on my right. A strange woman stared back at me. I looked to the left. Ellen was there, sound asleep. I closed my eyes again, listening to the muted sounds of the nuns going from bed to bed. Most of the women, like me, asked for a particular food—an orange, a poached egg, a cup of tea. Everyone taken into the convent had been put into bed. Some of the survivors were still fairly healthy, having recently come from camps where they were fed; some were barely alive. The process of examining us one by one had already begun, those healthy enough to be released referred to a distribution center.

From time to time, as I lay there, I would struggle up from sleep as if ascending through fathoms of water, finally breaking through to the surface. Opening my eyes, I gazed across the aisle at the women in the beds facing me. Several of these women were survivors of Auschwitz. They were of the same nature as those who had been in the locked cars with us, having learned to survive by becoming as merciless and ruthless as the SS guards who kept them imprisoned. They now sat up in their beds, alert, demanding.

Next to these Polish women were three sisters who were also fairly healthy and were passing the time calling back and forth to each other in Hungarian.

"Edith," one said the first morning, "the nun is coming back. Will you ask her this time?"

"Yes, sister dear, I'll ask," the woman next to her replied.

When the nun approached Edith's bed, inquiring if she could bring her anything, Edith answered, "Could you bring each of us a rosary? We would like that more than anything!"

"Have you converted, then?" asked the nun.

"Oh, yes, before the war. A priest gave each of us a rosary then but they were taken away from us when we entered the camp."

I hope the women from Auschwitz don't find out about this, I thought.

In a few minutes the nun returned, carrying three beaded chains, a small black cross dangling from each one. "Here you are," she said, handing them to the sisters.

"Hail Mary, full of grace . . ." the three began chanting in unison, their hands clasped around the beads.

"Look!" a Polish woman yelled in Yiddish. "Do you see what those bitches are doing? They've got a cross in their hands!"

"I see! I see!" another from Auschwitz yelled. "Can you believe it? They should be thrown out of here!"

"You bastards!" the first woman yelled at them. "Get them out of here. We don't want you. Get out!"

The three sisters kept chanting, unaware of the insults that were being hurled at them in a language they did not understand. This indifference seemed to anger the Polish women even more. The uproar increased, the Polish women shouting so loud that three or four nuns came running. The three sisters were taken out of the room immediately, still clasping the rosaries in their hands.

Several hours later, toward noon, a nun came through the aisles and announced, "In a little while we're going to bring in dinner. I want all of you to stay in your beds. We'll come around and give each of you your meal from the pushcarts." As she continued on down the aisles, repeating her announcement, I saw how the women began to sit up, to wait anxiously. For many of us this would be the first meal in years given to us gracefully, one human being serving another as if both were equal, deserving of consideration.

When the carts began to rumble from the far end of the room, the wheels to move closer and closer, the women crouched on the edge of their beds like cats, low to the ground, stretched flat, ready for the rush. As soon as the carts were a few meters from our beds many of the women jumped, pushing the nuns aside, fell on the food, thrusting their hands into the bowls, licking their fingers clean, and quickly grabbing more.

"Stop! Stop! Please! You're making such a mess!" a nun kept yelling, but the women would not, could not stop. The smells of steaming cabbage dripping with butter, of hot savory beef, forced them on. If I had been able to get out of bed I would have been with them.

When every scrap of cabbage, meat, and pudding was gone, some of the women began to carry the bowls back to their beds, licking them clean, their long tongues swirling over and over the surfaces. Finally a nun cautiously approached the empty cart and went from bed to bed, collecting the bowls, clucking her tongue repeatedly. Later in the afternoon the same nun, an older, rounded woman, came back and said very calmly and slowly, as if she were speaking to children, "We're going to be bringing your supper on carts soon. Please, please stay in your beds this time. There is plenty of food. If the cart is empty I'll take it back to the kitchen for more. You must believe me when I say that we have more than enough food. Remember now, stay in your beds." She left, confident that this time we understood her.

When the carts again began to rumble in the distance the women poised themselves as before, jumped, sprang on the food. Again I remained in bed, too exhausted to even raise my arm. Ellen, beside me, slept on, as tired as I. Even as the women were still stuffing food into their mouths, I fell back into darkness.

This time I went deeper into the sea of sleep, sinking down, down, the voices of the women becoming fainter, far away. The water hung azure, deep green above me, roaring faintly like the drone of a distant stream. At times I found myself adrift on the surface again and opened my eyes. There on the table beside me would be another bowl of creamed wheat, sitting beside the other bowls. I would not let the nun take any of them away. Once six bowls swam before me all in a row, gliding deep, down, to the bottom.

It is cold, cold. We have been working all afternoon on the ship, carrying crates of vegetables down the ramp to the cellar. The SS finally orders us to stop working and line up for the walk back to camp. As we are standing in our rows the guard suddenly struts to the front of the line and yells out, "Numbers 85803 and 85801, step forward!"

Those are Esther's and my numbers! *I realize with a jolt.* Why are they singling us out? Have they discovered that we are sisters?

As we leave the line, carefully avoiding looking at each other, the guard orders us to follow her to the SS headquarters. Several times I have seen women being carried out of the office, broken, dead.

Three SS supervisors stare at us. After a long, quiet moment one of them says in German, "They don't look like sisters."

"No, they don't," another replies. "But we can't rely on appearances. We'll have to question them separately." She points to me. "You, number 85803, go outside and wait."

I begin walking toward the door. Esther will be alone with them! If I try to stay with her they will be sure that we are sisters and send one of us to a different camp. If I leave her alone she may be hurt. The door closes. I pick up a broom sitting outside and begin to sweep, keeping as close to the door as possible.

Long minutes pass. I hear nothing except the quiet swish of the broom on the worn boards. Then a harsh voice shouts, "I asked you a question! Answer me! What is the name of your mother?"

Silence hangs in the cold air.

"Then tell me the name of your father," the voice continues. "You do have a father, don't you? Or are you a bastard like all the others? Answer! Answer!"

Esther's sobbing, halting voice drifts out to me. "My father was named . . . named . . . Her . . . Herman . . ."

"And your mother?"

"Ta . . . Tamara . . ."

"How many brothers?"

Silence.

"How many?" The sound of a fierce slap resounds through the air. I sweep faster, wanting to run in, throw myself in front of Esther. She is giving all the wrong answers, confusing our half brother Herman and his wife with our mother and father.

"I . . . I . . . There were two—no, three brothers . . ." Esther finally says.

"She's an idiot!" one of the SS women shouts. "We'll get nowhere with her! Take her out and bring in the other one."

Quickly I replace the broom and stand at the far end of the porch. The door opens. Esther stumbles out, tears running down her face. A large red mark spreads across one cheek. Passing by her quickly, I go into the office.

I stand before the three supervisors. One of them is the short, quick SS woman who often walks beside me as we go to work. When I glance at her she turns to the supervisor standing next to her and whispers, "Watch out for this one. She's shrewd. She never cries."

She turns to me. "What is your name?" she demands.

"Seren Tuvel," I answer.

"Your father's name?"

"Abraham Tuvel."

"How many brothers and sisters?"

"I have five brothers and four sisters still living."

"Which sister is in this camp with you?"

"I have no sister here."

"One of our men was on the ship this morning supervising the unloading. He recognized you as someone he used to know. He also recognized your sister. Do you mean to tell me that he was lying?"

A man in an SS uniform is watching me. He comes closer. I see that he is someone I went to school with in Fulehaza. He takes out a notebook and begins writing in it. Then he gives it to my priest teacher from Fulehaza, who walks up to the three supervisors and hands it to them. He stands to one side, smiling.

"Well?" the SS woman demands.

"I did not say that the man was lying," I answer. "I have not accused him of anything. When he knew me long ago in Fulehaza there were six girls in our family. It's true that one of these six was with me. But she died on the march through Hungary."

"You're lying!" a second SS woman shouts.

"No, I'm telling the truth. She died last summer."

"You rotten bitch! You're a filthy liar. Admit it!"

I surprise myself. I am not frightened. Saying no more, I continue to look the SS supervisor in the eye.

"Get out, you miserable dog!" the short woman who knows me yells.

I go outside. An empty wasteland stretches before me. Esther is nowhere in sight. My heart begins to charge against my ribs. They have taken Esther away. I know it! *I decide.* They kept me just long enough to take her to the crematorium!

I begin walking on my wooden clogs toward a tall, smoking chimney in the distance. Snow collects on the bottoms of my shoes. I become higher, higher. "Esther . . ." I call, looking out into the whiteness swirling all around me. "Esther . . . Esther . . ."

"WHAT IS IT? WHAT'S WRONG?" A VOICE ANSWERED. My eyes popped open. The older, rounded nun, Sister Maria, was leaning over me once more. "Is it cereal? Do you want more cereal?" she asked.

"Was I screaming?" I whispered.

"No, you were whispering a name over and over. I was passing by and

I saw you turn about so on the bed that I thought you might need something. Then I heard the name."

"My sister!" I said. "I can't find her!" I looked quickly at the bed next to me. Ellen was still there but Esther was nowhere. I had to find her. "I have to see my sister!" I said.

"All right. We'll have someone take you to her. I'll be back in just a minute with an orderly."

When the orderly came he wrapped the blanket around me, picked me up in his arms, and carried me into a smaller room off the main hall. "There she is," he said in a deep, kind voice. "See, she's all bandaged up."

"Esther?" I called. "Esther, is that you?" The woman in the bed was lying with her face away from me, her entire body swathed in bandages.

"She's had several operations," the orderly said, "but she'll be just fine."

"But it doesn't look like her," I said.

"We'll just have to move a little closer then," he answered, carrying me to the other side of the bed. Then I saw it—the thin, white face of Esther lying on the pillow, breathing quietly, eyes closed, mouth slack, one bandaged hand drawn up near her cheek.

"Well, is it your sister?" the orderly asked.

"Yes," I sighed. Leaning my head against his shoulder, I fell again into whiteness, into the silent sea.

FOR THE NEXT FEW DAYS I DRIFTED IN AND OUT OF consciousness. The bed became even softer, softer than I thought possible, and I thought again that perhaps I was in heaven after all where everything was as fine as goose down. Then the nun, changing my sheets one day, whispered, "We've put a comforter under you, my dear. It will help your skin heal."

Another time when I awoke briefly and opened my eyes I saw that I was bandaged almost as much as Esther, the white cloths winding all around my arms to the top of my fingers, down my legs and over my toes. Every morning a sharp pain speared me in the right shoulder. Gradually I realized that I was being given injections. Often I woke up to find myself being pushed through the corridor, and tried desperately to stay awake long enough to see where they were taking me, but always failed, sinking again into unconsciousness.

One morning, however, I succeeded in remaining alert and saw that I was being taken into a room full of machines. Milling about the room were many men, all speaking High German. Then my eyes fell shut again and I could not open them. The next thing I knew, I was back in my bed and it was late afternoon. All of the other women were gone somewhere. *That room!* I thought. *It was full of Germans. We're back in camp! They took us back when I was unconscious, the nuns as well. They mean to kill all of us with those machines. We'll have to get out of here.*

"Ellen," I called. "Ellen! Listen to me!"

"Seren? What is it?" she answered sleepily. She was also bandaged and conscious sporadically.

"We're back in camp! I'm sure of it! They all speak High German. Tonight when it's dark I'm getting out of here. Will you come with me? We'll get help and come back for Esther."

"If you want me to," she answered. "I've saved up some bread. We can take it with us."

"Good girl! We're on the second floor but I think we can climb out the window and jump down."

"All right. Wake me when it's time to go."

When night came it seemed to take forever for the women to all lie still, quiet, breathing evenly. Finally when the last one was asleep and the nuns had turned off the lights and left, I slowly began to climb out of bed. As soon as I managed to sit upright, placing my feet on the floor, a wave of dizziness washed over me, washed me down, down. *No!* I thought. *I can't faint. We'll be killed in a few more days if we don't leave.* I shook my head slightly, stood up, and walked to Ellen's bed.

"Ellen, wake up!" I whispered. "It's time."

She stared at me, wild-eyed.

"Remember?" I asked. "We're back in camp. We have to leave."

"Oh . . . yes. I wrapped the bread in a towel," she said, getting out of bed.

"You go first. I'll be right behind you," I whispered.

Inch by inch we shuffled across the room to the window. As we were trying to pull it up, Sister Maria was somehow right behind us. "No, no, no, no, no," she clucked. "You must not be out of bed like this. Come now. Back to bed with you. Here, lean on my shoulders."

She put one ample arm around Ellen and the other around me. We shambled back to our beds. As soon as I lay down again, I was asleep, even before I could plan our next escape attempt.

When I awoke I was in a different room, one with bars on the windows. *They put us in a cell so we can't escape,* I decided. Tears sprang to my eyes. *Ellen! Where's Ellen?* I thought. Then I saw her in the next bed. A wave of heat flashed over me, and then another. My head became thick, hot, melting into the pillow. Sweat poured from my forehead into my eyes, down my neck. Oh, it was too hot, too hot. Red-hot, blood-hot, the water burning, sinking over me . . .

WHEN I AWOKE AGAIN A DELICIOUS COOLNESS WAS spreading across my forehead, easing into my consciousness. I opened my eyes to Sister Maria, sitting beside my bed.

"Ah, you are awake!" she said. "Is the cloth on your head too cold? Shall I remove it?"

I moved my head slightly.

"You have been very sick," she continued. "Did you know that you had typhoid fever? We had to move you and your friend to isolation. We didn't want you to contaminate the others."

"Have I been in this room long?" I whispered.

"Yes—nearly four weeks. It's the end of May. You aren't thinking of running away from us again, are you?" She smiled, smoothing a fresh cloth across my forehead. "Please don't be afraid of us," she continued. "We want you to get well and then you can leave. Doesn't that sound like a better idea? Of course it does! You know, I never thought I'd be a nurse, but one day at the beginning of the war Hitler sent one of his SS men here. He told us that we had two choices: go to a camp or remain at the convent as nurses. Of course, we all chose to stay here. So you see, I enjoy taking care of you. I could have been you in that camp. The least I can do is help you get better. Do you understand?"

"Yes . . . but I heard German voices one day. I thought . . ." I couldn't finish the sentence; it took too much effort.

"You thought you had good reason to be frightened. Is that it? Of course! I should have known. Those voices belonged to wounded soldiers from the Wehrmacht. We are caring for them as well in another wing of the hospital. They won't hurt you. When they're recovered they'll leave too. Would you like anything to eat? It's a little past suppertime but I can get you some fruit or a nice bowl of pudding."

"Just some water. I'm so thirsty."

"Of course. I have some ice water right here, good and cold!"

Sister Maria talked with me half the night before I slipped back into sleep. When I awoke again, I realized that Ellen was no longer in the bed beside me. I was in a room by myself.

"Ellen!" I tried to shout. It came out as a whisper.

"What is it?" Sister Maria said, appearing out of nowhere.

I decided that this nun was not to be trusted after all; if Ellen had been taken back to camp I would soon follow. I said nothing.

"You wonder where your friend went, don't you?" she said. "I should have told you. She developed hearing difficulties after she came down with typhoid fever. We sent her to another hospital for an operation on her ears. They have some good doctors there—ear specialists. She will be just fine."

I am alone . . . I thought, closing my eyes. *After all this time I am alone . . .* Sister Maria was chattering on but I could not distinguish the words. A great weight was settling on my chest, pulling me back under the sea, under the heavy, black water.

THE NEXT TIME I AWOKE IT WAS EARLY JUNE. AFTER the typhoid fever abated, pneumonia had set in. Despite these illnesses, however, my body began to heal itself. The nuns faithfully took care of me, attending to me day and night, ever kind. One morning Sister Maria bustled up to my bed and announced, "We're going to take your bandages off today. Isn't that wonderful!" Slowly she and another nun unwound my right arm. The pink fingernails appeared first, white crescent moons shining at the bottoms, then the first and second joints, pale, whole, the bone covered, the knuckles wrinkled with new skin, the back of my hand, the wrist. Still unwinding, they reached my forearm. Oh, it had flesh! The upper arm as well! Holding it out in front of me, I gazed at the tender, soft skin, at the fine hairs curling as if I were newborn, a baby discovering her arm. When my other arm was uncovered it too was smooth, firm. And my legs! Was there fat on the thigh? There was! I could not believe it, lifting first one leg and then the other, wiggling my toes back and forth. Even my sore toe was healed, the missing part barely noticeable.

"How well you've healed!" Sister Maria was saying.

"Do you have a mirror?" I asked, suddenly remembering that I had a face too.

"Yes, we do," the other nun answered. "I'll get one for you."

Returning, she held the mirror in front of me. I glanced at it and quickly turned away. "You can take it back," I said.

"Oh, child, you will blossom again," Sister Maria said. "The face takes longer to heal than the body. The suffering is still there—lodged in the lines and furrows. But they will fade. You'll be lovely again. I can't wait to see how beautiful you'll be."

"You may have to wait a long time," I answered.

"I'll wait! In another week or two you should be well enough to go outside and sit in our garden. You'll see all the spring flowers."

EVERY DAY AFTER THAT I FELT SOMEWHAT BETTER than the day before. One afternoon as I was lying in bed, back in the large assembly hall again, Esther walked into the room for the first time. She came in hesitantly, her head still bandaged in white cloths wound completely around the back and top of her head, leaving only her pale face exposed. She had not regained all of the weight lost during the long months without food, her tall body no more than a long, slight line in the white pajamas.

"Esther!" I laughed as she reached my bed. "You look so funny."

"I do?"

"You look like a walking stick with a head!" I said, reaching out my hand to hers. "Oh, but I'm glad to see you again. It's been so long."

She sat down on the bed beside me and began to stroke my cheek with her fingertips. Tears slid from her eyes and plopped in the pillow beside me. "I didn't know if we were going to make it," she said then. "I wouldn't have if it hadn't been for you."

"Do you think I could have survived alone?" I asked. "Never! I needed you and Ellen as much as you needed me!"

We gazed into each other's eyes for a long time, unable to quench the thirst for the sight of each other. Finally Esther asked, "Where's Ellen?"

"She's been sent to another hospital. She had to have special treatment for her ears."

"Will we ever see her again?"

"I'm sure of it," I answered.

We sat quietly then, Esther smoothing the hair away from my forehead with her hands. When a large group of doctors and uniformed men suddenly came swinging through the doors of the hall and began walking down the aisles, we barely noticed them. Groups of people visited the hospital now and then to see if we were being given good care and were recovering. Some of the Jewish survivors, however, were either too ill to recover or died from putting more food into themselves than their emaciated bodies could digest during the first few days.

This particular group of visitors seemed to take a special interest in us. The nuns were fluttering after them like a flock of chattering blackbirds. Sister Maria flew to my bedside, her face flushed, hands up in the air. "It's General Eisenhower!" she said. "He's brought his whole entourage! I knew they were coming to visit us sometime but I didn't know it would be today." She stood beside my bed, hugging her round body with her arms and rocking slightly back and forth, watching Eisenhower walk down the aisle.

When Eisenhower's group reached the middle of the room they stopped and looked around. The doctors began pointing to various patients, speaking about their conditions in the language I now recognized as English. Then a doctor gestured in my direction. Immediately Eisenhower began walking briskly toward me, all the other men following closely behind. At the foot of my bed he stopped abruptly, his face turning red and angry, and stared at Esther. Not at all interested in the commotion, she was continuing to caress my face with her hand, trailing her fingers lightly over my forehead and down the side of my cheek.

Eisenhower barked a few words in English to the man standing next to him. Esther, looking up when she heard the harsh tone of voice, jumped slightly. Then the man standing next to Eisenhower, evidently his interpreter, pointed a finger at Esther and said loudly in German, "You! Tommy! Get out!"

Esther stood up slowly. "You want me to leave?" she asked. "This is my sister," she said, addressing one of the German doctors. "We haven't seen each other since we arrived at the hospital."

"I know," he answered, "but General Eisenhower thinks you're a man. I'll tell him who you are."

The doctor spoke to the interpreter and the interpreter to Eisenhower. He, in turn, glanced at me again, looked me in the eyes, and said something in English. Then he turned and marched out of the room, the nuns still flapping along behind him.

"Tommy!" I said, clasping Esther's hand. "Do you like your new name?"

"Why did he call me that?" Esther asked.

"It must be a nickname for a soldier in the United States," I answered. "He thought you were a man come to court me. As if one would!" I laughed.

"Well, I guess he can't see very well then," she answered, "even if he is a general."

"Tommy!" I said again. "I like it!"

GRADUALLY I BEGAN GETTING UP AND WALKING slowly around, holding on to the side of the bed with one hand. My legs and feet still had no sensation in them and I felt as if I were walking on two sticks of wood. Then one day in the middle of June, Sister Maria came up to my bed with a wheelchair. "It's a beautiful day!" she said. "Would you like to go outside and sit in the garden for a while? The sun is warm. The flowers are all in bloom."

"I would love to!" I answered.

"Good! Just climb into this and off we'll go."

She whirled me down the aisle and out into the bright light falling in white swaths on the green sea of grass, on the oak trees, on the daisies and irises curving along the sidewalks in shades of lavender and yellow. We stopped under a large shade tree.

"Summer has come while I've been asleep," I said. "I've missed the spring . . ."

"You'll catch up!" Sister Maria answered. "I'll leave you here for a little while. I must see to some other patients. Smell the flowers for me," she called as she walked back toward the hospital.

For half an hour or so I looked at the bunches of billowy clouds sweeping across the great span of blue, at the masses of daisies swaying as a breeze swept over them in waves. Other solitary women sat here and there on the wide expanse of lawn—frail bits of flesh stuck in metal chairs while around us the world swelled and dipped in glorious undulations.

I don't have to stay in this chair, I decided then, and stood up. I began to walk, creeping along over the grass, one foot slowly brought up to meet the other as if I were still in Ravensbrück, my legs two wooden logs. After a few minutes I stopped and turned around to see how far I had gone. The chair sat like a tiny spot so very far away, seemingly miles away. *How can I have gone that far?* I thought, sinking onto the grass. I looked at the chair again. *Oh, it's not that far. It's only about six meters from here."* I got up again and began moving toward the chair, looking down at the ground so that I would not stumble over a hidden rock, and then looking up again. The chair was not closer!

After an eternity of time had passed, minute by long minute, the sun on my face still, hot, indifferent, I was near enough to the chair to reach out and grab the sides. Cautious lest I tip it over, I reached for them, half turned, and lowered myself into the seat. *I have a long way to go,* I thought, *a very long way.*

Several days later the nuns began doing exercises with me. The prolonged exposure to cold weather, the daily freezings, had reduced the circulation in my legs. Every morning I sat with my feet raised for half an hour and then stood up until the stinging needles of pain shot out of my legs, one by one.

As I was hobbling around my bed one morning, gritting my teeth until the last needle was gone, I heard someone walk toward me and stop a few feet away from the bottom of the bed.

"Seren?" a voice asked.

I opened my eyes. "Joseph! You've come back!"

"I promised you I would."

He held out his arms. I fell into them, resting my head against his chest for a moment, his shoulders and head reaching up above me, arms wound around my back. When I pulled away I looked at him without saying anything, gazed at his face, at the deep crinkles around his dark, laughing eyes. I could not believe that this nephew of mine, this child of an older half brother who never paid much attention to me, would seek me out over and over.

Finally I asked, "Why me, Joseph? Why do you always try to find me again?"

"Didn't you know?" he answered.

"What?"

"You're my favorite aunt."

"I am?"

"You always have been."

"But I am so much older than you. Esther is more your age. I wasn't home anymore when you came to visit our house."

"You don't believe me? Well, I have proof!" He took what looked to be a tattered photograph from his pocket and handed it to me. For an instant I stared at the young girl smiling back at me, happy, full of health. I wondered who she was. Then I realized that I was the girl. The photograph was the one taken by Eugene just before Esther and Emma left Reghinal-Sasesc for Budapest to work in the lingerie factory. It had been creased into thirds, the images of Esther on the left and Emma on the right folded over me in the middle; while the two outer thirds were soiled and cracked, the middle section was smooth, clean.

"Where did you get this?" I asked.

"I carried it with me on the inside of my shoe. No one ever found it."

"You had it all during the war?"

"Yes. I knew that you, of all people, would survive. Now I want to give it to you."

The black-and-white image swam before my eyes. Again I heard Eugene's voice ordering, "Silence! . . . You must pay attention or I'll never get this picture taken!"; remembered how Rose and my mother had stood together, hand in hand to one side of him, wanting the moment never to come when their daughters would separate, leave them.

"Have you found out anything, Joseph?" I asked. "Have you seen anyone else from home?"

He looked down at the floor. We were now sitting on the edge of the bed, my hand in his. "No . . ." he answered softly. "I was with Rose's husband, Eugene, and also with Louise's husband in the labor camp. The three of us were taken to Auschwitz together and put in a work detail. But when they began evacuating the camp we were separated. I was sent to Turkheim where I saw you. I don't know where Eugene and Bela were sent."

"What about my mother? Was she still well when you left Reghinal-Sasesc?"

"Yes . . . but I heard that they cordoned off a section of the outskirts of town and put all the Jewish people in it after I left."

"I know," I answered. "I found out when Esther and I were in Budapest. We tried to send for her but by then all Jews were forbidden to travel."

"I'm going home!" Joseph said. "Mother and Father may be there waiting for me. Many Jews were put in work details at Auschwitz. We were fed well. Look at me!"

"Joseph . . ." I said, grabbing his hand tighter and looking into his eyes. "They may be all right. But please don't get your hopes up too high. So many died in the locked cars. So terribly many."

"I know. But I have to hope, don't I? I'm going to start looking for them and my two brothers as soon as I leave here. I was in a hospital too, but I've been released and I'm going home."

"Where will you go—to Reghinal-Sasesc or to Valea Uzului?"

"To both."

"Joseph, if you find anyone, anyone, will you let me know?"

"Of course. There are so many of us. Some of us will have survived. I know it! Remember all of your mother's brothers? Remember Uncle Louie?"

"Uncle Louie! How could I forget him? Whenever he needed money he came to work at the mill. Father could barely tolerate him. Every time we all went to temple he stood in the door and laughed at us. Father was always afraid he would be a bad influence on all my brothers. If Uncle Louie hadn't been Mama's brother, Father would have told him to leave and never come back."

"Well, I have to leave pretty soon," Joseph said then. "I want to see Esther and then I'll go."

"Wait, Joseph! How did you find me? You never said."

"Through the central office in Munich. The Jewish Council there has a list of all the survivors and where they can be located. Your name and Esther's name were on the list. The convent must have sent them."

"But no one else's name?"

"No one else's . . . I'm sure they don't have all the names. The war has been over for only two months. Everything takes time."

"Yes . . . Thank you for coming, Joseph. It means so much to see someone from my family."

"You're welcome, my favorite aunt. I'll see you again. Don't worry."

Twenty-five

IN LATE JULY, THREE MONTHS AFTER I HAD ENTERED the convent hospital, I was well enough to be transferred to a distribution center at Feldafing, Bavaria. Esther was still too ill to travel; I did not like leaving her but the nuns assured me that I could come back and visit her as often as I desired. When she was better she would be sent to Feldafing as well.

Early one morning a Red Cross leader accompanied me and the other men and women who had recovered to Feldafing. Still wearing our pajamas, we boarded Red Cross buses, feeling as if we were out in public in our underwear. The nuns assured us, however, that we would be given clothes when we reached the center, courtesy of the American people. As we pulled out of the hospital I saw only Sister Maria waving, her whole arm slowly moving up and down, up and down, the robe flapping like the wing of a great bird. I would never forget her kindnesses.

When we arrived at the center, a former Hitler Youth camp, we were driven directly to the main office to be registered. As I descended the steps from the bus I heard someone call my name. "Seren! Here! Seren." I looked up. There was Ellen standing directly in front of the office, her face radiant.

"Ellen!" I cried, hugging her close. "How did you know I was coming?"

"I waited here every day since I arrived. I knew you would get off that bus one day. And now you have! Oh, Seren, I've missed you so. It's wonderful to have you back! And you know what? We have dormitories here with bunk beds. I have a lower bunk and I saved the upper one for you. I remembered how you always said, 'Up we go! Up we go!'"

"You learned, didn't you?" I laughed. "Esther too. On the way over I decided to look at the hospital here. If I think it's good I'm going to ask if Esther can be sent too."

Ellen and I went to our dormitory, a large, modern building with clean showers and toilets, a spacious dining hall with a long table where we ate our meals, and a room full of bunk beds. There were twenty women in our dormitory. The center was very well organized, I soon realized. A number of the men survivors had come from an area located near the border of Poland and Lithuania that was known for its well-educated, intelligent Jewish people. These men had chosen leaders responsible for requesting food from the kitchens and bringing it to the dining rooms.

The next morning I visited the hospital at Feldafing and, satisfied that Esther would receive good care there, asked the central office if they would transfer her. I wanted her close; the electric trains were so erratic, stopping sometimes for hours when the current was shut off, that I did not want to rely on them to enable me to visit her. Three days later Esther arrived and was put in the hospital. The three of us were together once more.

As the weeks passed I began to grow restless. Every day I looked at the large bulletin board in the office to see if my name was listed among those who had received mail; I received no letters, not one. Every day I waited at the station for the trains to come in, thinking, *One of these days either Samuel or someone from my family will come. I cannot believe that only Esther, Joseph, and I survived. There are my brothers, my sisters, my mother, my aunts and uncles, all the children . . . Someday one of them will come and find me.*

On a hot afternoon in August I sat on the bench in front of the station, watching the passengers descend the steps from the train. Suddenly a tall, dark-haired man caught my attention. *I know this man,* I realized instantly, my heart jumping. *He's someone from my family! But who? No one in my family ever dressed like this!* On his head the man wore a large, round black hat like those of the Hasidic Jews. A long black beard flowed down the length of his chest, ruffling slightly in the warm breeze blowing in from the south, spilled over the black cassock that reached to his white socks and tall black boots. He came closer and smiled, his white teeth dazzling against the dark beard and mustache.

My God! It's Uncle Louie! I realized. Immediately I held out my arms to my mother's youngest brother, rushing to embrace him.

"No! No!" he shouted, holding me back with an outstretched hand.

I stopped short. "Uncle Louie!" I cried. "It's me, Seren!"

"Yes, my child. I know. But you must not touch me. It is forbidden." Only ten years older than I, he stood like a patriarch just come down from the mountain, the voice of God ringing in his ears.

"I don't understand . . ." I stammered.

"I'll explain, my child."

Uncle Louie escorted me back to the dormitory and sat down to tell me his story. Like Joseph, he had been at Auschwitz until it was evacuated. As they were leaving the camp an SS guard gave him a suitcase to hold, and they began the long, killing march through the frozen countryside. The weather was severe, the snow ceaseless; many of the prisoners fell down in the drifts and died or became lost in the blinding winds. Either the SS guard was also lost or he forgot who he had given the suitcase to; Uncle Louie was left with it.

After the liberation he was sent to Salzburg, Austria, still carrying the suitcase. When he finally opened it he discovered that it contained valuable jewelry—gold chains, diamond brooches, emerald rings—all stolen from the inmates of the concentration camps. He stored it away and declared himself to be a Hasidic rabbi, he who had never entered a temple before the war. Then he set out to find the surviving members of his family. Seeing Esther's and my names on the list from Feldafing, he came to us at once, primarily to indoctrinate us into Hasidism, an ultra orthodox branch of Judaism. As I listened to him talk, as I learned that his wife and two little girls had been killed at Auschwitz, I decided, *The poor man has lost his mind.* The war resulted in peculiar transformations; some of those who had been very religious before it started emerged afterward as disillusioned atheists, while some of the previous agnostics were now devout believers.

Before that day was over Uncle Louie had visited Esther in the hospital, marched into the central office at the center, and established himself as the leader of the Hasidim at Feldafing. He immediately gained a large following, he and his devotees soon driving everyone to distraction with their daily pronouncements. They created laws governing every aspect of our life, especially the preparation of food, and spent a great amount of time in the kitchen supervising the cooking.

I tried to ignore my uncle and his beliefs as much as possible, having always been one who took only the major Jewish laws to heart, until Uncle Louie began to focus his attention on me.

"Seren," he said one day. "It's time you were married. I take it upon myself as your uncle to ensure your marriage to a rabbi."

"What did you say?" I said, not believing what I had heard.

"I want you to marry a rabbi. It is the highest calling of a woman to marry a rabbi and bear him children."

Suddenly I remembered our grave, silent rabbi at the mill in Fulehaza. Although he was the father of many children, it was known that he and his wife slept in separate bedrooms. Zipporah and I used to giggle over this when we were small, wondering when and how these children came to be if the rabbi and his wife did not share a bed.

"I know," Zipporah said one day. "When the rabbi wants another baby he takes off his round hat and tosses it on her bed to let her know."

"Oh!" I would squeal. "Can't you see the hat twirling around before it falls. Maybe it even lands on the rabbi's wife's head!" We would then roll on the floor, convulsed in laughter.

How Zipporah still flits into my mind, I realized.

"Do you understand, Seren?" Uncle Louie was saying. "I will begin questioning several of the rabbis here to see if any of them are interested in a fine girl like you."

"No!" I answered. "I'm not a girl! I'm twenty-seven! I don't need you to pick out a husband for me."

"You will defy me, then? You will defy a holy man? Do you no longer believe any of what your dear mother and father taught you?"

"Uncle Louie, I became engaged to a man named Samuel before the war. We met in Reghinal-Sasesc. I haven't seen him for two years, but he may find me one day, just as you have."

"I meant to tell you something sooner," Uncle Louie replied. "I didn't have the heart until I realized that you were meant to marry a rabbi. I met your Samuel in Auschwitz. He told me all about you. One day before we evacuated the camp I saw him being taken to the crematorium."

"Ohhhh! He was dead?"

"He must have been. He was on the cart that took the bodies to the furnaces each morning. Did you have such a cart at Ravensbrück?"

I shuddered, remembering the piles of bodies, the frozen arms, the open mouths and eyes. It was too much. I put my head in my arms and began to cry, sobbing for Samuel, for his kindness, for the losses that had no end.

"It's all right. I'll find a rabbi for you very shortly," Uncle Louie continued. "Many of the men are anxious to get married and establish homes. Right now I must inspect the kitchen again. No one washes the dishes exactly as I have prescribed. Think about what I have said, Seren. I'm only thinking of your welfare."

As soon as he was out of the room I decided: I was leaving Feldafing. Esther was greatly improved and she and I wanted desperately to travel back to Hungary and then to Transylvania to look for our mother. I had not let go of the hope that she was still alive. If we persisted in looking we would find her. Drying my eyes, I went to tell Esther of my decision.

When I reached the hospital I was told that Esther had to be examined one more time before being dismissed. It was at this examination that our plans were thwarted. One of the doctors was not satisfied with her progress; her head was not healing properly. He advised that she be taken to Munich for testing. On the following day when she was examined, slivers of metal still inside her head showed up clearly on the X rays. She was operated on immediately and then brought back to Feldafing for recovery. For months she would not be able to leave the hospital. While I did not want to go home without Esther, my days became long, the ache of loneliness, of empty idleness, pressing against my chest, heavy and unrelenting.

Then I learned that a trade school was being established for displaced persons like us at Waldheim, a village located about twenty miles from Feldafing. I knew immediately that I wanted to go there and become a teacher in the dressmaking division. Like the other teachers, I would not be paid, but I would be involved again in sewing and out among other working people. I could not wait to go. Briefly I considered taking the train there each morning and returning again at night, but as the trains were very unreliable, it might take me an entire day simply to reach Waldheim. I decided instead to take accommodations given in return for teaching at the school. As these accommodations were with German citizens, I would be boarding with someone who surely still regarded me as the enemy. However, I was desperate to leave the communal life. I had had enough of living in camp situations. When I asked Ellen if she would go with me, as she was also an accomplished seamstress, she declined. She had met a young man at Feldafing from the area where she had been born, and they were growing very fond of each other.

Early one August morning I left for Waldheim by myself, promising to come back and visit Esther and Ellen on the weekends. As soon as I arrived I reported to the office of ORT, the Organization for Rehabilitation through Training. This was a women's organization founded in the United States to establish trade schools for all of the homeless persons who had survived the war. In the village of Waldheim this organization had obtained the use of a large hotel and set up classes in various assembly rooms. Mechanics was taught in one room, tailoring and dressmaking in another, carpentry in still another. The dining hall remained as it was; we were given breakfast, dinner, and supper there, as most of us had been assigned single bedrooms having no cooking facilities. The bedroom I was given was in the house of an elderly German widow who avoided me completely. While her attitude disturbed me greatly, it was almost bearable considering that at last I had a room of my own where I could close the door and be entirely by myself. The choice of having either solitude or being with others was like a gift. Sometimes at night, however, as I lay on my bed in the still room, the widow sleeping behind the locked door of her room, I thought, *I'm lonely . . . so very lonely. If only I had a friend . . .*

DURING THE DAYS MY WORK COMPLETELY ABSORBED me. Throughout the length of what had been the largest assembly hall in the hotel, sewing machines were set up on tables. At one end of the room I taught dressmaking to the few young girls who had survived; at the other end a man taught tailoring to young men. One day this man came over to me and said, "I've been watching you. You're very good with the students. Have you taught before?"

"A little," I answered, remembering how I had taught Emma and Esther in Reghinal-Sasesc. "Have you been here long?"

"I came here from Auschwitz as soon as the war ended," he said. "I had nothing to do, no books to read. When the school opened I volunteered as a teacher and the ORT office put me in this room. I enjoy the work but I'm glad that you've come too."

"Oh, I'm happy to be here! I have my own room. On the weekends I can see my sister in the hospital at Feldafing. I enjoy working very much. I can't stand not to work."

"That's exactly how I am! . . . How is your sister? Was she wounded?"

"Yes, in a bombing. We came from Ravensbrück to Turkheim and then Burgau. Finally they put us on a train again and left us in the locked cars. The train was bombed. She was hurt and has had several operations on her head. But she'll recover."

"I was also on a train for a long time just as the war was ending. We had been taken out of Auschwitz and were traveling west. One day the order was given to get out of the cars. The SS then lined us up by the side of the tracks and began shooting us. In the middle of it, when half of us were already dead, the American army came upon us and halted the shootings. I was so close to being killed! You must have been too! Tell me. Why was your sister injured and not you? Was it just luck?"

"No, it was a piece of bread. I saw it on the ground, squeezed out of the opening on the locked car, and reached for it. When the bombing started I slid under the train. The piece of bread saved me."

His face spread into a wide, open smile. "A piece of bread!" He laughed. "That's wonderful! By the way, my name is Meyer Bernstein. May I ask what is yours?"

"Seren Tuvel."

"I'm very happy to meet you, Seren." He held out his hand. I took it, looking into very dark eyes that for once were on the same level as mine. His hand was soft, gentle. I glanced at his curly, dark hair. "I'm very happy to meet you too," I answered.

OVER THE NEXT FEW WEEKS I GATHERED ONLY SMALL bits of information about the missing members of my family. One day Ellen burst into the room where I was teaching. "Seren, you've received a letter!" she called as she walked toward me. "I knew you would want it right away so I brought it to you. It came to Feldafing last night."

I tore it open. It was from my nieces Emma and Magda, Rose and Eugene's older daughters. Oh, I was happy to hear from them! I had regained two more members of my family. I skimmed through the letter quickly. Emma had been taken to Bergen-Belsen concentration camp after leaving us in Budapest. Some time later Magda was taken from Rose and Eugene at Reghinal-Sasesc and placed there. The two sisters were reunited.

I wrote back to her immediately, telling her that her father, Eugene, had been in Auschwitz with Joseph. I could tell her nothing about Rose.

Then Joseph came to see me one more time, bringing me news that there was no news. He had traveled all the way back to my former home in Valea Uzului, to the mill high above the valley floor, to the home of his parents, Herman and Tamara. He had found no one, nothing. The houses were empty, the furniture ransacked and broken, fragments of pottery scattered over the floors. My mother was not at our house, nor Shlomo, Eliezer, Meyer, Mendel, Rose, Berta, Louise, or any of their spouses or children. Joseph had hoped to find at least one of his brothers, Miksha or Ernie, but his home was silent, the only sound that of the wind blowing in through the open front door and out the back.

"It doesn't mean that they're all gone," he said. "Traveling is terribly difficult. They may be stuck somewhere, wondering if I'm alive. Or they may have gone to Palestine! That's what I think. They've gone to Palestine! I came to say good-bye, Seren. I'm going there too!"

"You are?" I asked, my voice full of sorrow. "I'm sad and happy for you at the same time."

"You'll always be my favorite aunt," he said then, touching my hand. "I brought you a farewell present." He unwrapped a package he had been holding in his hand. A length of green-flowered material fell out, spilled like spring flowers over the cutting table. "Oh, Joseph, it's beautiful!" I cried. "I haven't had material to sew a dress for so long!"

"I brought some for Esther too. I'm going to see her in Feldafing before I leave. Will you visit me in Palestine someday, Seren?"

"I would love to, Joseph! I would love to!"

"I'll be waiting," he called, and walked out of the room, waving at the door once, and then stepped out into the early-afternoon light and was gone.

AFTER JOSEPH LEFT, THE LONELINESS THAT HAD BEEN quietly building up like a great, white stone settled on my chest, weighing heavily on me all night long. I went back to my room, empty, silent, wondering, *How did it come to be that I, who have always been surrounded by friends, by sisters and brothers, by nieces and nephews hanging in and out of the front door and groups of cousins stringing along the lawn like a gaggle of geese, am so alone?* Except for the letter from Emma and Magda I heard from no one in my family; outside of Uncle Louie none of my relatives came to Feldafing. Years were to pass before I would be able to obtain any more information about my family. I never assumed that they were all gone. I never gave up hope. Nevertheless, I was by myself in a country that did not want me. If I or any other Jew entered one end of a train car, the German civilians on board rushed to get off the car at the other end. Despite this, I traveled back to Feldafing to see Esther and Ellen every weekend.

Then, little by little, Meyer and I came to know each other, talking over dinner, over supper, after the work for the day was done. One day he asked if he could accompany me to Feldafing. On the way there I told him all about Uncle Louie, as we were sure to come across him. Although I tried to avoid Uncle Louie as much as possible, he sought me out constantly, reminding me repeatedly that he expected me to marry a rabbi. Fortunately Uncle Louie felt he had to be everywhere, supervising everyone, so he could not spend a great amount of time with me. Still, it was almost enough to make me stay away from Feldafing.

When we arrived my worst fears materialized; Uncle Louie was waiting for me at the station, his long robes flowing in the September wind. He stood by himself, separate, removed from all those who were not allowed to touch him, his hands folded together on his chest, smiling slightly like a benevolent dictator. As soon as he saw that I was with a man his smile faded, his eyes darkened, and he strode up to us quickly.

"Whom have you brought along, Seren?" he asked. "A friend of Esther's perhaps . . . or Ellen's?"

"Uncle Louie, I would like you to meet Meyer Bernstein," I answered. "He teaches tailoring at the school."

Meyer held out his hand. "I'm very happy to meet you," he said. "Seren has told me a great deal about you."

My uncle ignored the hand. "You sound as if you might be from Lithuania, Mr. Bernstein. Is that correct?"

"Yes, it is. I come from an area in Lithuania near the border adjoining Poland."

"I see. And are you a rabbi who perchance has decided not to dress accordingly?"

"No, no, I'm not. I see that you are, though. At home we had a number of learned men who were always arguing over the interpretation of Judaic law. Perhaps you could settle a question that—"

My uncle turned abruptly to face me. "I have met a suitable rabbi, Seren. You are well aware of my meaning."

"I'm in a hurry!" I answered. "Meyer wants to visit the hospital with me, and Esther is not always in her room. They often take her away for tests or examinations. We want to spend as much time as possible with her."

"Please remember who I am!" he answered, his long beard quaking. "I am your dear mother's brother! I am responsible for you. I take that responsibility very seriously!"

WHEN I RETURNED THE FOLLOWING WEEK, ALSO with Meyer, Uncle Louie became furious. He followed us into the dining hall and immediately began reminding me of my obligations as a Jewish woman. Almost before I realized it, Meyer entered the conversation, citing one law after another from the Torah, reciting it first in Hebrew and then in Yiddish. Although he had told me that he spoke and read Hebrew, I did not realize how thoroughly he had studied the Torah. I sat back and watched as Uncle Louie stumbled around in Yiddish, grasping for the fragments of knowledge he had picked up here and there. *This is wonderful!* I thought, a smile spreading across my face. *The young man who so angered my father as he stood at the window taunting us as we walked to temple, who now insists that I marry a rabbi, is revealing himself to be almost totally ignorant of Judaic law.* Of course, I realized that Meyer was deliberately trying to embarrass Uncle Louie.

Finally one Sunday afternoon Uncle Louie approached Meyer and me as we were descending the hospital steps hand in hand, skipping down like children. When we reached the bottom he said, "I have reached a decision. Since you continue to defy me, Seren, since you continue to see this young man, I insist that the two of you be married here in Feldafing as soon as possible. I will marry you!"

I burst into laughter, knowing exactly what my uncle was thinking: that as a nonbeliever I would not hesitate to move in with Meyer without benefit of a marriage ceremony. But I was still my mother and father's child; I would never go against what they had taught me. Obviously, however, Uncle Louie did not understand this.

"Is it so funny?" Uncle Louie asked then. "Am I too late?"

"No, no . . ." I answered, looking at Meyer. The two of us had an understanding, more unspoken than otherwise, that we would marry someday.

"It could not please me more," Meyer said, looking into my eyes. "Why should we wait? What is there to wait for?" He looked down at his wrist briefly, fingering the tattoo with his free hand. He had been left with no one from his family, not one living relative. Turning to my uncle, he said, "We would be honored to have you marry us."

At the beginning of October, less than two months after we met, five months after I entered the hospital at Saint Ottilien, Meyer and I were married. Before the ceremony Uncle Louie took me to the *mikvah*, the bathhouse, where it was determined by a Jewish matron that I was at a time in my menstrual cycle suitable for marriage. When we returned he arranged for a *chuppah* and I chose my wedding dress. Two dresses were all I owned at the time, the one I had made from the print material Joseph brought me and a beige Empire-waist dress with a high neckline and long sleeves that had been given to me at Feldafing. "Which one shall I wear?" I asked Esther as she sat in her hospital bed.

"The beige one," she answered. "It's so becoming on you."

"Really? I can actually look becoming? If only my hair had grown out more. A man was always attracted to my hair first. Meyer has only seen it short."

"Maybe he loves you, not your hair," she answered, smiling. She still wore the bandages all around her head. "He's a very lucky man."

I hugged her close, thinking of all we had been through together. She also had met a man who cared for her, bandages and all. "No, it's your young man who is lucky. He doesn't even know how lucky . . ."

As time for the wedding approached rain began pouring from the sky in great, gray streams. Ellen and I waited in Esther's room, Uncle Louie outside the door pacing up and down, his beard flapping behind him. Meyer was late. He had traveled to a neighboring village on the unpredictable train to accompany his attendants back to Feldafing. Every few minutes Uncle Louie charged to a window to see if Meyer and the other two men would materialize out of the falling water. I was not worried; I knew they would come. Uncle Louie, however, did not. "It's disgraceful!" he said over and over. "To be late for one's own wedding. It's entirely disgraceful."

Finally, an hour after the wedding was to begin, Meyer and his two friends came up the steps and into the hospital. The train had been stalled somewhere between the two towns. Immediately Esther, Ellen, and I lifted up the *chuppah*, went out into the drenching rain, and crossed the street, the men following behind. We all gathered in a small park across from the hospital. I donned a double heavy veil, as was the custom. As Esther, Ellen, and several other women who had come to watch us took me around Meyer seven times, I stumbled repeatedly, blinded by the veil and caught by the mud oozing at our feet. Several times I would have fallen into the puddles if Ellen or Esther had not caught me.

At last my uncle began to intone the ceremony, the rain drumming against the top of the canopy, Meyer beside me, his hand in mine, Esther with her bandaged head on the other side, Ellen next to her. *We have come a long way,* I thought as Uncle Louie's voice chanted above the rain. *We are almost whole again. If only my mother were here . . .*

And then I remembered. How often had she said, "If you don't stop noshing from my pots it will pour on your wedding day!"

She is here after all, I realized. *After all of it, she is here . . .*

Twenty-six

NOW THAT I WAS MARRIED, NOW THAT I HAD SOME-
one with whom I could build a new life, I wanted only one more thing—to
be able to leave Germany. Living in a country ravaged by war was difficult
in itself, as all goods were scarce and strictly rationed. But this would have
been bearable if it had not been for the realization that Meyer and I, as well
as all other Jews, were still not wanted. Overwhelmingly, the German citizens believed that it was not for nothing that their Führer had shipped us
to concentration camps; we were murderers, we were thieves, we were
"spoilers of the race," and it was to save mankind that we were starved or
worked to death or died of utter despair.

One bitterly cold, late afternoon shortly after our marriage, Meyer and
I decided to ride the streetcar to the new room we had been given. As we
boarded it, two German men at the other end of the car started for the rear
exit, as often happened when any Jew entered, but stopped near the door.
The severe weather must have detained them. As we sank into the nearest

seat, one of the men turned to the other and said in a loud voice, "Well, the war's over."

The second man glanced in our direction, pulling his black leather cap down over his ears. "Yes. Now the damn Jews have it all!"

That night as we sat over our dinner I said for the third time since breakfast, "Meyer, we've got to leave here."

He looked at me, put his fork down slowly, and rested his hand on my shoulder. "Seren," he began, "I want to leave as much as you do. We've applied for visas to the United States. We've been placed on the waiting lists. What more can we do?"

"There must be something! How can we wait until our names reach the top of the list? It will be fifteen years!"

"The quotas have been set. If we had someone in the United States to sponsor us, we could be placed on a preference list, but we don't."

I turned slightly from him, looking out into the dark night. "Sometimes I'm afraid. We're still in the same country as the camps. We're with the same people. Who is sure that it won't all begin again?"

"No one," he answered, dropping his hand. "No one."

If we could have lived in our own apartment, however small, we could have created a quiet haven in which to wait out the fifteen years. Rather, Meyer and I were given a room, only slightly larger than the one I had as a single person, in the home of a German family. As soon as the head of the house learned that we were to be living in his spare bedroom, he walled off his living quarters from us, dividing the house in two. On his side were the rooms for him and his family, on ours the room of an elderly German widow, our room, and a small, shared kitchen where the widow and I took turns cooking.

We did not see the face of the widow for two months. Early every morning she rushed into the kitchen as soon as the gas lines were turned on. The gas was rationed and available only for an hour in the morning and an hour again in the evening. After hurriedly fixing herself breakfast, the widow scurried back to her room, plate in hand, as soon as she heard my footsteps approaching the kitchen door. I entered the kitchen to the sounds of her door being banged shut quickly, followed by the clicking of a lock and the gliding of a heavy metal bolt.

Partly I understood the widow's fear of us, as she, like many other German people, appeared to be quiet and refined, preferring an orderly, reserved life. Suddenly thrust upon her had been Meyer and me and the other displaced Jews, some of whom were young, unruly men of seventeen and eighteen. These men had been young boys of thirteen and fourteen when they were taken into Auschwitz and had learned to survive by becoming rough and somewhat crude, frightening the Germans with their rowdiness even though they did not harm anyone. What angered me was the widow's assumption that Meyer and I were like these young men and, given the chance, would pounce upon her demanding exclusive use of the kitchen. As it was, she often left me with only a few minutes to cook while the gas was still flowing.

Many times even if I did have gas to cook with, I did not have any food to prepare. Everyone, Jew and non-Jew alike, was given ration cards to be redeemed for such things as butter, eggs, milk, vegetables, and meat. Every night after leaving the training school I stood in long lines at the markets. Meyer and I could have continued to eat at the dining room of the training school in lieu of receiving coupons, but after all the years of eating mass-prepared food amid hundreds of other people, I wanted so much to make dinner for just the two of us.

As I waited in these lines for an hour or two each evening, slowly moving to the front, I saw each of the German housewives ahead of me present her coupons and receive the groceries. But almost every time I reached the head of the line, the clerk behind the counter told me he had just run out. The village being quite small, everyone knew who I was. There was no point in arguing with him, for I had no way to prove whether or not he was, indeed, out of food.

One chilly, damp evening in late November, nearly two months after Meyer and I were married, I climbed the stairs to our room feeling completely discouraged. After I had stood in the butter line for an hour, seeing every German woman in front of me receive her one-fourth pound ration, the clerk announced to me, "I just ran out." When I reached the head of the meat line the clerk took the coupon from my outstretched hand, glanced up at my face, and then handed it back to me. "Out!" he said quickly.

Then, as I reached the top of the stairs and came into the kitchen, wondering what I could scrape together for dinner, the widow ducked her head and began to run toward her door. Something in me snapped. In a rush I dashed in front of her and planted myself in front of her door, blocking her exit. She stopped abruptly and drew her arms around herself, trembling.

"Now you listen to me!" I began. "Ever since we moved in here you've been acting like I'll attack you with a butcher knife. If anyone should be frightened, it's me! It's your people who brought us here in locked cars. It's your people who killed my people. I didn't ask to be brought here. I was perfectly happy in my home in Transylvania!"

I stopped. The widow was now covering her face with her hands. "Please look at me," I continued in a softer tone, knowing she was terrified. "I have hands, like you. I have a face, like you. I am human."

She looked me in the eyes for the first time. "Why do you run away from me?" I asked.

"I'm sorry," she whispered. "I thought you might harm me . . . I'm very sorry." Then she went into her room.

The next morning, however, she did not flee the kitchen when I entered. Gradually we began conversing politely. When she learned how I was turned away in the markets, she offered to take my coupons and redeem them. When she realized what an inept cook I was, she said one evening, "Why don't you let me prepare dinner for the three of us. You must be tired after teaching all day. Let me cook." Of course, I let her. She was an extraordinarily good cook, having worked in the kitchen of a German baron most of her life. Little by little, she even taught me how to prepare delicious meals. Some of the dishes I cook today are ones she taught me how to make—chicken with egg noodles, potato and cheese casseroles, delicate cabbage rolls.

By spring of the new year I knew that I was with child. The widow, Anna, was overjoyed. I was not so sure of my feelings, of bringing a child into the midst of a people who would regard him or her as one of the enemy.

ONE DAY THAT SAME SPRING I CAME HOME TO FIND A letter waiting for me. While I did not recognize the handwriting immediately, I felt instinctively that it was from someone who had known me before the war. Small miracles still happened: a man finally traced his wife to another country where she had been taken after liberation, a sister discovered a sister in a remote village, a friend found a friend. Maybe the letter was from Eugene or Berta's husband or even from one of my brothers. I tore it open. "My dearest Seren," it began. It was from Samuel!

> I am so very, very happy that I have found you again! After liberation from Auschwitz I went to your apartment building in Budapest looking for you. No one was there. But I never gave up hope that you were still alive. I found out that Lily's mother was in Sweden and I wrote to her there. She replied that you had written her about Lily's death (I was so sad to hear that) and gave me your address. I knew you would make it! I can't wait to see you again.

Slowly, I folded the letter and placed it back in the envelope. How could Uncle Louie have told me he saw Samuel's body on the cart going to the crematorium? Perhaps he did not see it at all and made up the story so I would marry a rabbi. But then again, maybe he thought he saw Samuel's body after all. The war had so interchanged life and death that they were almost indistinguishable.

It did not matter. I was married to Meyer. In a few more months our child would be born. Sliding the letter under several scarves in a bottom dresser drawer, I whispered, "Find someone else, Samuel. Be happy . . ." I did not look at it again.

SHORTLY AFTER MEYER AND I WERE MARRIED, ESTHER had finally been discharged from the hospital at Feldafing and had moved into my old room in Waldheim. Both she and Ellen, who remained at

Feldafing, could talk of nothing but the young men they had met in the hospital. "Sidney needs me," Esther said one Sunday afternoon over tea. "He lost his wife and two little boys at Auschwitz . . . And I need him."

"So what are you waiting for?" I asked. "Marry him!"

She laughed, blushing, looking so healthy and happy that I could not quite believe it was her. "We wanted to be married by a rabbi—"

"Not Uncle Louie!" I interrupted.

"Not Uncle Louie!" she answered. "The only other one nearby is in Munich. Will you and Meyer come with us if we are married there?"

I grabbed her by the cheeks and drew her to me across the table. "We would love to!"

"Ellen and Ben are engaged too! I think we will all be married on the same day, but they're going to be married at Feldafing."

"By Uncle Louie?"

"By Uncle Louie."

"Well," I answered, "we'll have to wish them the best!"

On the one day between Passover and Pentecost when marriages are allowed, Meyer and I accompanied Esther and Sidney to Munich and back. When we returned a friend of Esther's and I prepared a wedding dinner with food that Meyer had purchased on the black market. Previously, I had refused to have anything to do with this corruption, but for this occasion I relented. To the four pounds of beef Meyer brought home I added struetzels made of flour and fresh eggs, creating a wonderful Hungarian stew. We invited a few friends, uncorked a bottle or two of wine, and feasted long into the night. As Esther, beautiful with her hair growing back in light brown curls around her face, rose from the table to go, she said very softly, "This was the nicest wedding anyone could ever have . . ."

A FEW MONTHS LATER, IN SEPTEMBER, AT THE BEGINning of the eighth month of my pregnancy, our baby was born. Meyer accompanied me to Saint Ottilien, the hospital where I had recovered after liberation, as soon as the contractions started. There I gave birth to a boy. He was so small in my arms, his dark, dark hair brushing against the white pillow. He was absolutely perfect, the doctor assuring me that he showed no signs of prematurity. We had decided to name him Jacob, after Meyer's father.

"He's the very image of you!" I told Meyer when he came to visit. "Look at his eyes!" They were a deep brown, as dark as the burl of a tree growing high on a mountain slope.

"Yes," he answered. "Yes . . . like my father's."

And when I looked again, I saw my mother's eyes as well.

The doctor would not allow me to take Jacob out of the hospital when a week had passed and I was more than ready to return home. "You must leave him here," he said. "He's too small. You can take him home when he gains another pound. He only weighs four pounds now."

"Absolutely not!" I said. "If I go home, so does my baby!"

"I must insist that he stay here," the doctor answered. "It is our policy to keep a premature baby until he attains a weight of five pounds."

"Then I'll stay with him. I won't leave him."

The doctor shrugged and walked out of the room.

After another week Jacob and I went home together. He thrived, snug in his basket at the school where I continued to teach part-time. In the evenings he was rocked to sleep in the arms of Anna. On Sundays Esther and Ellen fought over him all day long.

THREE MONTHS LATER, IN DECEMBER, ESTHER AND Sidney received permission to emigrate. A friend of Sidney's in the United States had agreed to sponsor them and they would settle near Chicago where a job was waiting. "Oh, Esther!" I cried when she told me. "I'm so happy for you!" In the deepest part of my heart, I was overjoyed that they would be able to leave Germany for the freedom of the United States. But I knew I would miss her terribly, and a part of me already grieved. She would be an ocean away from me. A week later Ellen and her husband received word that they would be able to leave as well.

As soon as Esther and Sidney were settled in Hyde Park, a community on the south side of Chicago, she began sending me packages—woolen pants for Jacob, warm scarves for Meyer and me, exotic canned goods that she purchased in this brave new world. "I know you will be able to leave Germany someday too," she wrote. "Please don't give up hope . . ."

"No, I won't give up," I answered in my letters, but in fact, I had. How could we keep on hoping when the quotas remained unchanged, when neither of us had anyone to sponsor us, when every month a fellow survivor left for the United States or Canada or South America? A few others continued to enter Palestine clandestinely, but I would not even consider the risks involved. I could not bear the thought of being caught and put into a detention camp in Cyprus, of having Meyer and Jacob taken from me.

I continued to teach part-time at the training school, to care for Jacob, to spend an evening out with Meyer once in a while. Anna had become entirely devoted to Jacob and he to her. When he began to crawl he would thump his little body to her door as soon as I put him down on the floor and then pound on it with both fists. She would open it immediately, as if waiting for him, and scoop him up in her arms, crying "Jacob! Jacob! Jacob!" The first word he said was her name, "Ann . . . nah!" Often she chased us into the night with a "Go! Go! Enjoy yourselves!" so she could have Jacob all to herself.

We would walk to the theater, watch a light comedy, even laugh, come home, retrieve Jacob, and go to bed. But I seldom slept through the night. Again and again I sank into a deep sleep, into a pit, hearing above me the pile of frozen bodies begin to topple, seeing them fall one after the other, stiff arms and legs coming closer and closer, the eyes still open.

"No! No!" I screamed, waking in a cold sweat. Meyer would draw me to him and assure me that it was only a dream. If I fell asleep again, I dreamed of ghosts running in the rain.

Spring finally came again . . . even summer. I went to the school each afternoon, carrying Jacob in my arms, and continued to teach. But my heart was not in my work. One by one even my students left for Australia or South America, the bravest ones to Palestine. Fall came and Jacob began to walk. When winter returned once more, I wanted to retreat into our room, close the door, and crawl under the covers to wait. I could not bear the thought of year after year going by and the three of us remaining in such a hostile land with no family, little work, and no hope.

Then one evening Meyer bounded up the stairs and into our room while I was putting Jacob to sleep. "I've just come from the American army office!" he said. "And you know what?"

I stared at him, waiting for him to continue. His eyes were sparkling and bits of snow glistened in his dark hair. He was smiling at me, waiting for me to ask. "No, of course I don't know what! Tell me!" I said.

"The officer had just posted a few notices when I came. They said that the Amalgamated Workers Union of Canada wants to sponsor tailors. They're giving a test at our school next month. Whoever passes it will be able to immigrate to Canada!"

"Meyer!" I shouted, waking Jacob, who began to cry. "Is this true? Are you sure? You wouldn't tease me, would you?"

"It's true! I read the notice three times to be sure." He grabbed both Jacob and me and swung us around and around the room until we all collapsed on the bed.

"Will you pass the test? Will it be difficult?" I asked, suddenly afraid.

"Am I such a bad tailor?"

"No. No. I just can't believe it."

"So, we'll see," he answered. "We'll just have to wait and see."

The test was given and while Meyer was confident that he had passed, I was terrified that he had not. The test had been only for men, or I would have taken it too. Jacob was growing older and I so wanted him to spend his youth in a country where he could live without fear, without seeing hatred in the eyes of every passing stranger.

Finally the results were announced. Meyer had passed. Immediately the Canadian government applied for our visas. When they arrived we were asked to come to the Canadian consul in Munich. As we walked out of the office, the visas in our hands, I felt as if even impossible longings can be realized.

In the late winter of 1949 we said good-bye to Anna. Tears streamed down her face as she asked over and over, "You will write, won't you?"

"Yes! Yes!" I answered her each time.

After taking the train to Bremen-Hofen, we boarded a large military ship, the *General Sturgiss*, for the eleven-day journey to Halifax, Nova Scotia. Over two hundred other families were on the ship as well, one hundred and twenty Jewish families and the remainder non-Jewish, all emigrating to Canada. As soon as we were aboard, the families were separated, the men put into cramped quarters in the bottom of the ship and the women and children in small cabins. It was almost as if we were in a camp once more, for every morning a large, rough Polish woman, reminding me almost more than I could bear of an SS woman at Ravensbrück, checked each cabin. The room had to be spotless and I spent most of my time trying to keep it so.

Meyer was equally frustrated, for even though our fares were to be deducted from his pay once he began working in Canada, all of the men were expected to paint the ship every day. On the second day of our voyage he came to my cabin early in the morning and said, "Give Jacob to me. I'll take care of him." Thereafter when anyone asked why he was not painting, he replied, "My wife is so ill. The trip is very difficult for her. She hasn't been well." He did not have to paint again.

The voyage was quite rough, the ship heaving back and forth all day long and throughout the night as well. While I was not sick as Meyer said, not becoming ill ever again once I was out of the camps, I could not rest. Jacob was in a crib beside my bunk and as the ship tossed, it rolled back and forth, back and forth, back and forth. I was afraid that the crib would crash into a wall and Jacob would be hurt.

One night I decided, *This has to stop!* I jumped out of bed and searched through a trunk until I found a length of rope. With three strong knots I tied the crib to my iron bunk bed and it stood firm while the ship swayed. With a sigh I climbed back into bed, confident of finally sleeping through the night without hearing the bed rolling.

A few hours later I woke up, sensing that something was wrong. In the pitch-black I reached out my hand toward the crib. Nothing was there. How could it have disappeared? My heart pounding, I crawled out of bed and hurriedly found a flashlight in my suitcase. Flicking it on, I moved the beam of light over the floor. Here was one side of the crib, there another, there still a third. The crib had been torn apart by the ship's rocking. But where was Jacob? Then my beam of light found him sitting in the middle of the floor, smiling. He was pointing one finger at the flickering ray. Sweeping him up in my arms, I took him into bed with me. The rest of the voyage I kept him with me every night.

On a clear, icy morning, the wind whipping across my face in an unrelenting stream of frigid air, I stood on deck waiting for the first glimpse of land. It was the eleventh day. I could not quite believe the long years of waiting would be over in an hour, two. Meyer was beside me, one hand in mine, the other holding Jacob to his chest. "Is he too cold?" I asked. "Feel his face."

"He's fine!" Meyer answered. "He'll be a big, strong boy, won't you, Jacob?" He wrapped the scarf around Jacob a little tighter.

I gazed out across the slate gray expanse of ocean and air, my mind easing out past the water, the wide, rolling sea. A memory began to drift over me, mingling with the sea spray, the wind. Once again the Gypsy fortune teller was sitting in my mother's warm kitchen holding my hand in hers, her silver bracelets jingling, my mother smiling at me from across the long table. "You will cross a big body of water someday," the Gypsy said.

Meyer squeezed my hand. "Are you all right?" he asked.

I nodded my head.

"Look!" he shouted then, releasing my hand and pointing into the distance. "I think I can see it. Over there! It's very dim, but I think that's the land."

And there it was—our new home slowly taking form out of the air, the mass of land becoming dark and clear on the light horizon.

"Do you see!" he asked, throwing his head back, his eyes bright in the cold wind.

"Yes!" I answered. "I see!"

Fifteen Years Later

JANUARY 1964

CANADA BROUGHT US GOOD FORTUNE. NOT IN MONEY, but in great happiness. During our first year in Montreal, we were invited to a large fund-raising dinner for Israeli bonds. Meyer and I put on our best clothes. We did not go out often, and this was a chance to get away together from the hard work of our everyday life raising children and building our businesses.

Samuel Bronfman was the guest speaker that night. He showed us slides demonstrating how the Canadian and American money was being put to good use in the new Jewish state. I was paying close attention; I had never been to an event like this. Suddenly, I was shrieking, my legs were trembling, I was sliding under the table in a complete faint.

I came to quickly. The room was absolutely quiet as the lights were turned on. "That's him, that's him," I was babbling to Meyer. The last slide had been of Ben-Gurion, the prime minister of Israel. Seated next to him was one of his agricultural administrators. "That's Shlomo! That's my brother!" Meyer was dubious, but I knew I was right.

In the next days the Jewish Federation contacted the Israeli Agriculture Department; it was confirmed that the man was indeed Shlomo.

And so one bitterly cold afternoon in early 1951 I went to the mailbox in the foyer of our apartment building in Montreal and found a letter from Israel waiting for me. Anxiously I tore it open and turned to the last page to read the signature. "Your brother, Shlomo," it read. Oh, it was from Shlomo! One of my brothers had found me again! The last time I had seen him was in 1935 when he left home to marry a woman in a distant village.

I read the letter slowly, almost unable to understand the written words. I kept seeing Shlomo's face, my eyes focusing briefly on the letters which then dissolved again into the contours of his wide eyes, his long, straight nose. "Eliezer is here as well," I managed to read. "He and his wife live not far away."

I slumped against the wall of mailboxes, tears washing down my face and running onto the page. Two brothers were alive to me once more. Going up the stairs to our apartment, I found a quiet corner near the front windows of the dining room where Jacob and his baby sister, Marlene, would not disturb me, and read the rest of my letter, the pale light from the snowy sky falling across my hands, across the blue inked words:

> I lost my wife and son in Auschwitz, but I have remarried. Her name is Zella. We have a good life together.
>
> Rose's surviving daughters, Emma and Magda, wrote to me from Sweden and gave me your address. I was so relieved to learn that both you and Esther are alive and well. Herman and Tamara's three sons also survived and are all here in Israel.
>
> It would make Zella and me very happy if you could come to visit us. Our home is always open to you and your family. We are all here waiting for you.

When Meyer returned from his tailoring shop later, I showed the letter to him. "I would like for you to go more than anything," he said. "I have no one left. Now, you do. I wish you could go."

"I'll go," I answered. "Not now. We have so little money. But someday, I'll go."

The airfare accumulated bit by bit in an oak box I kept locked in a dresser drawer. Every time I pulled out the slim, brown box and deposited a few more dollars in it, I thought, *I am that much closer to Israel.*

NOW, THIRTEEN YEARS AFTER GETTING SHLOMO'S letter, I sat on an airplane, preparing for our imminent descent to the airport at Tel Aviv. In a few more minutes I would be reunited with Shlomo and Eliezer, holding them again after almost thirty years. I could not quite believe that it would happen. As the plane descended through canyons of air, the wide, blue sea looming closer and closer, I wondered if I would be able to find them in the airport crowd, if they would be able to find me. Finally the wheels touched down, bumped up once, twice, and then rumbled along the runway, my stomach whirling over and over on itself.

Upon leaving the plane, I entered a long, tunnellike ramp and then began to climb the stairs to the main part of the terminal. As I reached the top, I saw a large number of people, most of them quite tall, grouped in the center of the terminal and looking expectantly at the arriving passengers. *An important person must be on this flight,* I thought. *Maybe a famous celebrity. I wonder why I didn't notice anyone like this on the plane.*

Then my heart began to race wildly. Herman was standing in the crowd! No one had told me that he survived. It had to be him! He still looked so much like our father—tall, fair, his light hair glinting in the sun that poured in through the windows. I picked out another face—Shlomo! And beside him—Eliezer! All the other people seemed to be with them. Suddenly I realized that the entire crowd was for me, all these people had come to see me. In one way or another they were all mine, all my relatives. After so many years I had a family again.

Herman began running toward me. "Aunt Seren! Aunt Seren!" he called.

"Why does he call me 'Aunt'?" I said aloud. Then he had me in his arms.

"I'm Miksha," he said, holding me tight. "Do you remember me? I'm so happy to see you!"

I had been confused. It was Herman's oldest son who had me firmly in his arms. He looked exactly as Herman had the last time I saw him.

Then I was passed to Eliezer, who was as I remembered him—quiet, calm. "Welcome," he said softly, looking into my eyes.

I went from him to his wife and daughters to Herman and Tamara's other sons, Ernie and Joseph, to the two sons of Berta and Morris, to wives, children, and grandchildren. Finally I fell into Shlomo's arms, his chest and shoulders reaching high above me like my father's once had, and let the tears that had been welling higher and higher fall.

"So you've come," Shlomo said.

"Yes! Yes! Why should I be crying? I'm here!"

He held me close for a long moment. "You look well," he said then, wiping the tears from his own eyes. "I'm so happy you are here."

Shlomo and his wife took me back to their home. Everyone else followed, pouring into the house, spilling out into the yard and lawn, eating and laughing and getting reacquainted all afternoon and long into the night. Shlomo's wife, Zella, was a lovely young woman who kept bringing in chocolate cake, apple pie, and dark bread with cheese as we talked. I would not finish chatting with one nephew or his wife and another would come up to me.

"Seren," Joseph said, drawing me to him again. "I knew you would come someday, just as I knew you would make it through the war. Do you remember the times I found you? Do you remember the photograph I carried in my shoe?"

"Oh, Joseph," I answered, cupping his beautiful face in my hands, a face combining Herman's fair radiance and Tamara's laughing grace. "I've never forgotten you. Never!"

"You're still my favorite aunt," he said. "Do you believe that?"

"Yes, yes, I believe it."

"Good! The day after tomorrow, when you've had a chance to rest, I'm going to come in my car and we're going sightseeing! Is it all right?"

I nodded my head, beginning to cry again.

Eliezer approached me quickly and held out his handkerchief, looking at me with moist eyes but saying nothing. I laughed despite the tears. "Eliezer," I said, "you are still a *la ceas lingurita* . . . a teaspoonful every hour. That's how many words you give us. Do you remember when Mama called you that?" I asked, taking his hand.

"Yes . . ." he answered softly, looking above me into the group of people milling all around us. "How was your flight?" he asked then.

"I could hardly stand it, it was so long! Tell me, Eliezer," I said then, "how are you? I've thought of you again and again. You were always my favorite brother at home. I was so proud of you when we walked to school together."

Again he looked away from me, staring at the gathering dusk for a long moment. Finally he said in his slow, careful way, "I don't think about the past—ever. I live in the present. I have a good job with the Agricultural Administration. I enjoy working with the farmers, teaching them how to grow better crops, how to take care of their animals. It's a quiet life. Sylvia and I have been blessed with our daughters, Judith and Rivka . . ."

"They're wonderful girls!" I interrupted. "And they've married and given you grandchildren already!"

"I am content," he said quietly. Then he rose and walked away. For years I had wondered exactly what had happened to the brothers and sisters who did not survive, and I felt sure that Shlomo and Eliezer knew more than I did. *Maybe Shlomo will tell me about everything,* I decided.

Finally, well past midnight, everyone went home, promising to return often during my two weeks' stay. I fell into bed exhausted but quite unable to sleep. All these people were my family. I had never felt so important in my life.

In the morning, Shlomo and I sat together over a leisurely breakfast. Shlomo had taken a vacation from his managerial position in a *moshav*, a cooperative village, so that he could have all of his time free while I was in Israel. This overwhelmed me, for I had always felt closer to Eliezer. Perhaps Shlomo and I would have been friends at home if our father had not sent him to the yeshiva at the age of eight.

Now he sat across the table from me, smiling, asking questions that any brother might ask a sister, pretending that it had not been thirty years and so many losses since we had last seen each other.

"How is Meyer?" he asked. "I hope he is well."

"He's fine," I answered. "He works hard. His tailoring shop always has a customer waiting for him when he comes in the morning."

"That's good. And the children?"

"Jacob is almost seventeen already and Marlene is thirteen. You should see her. She is beautiful like our mother, like her grandmother. I named Marlene for her . . . Oh, I just remembered! I brought a present for you from all of us. I forgot to give it to you last night." Jumping up from the table, I ran to the bedroom and came back with the gift.

"You didn't have to bring me anything," Shlomo said as I handed it to him. "I want to see you. I don't need anything, just you—having you here with our family again."

"It's nothing! Open it."

Slowly he unwrapped the present. A pair of pajamas was exposed bit by bit—first the black stripes, then the white spaces. He handed the package back to me. "Here," he said softly. "You give these to someone who can use them. I don't need them. I have everything I need. You're here. That's fine."

Instantly I realized that I had given him pajamas with stripes. Surely he had worn similar ones in Auschwitz, worn them as his wife and son were fed to the ovens. I had not even thought of the stripes when I bought them; they were simply something I could afford.

"I'm sorry," I said. "I didn't even think!" I took the package from him. "Please forgive me."

"It's fine," he said. "Truly, I need nothing."

"Shlomo," I began then, unable to wait any longer. "Did you ever find out what happened to Mama? Was she taken to one of the camps?"

He rose quickly and went to the kitchen door. "I told Zella that I would do some shopping for her this morning," he said, opening the door. Then he paused, turning back to look at me. "I'm sorry I can't answer your questions, Seren," he said. He went out, closing the door behind him.

Zella, who had been kneading bread at the other end of the room, came up to me. "He really won't talk about the past," she said. "He's told me very little. I know that he lost his wife and son in Auschwitz, but that's all. He asked me not to question him, so I don't."

"But there are so many things I want to know. If Shlomo doesn't want to talk about the war, I won't ask him to. But who will tell me?"

"Someone will. You'll see." She rose from the table. "I must get back to my baking. Shabbat will be here before we know it."

"Why are you baking so much? You'll be exhausted! Please don't do it because of me."

"You just wait until Saturday," she said, smiling.

On Saturday I soon realized what Zella had meant. Early in the morning, as we were still sitting at the breakfast table, people began arriving. All morning, throughout the afternoon, and long into the evening men and women who had once lived in our area of Transylvania came to visit with me—business acquaintances of my father, friends of my sisters, neighbors, classmates of my older brothers. Once again I was "a Tuvel girl" surrounded by loving family and friends.

As I stood among everyone, often laughing and crying at the same time, a small, older woman, her gray hair curling in fine wisps from the edge of a deep blue scarf, came up to me. "Please forgive me," she said. "I know you have your family here. I wanted to say hello and then I'll be on my way." She paused and looked down at her hands, clasping and unclasping them several times. "I went to school with your mother," she said then. "She was a dear friend . . ." Her voice choked. She patted my hand twice with her soft, light fingers and turned to leave.

"Wait," I called, touching her on the shoulder. She turned back, her eyes misted, dim. I pulled her to me, held her as if I had my mother once more in my arms. "Thank you for coming," I said. "Thank you for everything."

The next evening Joseph and I sat together at the dining room table. I was becoming exhausted from all the visiting, but I welcomed the opportunity to talk to him privately. "Joseph," I began, "there are so many details about the war that I don't know. I have been in Canada all these years, not knowing. In their letters Shlomo and Eliezer write only of their work or of the weather. Can I ask you? Will you tell me?"

He took my hand. "My wife and I have to leave for home in a few minutes. I'm sorry. But someone will talk to you."

"Will I see you again?"

"Of course."

Late that night Miksha and I found ourselves together in the living room, everyone else having gone to bed. Sensing that he had remained to talk with me, I moved my chair closer to his, watching the fire quietly burning in the grate before us, and waited.

"I thought you might have some questions," he said after a few minutes. He glanced at me and then settled back into his chair.

"I do," I answered. "I thought no one would ever let me ask."

"It's very hard for Uncle Shlomo and Uncle Eliezer to say anything about what they have gone through. They have tried to forget the war and the years immediately after it. But you should have seen Uncle Shlomo in Cyprus! He administered all the Jewish schools on the island."

"Shlomo did this? I know nothing! Tell me everything!"

Miksha laughed and poured himself a cup of tea. "I've learned these things in bits and pieces . . . a little here, a little there. I know that Uncle Shlomo was taken into a labor camp like all of us and then sent to Auschwitz, but I'm not sure when. His wife and son were arrested later. Uncle Eliezer was also taken to Auschwitz after he was caught by the Hungarian army. This was sometime after he deserted."

"I remember when he did. We were so afraid he would be captured and shot."

"I think the two of them saw each other at Auschwitz, but they were not able to remain together. After the war Uncle Shlomo went to your home in Valea Uzului to see if anyone had come back, just like my brother Joseph did. He found no one . . . only the empty house, the jars of fruit that your mother had canned broken and rotting. So he left and secretly boarded a ship for Palestine. Uncle Eliezer did the same, but he sailed on a different ship. Both ships were seized and the passengers taken to Cyprus. There Uncle Shlomo immediately became involved in governing all the Jewish prisoners and set up schools for the children. He was on the *Exodus*, the ship full of children that sat in the harbor for weeks until it was finally allowed to sail for Palestine."

"Shlomo did this? I should have known! He was always getting into something! He and my sister Zipporah used to fight constantly because they were so alike. They both wanted to be in control."

"I remember her very faintly, but it seems she was very beautiful."

"She was . . . oh, she was so full of life . . . I couldn't save her. I wanted to desperately, but I couldn't. She was shot, you know."

"Yes, Joseph told me. It does no good to feel guilty. I couldn't save Mama and Papa either. I was in prison when they were taken." He took my hand in both of his and held it firmly.

"You look so like Herman, like your father. Has anyone ever told you that?" I asked.

"Yes . . . often. Our first son is named Herman after his grandfather. I wish you could meet him. He's in the Israeli army."

"Were you here for the war of 1948?"

"Yes, we fought in it."

"All of you?"

"Yes, for Israel. In the war of 1956 as well."

"Did you ever find out what happened to your mother and father?" I asked.

"They were taken from the ghetto in Reghinal-Sasesc, probably in 1944. I was arrested much earlier, before the ghetto was made, and taken to Budapest. Emma and I were in the same prison. Once I caught a glimpse of you and Esther when you came to visit Emma."

"Miksha," I said then, looking into his blue eyes. "I saw your mother's coat—the jacket I made for your mother, Tamara—at Ravensbrück. One day I was standing in the counting lines, and I saw it on the back of a woman who had just been sent from Auschwitz. I would have known that coat anywhere."

Miksha hid his eyes from me, but then when he looked at me, he said softly, "Thank you for telling me this. I always knew this is what happened to her, but for just a moment I felt closer to her than I have since the war."

"Miksha," I said. "Now, I must know about my mother. Everyone I ask turns away. No one will tell me what happened. I know you know something."

Miksha took a deep breath and slowly said, "You know Alfred was only fifteen years old, but he saw everything. No one likes to talk about it because it was so horrible—for your mother and for Alfred.

"One day the soldiers came and rounded up everyone who remained in the village. There couldn't have been many people left. They were all given shovels and told to dig a long trench, six feet deep and four feet wide. As soon as the trench was completed everyone was shot—except for your cousin, who was hiding in the woods."

This young boy was now a man. He'd fled from the slaughter and found refuge in a convent. Eventually he was sent to Israel and reunited with some of his relatives. There he'd changed his name to Yacov; like all of us, he had worked hard to adapt himself to his new country. He had greeted me without saying a word about what he'd witnessed. I was sure he'd be relieved that Miksha had told me what he had seen.

Miksha was silent now. We both knew the truth. His hand tightened on mine until my fingers ached, but I did not try to pull away. We sat for a long time, staring into the fire, tears running down our cheeks in silent streams.

"I think of my mother and my father every day," I finally said. "I miss and love them so deeply. If only I could have told them one last time how much. . . ."

"They know. I'm sure of it," he answered, kissing me on the cheek.

WHEN THE TWO WEEKS OF MY TRIP WERE OVER, TWO of the most joyous weeks in my entire life, I left them all—my brothers, my sisters-in-law, my nephews and cousins, promising to return with Meyer and the children soon. As I looked back at them standing in the airport terminal as they had at my arrival, I thought, *How can I leave them? I have my family back again!* I waved once more and walked into the plane.

Epilogue

Seren, Jacob, and
Esther; Meyer and
Sigmund, Esther's
husband, standing. This
photograph was taken
in Montreal, Canada,
shortly after Seren and
Meyer arrived there
from Germany.

Seren's family in Israel in the 1950s: nephew Miksha, left rear;
stepsister Berta, fifth from left, and her son, Yosef, who
carried her photo in his shoe, fourth from left; and brothers
Eliezer and Shlomo, fourth and fifth from right.

1980

For many years I could not think about the war. Every time I closed my eyes, especially while we still lived in Germany, the images of those ghostlike skeletons running in the rain after our train was bombed floated before my eyes. On my second trip to Israel I learned that Shlomo and Eliezer had both been in a rear car of the same train as I. Perhaps this is why that nightmare continued to haunt me. My brothers had been only a few meters away from me, but we would not have recognized each other even if we had found one another. My brothers were the skeletons.

As the years went by and I became the mother of another child, merely taking care of the two children filled almost all of my time. If one was not ill, it was the other. I continued my dressmaking business as well, sewing at night when the children were asleep. When they grew older I opened my own shop. If I had been forced to do nothing I might not have kept my sanity. I will always be grateful to my children and to my work.

I am somewhat proud of Esther, Ellen, and myself. We did not let ourselves be dragged either into selfishness or into despair. Then again, in so many ways, we were simply lucky. Life was abruptly taken away from so many. We were fortunate in that we were allowed to live, however minimally.

I continue to work, to enjoy being with my husband and children, to see Esther and Ellen and their families as often as possible. In 1960 we were allowed to emigrate to the United States and moved to Chicago near Esther and Sidney and their two sons. Ellen and her husband live in Philadelphia, where their oldest son is a student at the yeshiva. Whenever they come to visit me we sit together around my dining room table, the dirty dishes left sitting as they are, and reminisce.

"I can still see you walking around with that black kettle on your head in labor camp!" Esther will say.

"Oh, I thought of that last week," Ellen will answer. "I burst out laughing just thinking of it."

"I didn't lose my head to a bomb, did I?" I ask.

"No," they agree, and we all laugh again.

These are a few of the things Meyer and I will not do: stand in long lines, use metal dishes, eat turnips, read books or watch movies about the Holocaust, or watch any violent movies. The Vietnam War sickened me at heart. I could not bear to watch the news again until it was over. Otherwise we go about our lives quite peacefully.

Best of all, we have been blessed with a grandchild. A girl, Rebeccah, was born to our son Jacob and his wife, Linda, last December—a Hanukkah baby. I am probably the most outrageous grandmother you may ever see, singing Yiddish rhymes, clapping my hands at her hour after hour. I cannot get enough of her! Others tell me she has the same eyes as I—always full of adventure and asking, *What can I do next?* She is a wonderful, delightful gift to me after so much, after all these years. I am happy simply holding her hand.

Afterword

ABOUT SEREN TUVEL BERNSTEIN
BY MARLENE BERNSTEIN SAMUELS

In 1967, I was seventeen years old and a junior in high school. There was a particularly difficult elective course for which I had registered, Oriental History. At the close of the previous session, the teacher had announced his intentions: he planned to call upon six students randomly (out of twenty-five) during the coming three classes who would then present their term papers orally before the class. I was filled with such dread at the prospect of being called up before the entire class that as the evening wore on, my anxiety grew and my stomach reached a new height of turmoil.

It was shortly after supper. My mother stood at the sink washing dishes. I sat morosely at the kitchen table. "You ate nothing, are you sick?" my mother asked, quite unaccustomed to me limiting my food intake. With great effort, I relayed the teacher's proclamation, and that this was the source of my terrible anxiety. "If I get called on to present tomorrow, I'm just going to die!" I said in a typical high school girl way. Sara turned her head from her dishes, looked at me, and smiled a slight smile. Calmly and quietly she said, "You know, it's not so easy to die."

For many years, I was not able to read my mother's manuscript, despite the fact that several copies of it had made a permanent, dust-covered home on the top shelf of my library. Growing up as I did, with two Holocaust survivor parents, created in me a subconscious avoidance of all matters Holocaust-related—books, movies, articles, museums, lectures, television shows, and so on. Those close to me who had read it would always remark how unbelievable it was that I had not. To the contrary, it is truly believable. The manuscript was first prepared in the early 1980s, possibly 1981. Sara prepared an outline for herself to follow, and while she worked in her sewing room, she would record herself as she spoke about the various segments of the outline. She dreamt of having it published, and it was only several years after her death that, through a series of fortuitous coincidences, I was able to get this manuscript into the hands of Edgar Bronfman, who got it into Putnam's and my mother's dream became true.

When I was about ten years old, my parents emigrated to the United States, finally. Their dream came true. Throughout my childhood I would hear about "the States." Esther, my mother's only surviving sister, was living in "the States." That is how we happened to move to the Chicago area.

This is a picture of Seren's children Jacob and Marlene, taken at their Montreal home when Jacob was 4 and Marlene probably close to 6 months old, sometime at the end of 1950.

MY FATHER, MEYER BERNstein, was also a Holocaust survivor, having lived through four years of nightmares at Auschwitz. Meyer was born in Poland and attended yeshiva, planning to become a rabbi. When war broke out he was drafted into the Polish army, and when his unit was captured by the Germans he was taken away as a prisoner of war. He was sent to the camps as the soldiers were sorted by religion, political convictions, and national origin. While it is fair to speculate that in another kind of life Seren and Meyer might never have paired off with one another, in their lives as survivors they quickly recognized their common bond.

It seems apparent, now, that the only marriage partner my mother could ever have taken was one who, like herself, had experienced and prevailed over such horrors. Even in her role of wife, she remained committed to protecting and caring for those in her charge. My brother and I often joked about the extent to which she doted on our father, almost as if he were another child in the family, taking care of him, protecting him from unpleasant experiences and bad news, waiting on him hand and foot. Her role as caretaker and guardian had become so ingrained during the course of her camp experiences that she never succeeded in letting go of that posture, even to the slightest degree.

As children, we have little if any knowledge about the dynamics of other families and naively assume that our family is the same as all families. "The camps"—or "Lager," as my parents and their survivor friends referred to it—was an abstraction that, when I was very young, I believed all adults were required to endure. I came to believe that all adults experienced some terrible internment—a right of passage, a "coming out" event. How terrible to be an adult, I often thought. In fact, because the community in which we lived when I was a child was made up almost entirely of survivors, my parents really had no friends or neighbors who had not been in the camps. In my world all adults were Holocaust survivors.

During the occasions when adult company would visit our home for dinner, my brother and I would often overhear the discussions and stories of the war once dinner was finished and coffee had been served. In retrospect, it is difficult to imagine that when I was born, my parents' liberation and entire Holocaust experience was only four or five years removed. More amazing, though, is the fact that these stories were often accompanied by laughter from the dining room as the adults recalled tales of survival that in the present made them laugh and at the same time cry. How strange adults were, I believed as I sat on my father's or mother's lap during these times, hearing their laughter and at the same time watching their tears.

When I graduated from college I bought a yellow Volkswagen Beetle.

It was an exciting moment, the day sunny and fresh, early in June. I got into my very first brand-new car. Proudly, I drove it to my parents' home, and pulling into the gravel driveway, I honked loudly. My mother appeared promptly on the front porch steps, waving and smiling. Climbing up the steps to meet her, I asked, "So, what do you think of it? Pretty cute, isn't it?"

"Well, it is really cute," she said contemplatively with her Romanian accent, rolling r's, and v's instead of w's, "but one thing I don't understand. If you had to buy a German car, couldn't you find another color besides yellow?" She said all this with a wry smile on her face. The subtlety of this comment went right past me for a moment or two as I stood next to her thinking this over. Perhaps she thought little cars needed to be red. It was the subsequent realization of her experiences with the yellow Star of David that left me thinking the word "oops" for what seemed to be a fairly long while.

I was destined to think about that comment for the entire time I would own that car, when it was parked with a valet service and I needed to inform the attendant, "Yellow Volkswagen, please"; when I retrieved it from the repair shop, "Yellow Volkswagen, please"; or when it was vandalized and the police report was filed, "Oh, it's a yellow Volkswagen." And many years later, when I made the phone call to arrange a newspaper classified ad, I thought to myself, "Yellow Star of David for sale," while the nice lady on the other end of the telephone wire asked, "And what color is it, miss?"

How would another woman with her background have reacted to her very own child purchasing a German car in yellow? Would she have refused to sit in the car, been angry, cried? Who knows? My mother did ride in the car quite often and the subject was never mentioned again after that first moment, but I always knew it was in her thoughts each time she saw me appear in the driveway. In fact, the summer after I graduated from college she rode with me all the way from Chicago to Philadelphia to visit her friend, Helen, whom she called Helinka, who had survived the camps with Sara and Esther. The term "friend" held an entirely different meaning for them than most of us could ever imagine. It was difficult for me to assess Helen's reaction to the bright yellow German car as we arrived in the affluent suburb of Philadelphia, just before sundown on Friday afternoon, thank goodness, just before Shabbat begins.

Helen had married another survivor who had an uncle in the United States—an American citizen. He had sponsored their move out of postwar Germany. They had moved to South Philadelphia upon their arrival and purchased a little mom-and-pop neighborhood grocery store with money borrowed from the uncle. As the neighborhood deteriorated throughout the late fifties and early sixties, they persisted, buying up numerous such little stores and continuing to live in the drab little apartment above their first store. This was a fairly common practice among many of the survivors, both here and in my old neighborhood in Canada—the idea of living within the same confines as one's business whether that was grocery store, or dressmaking, watch repair, or beauty shop. Ultimately, they sold all these little stores and purchased several new, very large, "supermarkets" in an affluent suburb.

By the time Sara and I visited, they were living the good life in a large modern suburban house and had three sons. The youngest, who was probably fourteen at the time of our visit, was in the midst of a yeshiva education, devoting almost all of his waking hours to study of the Torah and Talmud, and to very serious daily praying. Helen herself had become devoutly Orthodox, and so staying in their home over the Sabbath meant experiencing old eastern European Judaism. From sundown on Friday to sundown on Saturday, the telephone was not answered, lights were not turned on manually but rather by electrical timers, even the light in the refrigerator was unscrewed to prevent turning it on inadvertently as a result of opening the refrigerator door. The car was not driven and any contact with specific types of metal was avoided, metal representing the material of both warfare and commerce. Even the top of the house key was wrapped in a special leather fob. Although my mother was raised in a religious home, her level of observance in adult life had been affected dramatically by her wartime experiences. It was during this visit to Helen that her cynicism about religiosity, and more specifically about Judaism, was undeniably revealed.

This experience is indelible in my mind, for while the family was at Saturday morning services, my mother and I strolled around the picturesque streets of that quaint little community. (She loved taking little walks, or strolls as she called them . . . "Let's take a little *shpatzier*," she would often say after dinner during the warmer times of the year or on a weekend morning that was particularly sunny.) "You know," she said, "I really don't understand all this religious observance in other people like us." This was her euphemism for other camp survivors, "people like us." "I have paid for the right to be a Jew many times over. So whom should I have to prove this to anymore? Do I really need to be a religious Jew to still be a good Jew?"

At first I naively thought she was referring to the dilemma of being a religious Jew in America, and then, after we walked in silence for a long time, she spoke again. "Some people, like Helinka, became very, very religious after the liberation. They believe that a Jewish God helped them to survive the nightmare of the camps and that they should thank God now for all their remaining days by being religious. But not me. I think now, how could any God, Jewish or not, have let such horrible things happen, such inhumanity of man against man no matter what their religion? How can I be a pious Jew after what I have seen?"

I was surprised by her comments, since when I was growing up, she kept a kosher home, and cleaned and cooked fervently the day before each Passover began. She fasted every Yom Kippur, but would not permit us, even as teenagers, to fast. "I have fasted enough in my life so that you should never have to fast as long as you will live!" she would say on Yom Kippur morning. Now, as if she read my thoughts, she went on, "You know, some things you do because they're comfortable, or you're used to it so it feels funny not to do it, like not mixing the milk with the meat, or keeping Passover. But this religious obsession—maybe those people are better Jews than I or maybe they know something that I can't see. I know for sure that if it turns out that they were right and I was not, or if it turns out that there really is a hell, it will be not so bad compared to what I have lived through, so I can't worry about it."

During such moments, she had a very keen ability to drop the conversation, changing the subject as though it had never occurred. It was truly amazing.

"Come," she said, taking my hand as if I were still five years old. "There is an ice cream shop. We should each have an ice cream cone and I want that green one with those little chopped-up nuts in it." Pistachio, her favorite. Any *shpatzier* with Seren was generally bound to be an emotional roller coaster, often with a surprise at the end. Most of the time, however, she was really quite upbeat and cheerful, something that perplexed me all of my life while she was alive and that I am only now beginning to understand. It was her optimism that compounded any personal depression I might have been experiencing with a sense of guilt over feeling depressed. In fact, one was not permitted to feel depressed or in any way unhappy around her, since what, after all, did I have to be depressed about compared to her life?

When I was in my late twenties, my parents bought a retirement home in St. Petersburg, Florida. They spent most of the unpleasant Chicago winter there and I relished visiting as often as possible. It was an opportunity to experience total pampering, for my mother still hovered over me as she did when I was a small child. "Come, sit," she would say in the mornings. Then she would pour me some coffee, putting a small amount of cream in it and even mixing in the sugar for me. Then she would prepare my breakfast, never asking what I wanted but rather making what she thought I ought to be eating: two softly scrambled eggs with butter of course, toast with raspberry jam and butter, or bagels with cream cheese and smoked fish. "How about a nice little piece of coffee cake your father bought this morning? You're too thin!" she went on. If I declined she would issue her standard edict. "You know what, at home you can diet, but here you should eat!"

AFTER BREAKFAST WE WOULD GO FOR OUR LONG morning walks on the beach. One particular time I was relaying a single woman's "Ask *Cosmopolitan*" type of dating dilemma to her. "Well," she said after much thought as we walked barefoot on the beach, "what can I tell you? I don't know what you should do. When I was your age, I was thinking about how I was going to stay alive through the night and into the next day. So what do I know of these kinds of things?"

She bent down and picked up a seashell, holding it up for me to inspect. "Look, isn't this a beautiful one? Isn't it amazing that there are such things?

You know, if you want to find the really big and beautiful ones you need to come out here around five or six o'clock in the morning. That's when the beach is full of beautiful shells. But there are a lot of people who make a living from selling these shells, so you have to come when they come. Or maybe you should sleep late when you are here, and if you want the nice shells let's just go buy some at those little shops. Then you don't have to take away from their livelihood, you sleep late, and everyone is happy." It was one of those conversations that she presented so matter-of-factly we might have been discussing the virtues of one coffee brand over another. She always considered the ramifications of every act, no matter how small or seemingly insignificant. Each action resulted in a reaction that might have unanticipated results. One always had to be prepared, always had to think ahead!

Many years after I had left home I was plagued by her ability to be optimistic, even in the face of her own premature and imminent death. It was only several weeks before I was to be married, a long-awaited event for my mother. I was close to thirty-four and still never married, unheard of for a Jewish girl with my background. My mother, Seren Tuvel—a nonsmoker—was diagnosed with terminal cancer that had begun in her lung and spread very rapidly through her body. It was described by her oncologist as "one of those red herrings we see so often in concentration camp survivors." She was sixty-five years old. The marriage ceremony was particularly difficult since I knew she would die very shortly afterward. All of us who knew how tenacious she could be remain convinced to this day that it was her sheer determination to see me married that kept her alive those few extra but critical weeks.

It was not long after my husband and I were married. The rabbi who had performed our marriage ceremony had become close to and quite fond of my mother. Fascinated by her life and her strength of character, he visited her daily in the hospital during what were to be the last few days of her life. Her untimely death was an irony that was particularly tragic in light of the hardships over which she had prevailed. "How is it that she can be so optimistic, so free of regrets even as she is dying? The frustration of having survived one of the world's most horrible events and then dying so early must be the ultimate disappointment!" I said to the rabbi as he came out of her hospital room.

We sat in the hallway outside of her room and spoke in whispered tones. The rabbi said after some moments of silence, "You know, I asked your mother if she has any regrets about her life, if she is afraid or if she feels as though she has any unfinished business."

"So what did she tell you?" I asked, unable to imagine how she might have answered those questions, what she could have possibly said. I was very curious but could not ask her to tell me herself.

"Well . . . when I asked her if she was afraid," replied the rabbi, very slowly, taking his time to remember the answers word for word, "she asked me instead, 'So, what's to be afraid of? There is nothing I am afraid of anymore, only dogs. I am always afraid of the dogs.'" The rabbi continued, "She told me she had no regrets, that she had always tried to do the right thing, to be a moral person, and that she felt she had been more productive in her later life than most people she knew. Your mother said that her life was like her sewing, that she had succeeded in making something from nothing. Her only sorrow is that she will not be here to be a grandmother to your children, but she knows you will try to be a good mother because she taught you what is most important in life."

We sat quietly and drank our lukewarm hospital coffee—too early in history for gourmet coffee and travel mugs. I got up slowly and went into her room. She was dozing quietly but opened her eyes as I sat down on the bed next to her. We held hands and she said to me, "You know I'm not going to be around for much longer, and now I am lying here thinking of some secrets that I should have told you sooner."

"Like what?" I asked expectantly.

"Well, like for example"—she became very serious—"let's say someday you're making chicken soup and you taste it and think, *Aach, it has no taste . . . it's not like my mother's. What to do?* Well, I'll tell you what to do now, and then when you're making chicken soup for Larry or for your children sometime, a long way from now, you will always think of me and about our conversation when you're standing by the stove." She continued: "When I taste the soup and it's not chicken soupy enough, I take a little squeeze of lemon and add it to the soup. And remember, you shouldn't put too much water over the chicken. Everyone is always putting too much water and that's why so few people can make a really good chicken soup. So, you'll always remember this, what I am telling you now, okay?"

She squeezed my hand and smiled a tiny little smile, her eyes halfway open. Her fingers were dry and cool—not cold, not warm, but cool. She dozed off again and I left her room for home, for my new husband, after what was to be the last time I would ever see her. It is only in writing this epilogue about Seren Tuvel, my mother, that I have remembered so many of the little details of daily life that for me as the child of two Holocaust survivors resulted in a childhood, an adolescence, and adult perceptions that are not what we perceive as typical American ones.

We think of survival in terms of living through life-threatening events, survival of the physical being. There are many chronicles of the dramatic acts undertaken to cling to life; the psychological exercises practiced to maintain hope and optimism. The majority of these tales, however, deal with short-term, intense crises: surviving an airplane crash for three weeks, living in a life raft without food and water for two weeks, being trapped in a cave for five days after the walls have collapsed. Looking at the protracted version—four years of physical and emotional dehumanization—alters any perceptions we may have had of those who survived daily events in the camps.

Few have examined the concept of spiritual survival. People would often ask my mother, "Well, how did you live for so long when so many died?" For the most part, it seems they considered only how her physical being clung to life. Not enough attention has been devoted to considering mental strength and emotional stamina and the role of hope in the triumph over such horrific evil. Put less melodramatically, surviving with spirit fully intact. One of the qualities that made my mother unusual, if not unique, was her ability to experience real, uninhibited laughter, a capacity for pleasure and joy. While it would be an untruth to say she was not severely scarred, physically and psychologically, by her experiences in the camps, the bitterness she might have harbored had never evolved into absolute cynicism. But it might also be fair to say that skepticism was a lifelong attribute, one I believe existed well before the experiences of the Holocaust transpired, and one of those personal characteristics that very well may have aided in her survival.

The fact that she was able to become a mother in every sense of the term is really quite remarkable knowing what we now know of the camp experiences, and for me, with my own two children, knowing what I now know about being a mother. Posttraumatic stress syndrome was not a concept that existed in her world. It was always quite clear that thoughts of her experiences and their effects not only were part of her daily life but also have permeated much of mine. As children, they often left us feeling somehow inadequate—there was nothing we could do to "fix" the damage that had been done to her, the opportunities that had been taken away forever, but worse, one could never quite anticipate situations that might evoke some unpleasant memory. Sara Tuvel was a far cry from the "June Cleaver" mom.

Recently, on a winter trip to Idaho, I took my early-morning walk with my very large hunting dog. There had been reports that the elk had migrated closer to residential areas due to sparsity of food. They were becoming aggressive. During the prior week they had charged at several women, hurting one. The local newspapers suggested exercising great caution. As I walked on, my dog stopped suddenly and began to growl, baring his teeth. He refused to move and continued to growl. Suddenly, I realized that during the entire walk I had been scanning the roadside, the trees, the surrounding terrain for places that might serve as protection, instantly, should danger present itself. I had been doing this unconsciously for at least half an hour but became aware of it only as the dog began to react.

The dog had spotted some elk only twenty feet away, yet my anticipation and planning ahead had been in progress much earlier than his warning—in fact, from the moment I had walked out of our driveway. I could not help but think of my mother at that moment, realizing how, so many years later, there are so very few aspects of my daily reactions to people, to my children especially, and to life's events that have escaped her subtle teachings: Always be prepared, always plan ahead, anticipate, be ready, don't depend on anyone but yourself, be inconspicuous, be observant, and always stay alert.

Index